NEW CIVIL-

MILITARY RELATIONS

NEW CIVIL-

MILITARY RELATIONS

The Agonies of Adjustment
to Post-Vietnam Realities

edited by

John P. Lovell

Philip S. Kronenberg

ta

Transaction Books
New Brunswick, New Jersey
Distributed by E. P. Dutton and Co.

Copyright © 1974
Transaction, Inc.

Transaction Books
Rutgers University
New Brunswick, New Jersey 08903

Library of Congress Catalog Card Number: 72-94547
ISBN: 0-87855-075-5 (cloth); 0-87855-571-4 (paper)

Printed in the United States of America

To Joanne Granger Lovell and June Fell Kronenberg

CONTENTS

FOREWORD

Not too long ago discussion of civil-military relations was the preserve of a handful of academics and sundry "defense intellectuals." If there has been one positive outcome of the Vietnam agonies, it may be the democratization of public awareness of the role of the armed forces in American society. The timely and relevant thrust of this volume is to remove discussion of this controversial topic from the quagmire of ideological slogans into the realm of informed and empirically based understanding. This volume represents a commitment on the part of its contributors to move toward that goal.

It should be made especially clear at the outset that the conceptual question of the independent versus dependent relations of the military and civilian orders does not always match up with predetermined ideological stances. Indeed, we find diverse viewpoints on the conceptual question criss-crossing political positions. Thus, supporters of the military organization

have argued both for and against greater congruence between
military and civilian structures. Likewise, the harshest critics
of the armed forces have variously claimed the military establishment is either too isolated from or overlaps too much with
civil society. The point here is that a conceptual understanding
of civil-military relations can be analytically distinguished from
a political position. Of course, this perspective will please
neither the antimilitary polemicists nor the apologists for the
warfare state who have heretofore dominated the debate on the
role of the armed forces in American society.

The contrast in political evaluations and public reactions
toward the American military establishment over three wars is
revealing. In World War II, which was popularly supported,
the American military was held in almost universal high esteem.
Conservative and isolationist sectors of public opinion were
quick to fall in line behind a liberal and interventionist national leadership. In the aftermath of the Korean War, defama-
tory images of the American serviceman were propagated by
right-wing spokesmen who also charged the services with being
soft on communism. Liberal commentators, on the other hand,
generally defended the qualities of American fighting men and
the armed forces. A still different pattern has emerged from the
war in Southeast Asia. Although initially the responsibility of
a liberal administration, the pursuit of the war came to be supported by political conservatives. At the same time, the severest
attacks on the American military establishment now emanate
from the political Left.

It is cruel irony that so many of our national leaders and
opinion shapers who were silent or supported the original military intervention in Vietnam have come to adopt moralistic
postures in the wake of the horrors of that war. There appears
to be emerging a curious American inversion of the old "stab-
in-the-back" theory. Where the German general staff succeeded
in placing the blame for the loss of World War I on the ensuing
civilian leadership of the Weimar Republic, the liberal establishment in America seems to be placing the onus of the Vietnam adventure on the military. It is only a slight overstatement

to say that antimilitarism has become the anti-Semitism of the intellectual community. Rather than shortsightedly castigating the men in uniform, we ought to make the civilian militarists and the social structure that produces them the object of our critical attention.

Operating somewhat independently of events in Southeast Asia have been a host of other developments serving to tarnish the image of the American military in recent years: racial strife within the armed forces, widespread drug abuse among troops, breakdowns in discipline in many commands, corruption in the operation of post exchanges and service clubs, and military spying on civilian political activists. But even beyond Vietnam and factors unique to armed forces and society in the United States, the public depreciation of the American military establishment may well be part of a more pervasive pattern occurring throughout Western parliamentary democracies. Researchers on contemporary armed forces in Western Europe, the United Kingdom, Canada and Australia have all noted a sharp decline in the military's standing in those societies. Indeed, I am persuaded that Vietnam is a minor factor in explaining the turmoil within the American armed forces. The American military, like its counterparts in other Western post-industrialized societies, is experiencing a historical turning point with regard to societal legitimacy and public definition.

Thus, as we move into the post-Vietnam period, the relationships between America's civilian and military structures require especially informed and sustained examination. In particular, the implementation of an all-volunteer force raises pivotal questions on the social organization and social composition of the emergent military. Although interrelated, each of these new dimensions of civil-military relations deserves separate comment.

The social organization of an all-volunteer force is yet to be ascertained, but we can already identify two opposing tendencies. There may be the ascendancy of a predominantly civilianized military; the culmination of a several-decades-long trend toward transforming the armed forces from an institution into an occupation. But there are also signs that the military is undergoing a fundamental turning inward in its relations to civil society; a return to more conventional and authoritarian social patterns. The dialectical nature of the emergent military is reflected in the internal contradictions of the two polar types. A predominantly civilianized military could easily lose that élan so necessary for the functioning of a military organization. A military force uniformly moving toward more recognition of individual rights and less rigidity in social control would in all likelihood seriously disaffect career personnel while making military service only marginally more palatable to its resistant members. A predominantly traditional military, on the other hand, would most likely be incapable of either maintaining the organization at its required complexity, or attracting the kind of membership necessary for effective performance. More ominous, a traditional military in a rapidly changing society could develop anticivilian values sundering the basic fabric of democratic ideology.

The related question of the social composition of an all-volunteer force is also yet to be definitely determined. Two reports, both issued in 1970, were supposed to give firm answers to this question. A Presidential Commission headed by Thomas S. Gates concluded that the membership of an all-volunteer force would be basically unchanged in quality from that realized through conscription. The other study, contracted by the Institute for Defense Analysis, differed on virtually all counts from the Gates Commission and predicted that an all-volunteer force would significantly tend to draw its members from the less educated and the minority groups of American society. Although such mutually exclusive findings may inform us as to the ethics of sponsored social science research (whose patrons want predetermined results), they tell us precious little about the kind of people who will constitute the military in the immediate future. It is reasonable to conclude, however, that an all-volunteer force will be less socially representative than the recent membership of the armed services, but, with the significant pay raises of 1972, nowhere near exclusively dependent upon the lower social and economic classes. Most likely, that is, the rank and file of a nonconscripted military will fall somewhere between the claims of the Gates Commission and the dire predictions of an "all black" or "all poor" force.

To raise the issues of the social organization and composition of the all-volunteer force, however, does point out a major limitation in the customary framework adopted in analyses of civil-military relations. This is the presumption that civil-military relations are primarily to be understood by looking at what is happening at the top levels of the civil-military hierarchy. Students of civil-military relations typically concern themselves with issues such as the interface between the Pentagon and the Congress or executive, or military-industrial linkages, or factors and personalities operating in the formation of national strategy, or the recruitment and socialization of the regular officer corps. The view from the top is a vantage point which I believe has generally characterized the political scientist more than the sociologist; and is one which pervades some of the chapters in this book.

Yet, if recent events have taught us anything, it is that social change can be as much an outcome of the actions of people at the lower levels of the social order as it is of the designs of institutional elites. Even within the armed forces it has become apparent that profound changes in civil-military relations have resulted from anti-authoritarian behavior on the part of many lower-ranking enlisted men. Efforts to eradicate racism in the armed forces are more a response to the actions of black servicemen than to altruistic decisions made on high. Steps to give the military a human face are coming to grips with a pervasive malaise in the ranks—whether as dramatic as "fraggings" in Vietnam or the more endemic forms of efficiency withdrawal. The new civil-military relations must take into account these populist features of the nexus between armed forces and society as well as the more conventional emphasis on civil-military elites.

In the final analysis, the basic premise that the military is a creature of the demands of national strategy must be expanded to incorporate the ways that strategy goals are constrained by the willingness to fight of the members of the armed forces. This is the lesson of the new civil-military relations in American society.

CHARLES C. MOSKOS, JR.
Northwestern University
Evanston, Illinois

PREFACE

Early drafts of most of the essays that appear in this volume were presented at a conference of the Inter-University Seminar on Armed Forces and Society held in Chicago in November of 1971 and co-chaired by the editors of this volume. Thanks are due to the Inter-University Seminar for its sponsorship of the conference, to the Russell Sage Foundation for funding the conference, and to Morris Janowitz, chairman of the Inter-University Seminar. Albert Biderman, Edward Bernard Glick, Charles C. Moskos, Jr., and Gary Wamsley, who chaired panels at the conference, each provided useful comments and criticisms which helped the editors to select and revise the papers which are included in this volume. We are indebted to Dora Fortado and Pam Beaulieu for typing the final drafts of the manuscripts and to Judy Granbois for the indexing.

INTRODUCTION

1

THE AGONIES
OF ADJUSTMENT
TO POST-VIETNAM REALITIES

John P. Lovell

The war in Vietnam has been the most costly emotional experience in the history of the United States since the Civil War. The scars are deep, for each additional year of American involvement has brought further disillusionment and alienation. One is reminded of Erich Remarque's plaintive reflection of the German soldier near the end of World War I:

> Had we returned home in 1916, out of the suffering and strength of our experiences we might have unleashed a storm. Now if we go back we will be weary, broken, burnt out, rootless, and without hope. And men will not understand us—for the generation that grew up before us, though it has passed these years with us here, already had a home and a calling; now it will return to its old occupations, and the war will be forgotten—and the generation that has grown up after us will be strange to us and push us aside. We will be superfluous even to ourselves, we will

grow older, a few will adapt themselves, some others will merely submit, and most will be bewildered;—the years will pass by and in the end we shall fall into ruin.[1]

As in post-World War I Germany, so in post-Vietnam America there is weariness, rootlessness and bewilderment—not merely among young veterans, but throughout most sectors of the society.[2] Some withdraw or "cop out" as an expression of their disillusionment; others vent their frustration in revolutionary sloganeering or more socially costly forms of political action. Policy-makers—civilian and military alike—are by no means immune to the confusion of the times. It is the gap between policy, or policy prescription, and changing reality that is of major concern to us here.

Although the Vietnam experience is but one of many causes or catalysts of change (and in relation to some aspects of change, is more symbol than cause) it provides an important landmark in American historical terrain. After Vietnam, one senses, many aspects of social, political and economic life in the United States will never be the same. The authors in this volume are concerned especially with civil-military relations. However, the key changes that are occurring in civil-military relations are so intertwined with a more complex pattern of change of social and political institutions that none of the authors has been able to limit his focus exclusively to interaction between the military and the civilian sector.

Indeed, it is clear that traditional concepts and descriptions of civil-military relations, like many of the policies themselves, have become anachronistic. Traditional descriptions tend to visualize the military "man on horseback" as a menace to society and to consider the maintenance of "civil control" of the military as the overriding goal to be sought in civil-military relations. Such descriptions vastly oversimplify the present pattern of relationships and in so doing, exaggerate some problems and neglect others, as several authors in this volume mention. One of the objects of this introductory essay, and this volume, is to present an alternative to the traditional conceptualization of "civil-military relations"—a revised framework which I hope more successfully accommodates complex and dynamic features of modern political life and currently relevant issues than does the traditional formulation of the problem.

THE CHANGING POLICY ENVIRONMENT

Although the Vietnam involvement has been a traumatic episode in American foreign policy and military policy (terms that can be used almost interchangeably for most of the past 30 years), the tragic dimensions of the involvement and the current implications for civil-military relations are fully apparent only if one views the Vietnam experience within the context of the evolution of American foreign policy since World War II. Ironically, the new concepts and theories which explained and justified those policy changes, plus the civil-military bureaucracy that grew out of them, evolved into rigid myth systems and an institutional behemoth which impeded further adaptation to changing reality.

Post-World War II Transformation

As early as the 1890s, important national leaders had begun to challenge the traditional view of Washington, Jefferson and their contemporaries, that the United States must steer clear of entangling political commitments with other nations. But until World War II, no firm consensus emerged for abandoning the traditional foreign policy posture. Instead, the imperialistic adventures of the Spanish-American War period, the subsequent partial retrenchment and the efforts to avoid involvement in World War I, the crusading entry into that war, and the disillusionment and withdrawal into "isolation" of the twenties and thirties represent vacillation of policy and division among national leaders and among the public at large. Only with World War II and the resulting deep commitment of the

United States to alliances and international organization was the tradition of political nonentanglement (misleadingly termed "isolationism") decisively abandoned.[3]

Arthur Vandenberg's shift in attitude and behavior from leadership in the so-called "isolationist" wing of the Republican party in the 1930s to promotion of bipartisan support for internationalism and American commitment to alliances and international organization in the early post-World War II period is symbolic of the shift that made a new foreign policy consensus possible. As Walter Lippmann noted, Vandenberg's change of outlook had special importance because

> when a sudden and tremendous change of outlook has become imperative in a crisis, it makes all the difference in the world to most of us to see a man whom we have known and trusted, and who has thought and has felt as we did, going through the experience of changing his mind, doing it with style and dash, and in a mood to shame the devils of his own weakness.[4]

In important respects, the postwar reorientation of American foreign policy was bold and innovative, as well as broadly supported.[5] Yet the complexity of postwar problems and the rapid pace of change throughout the world in the early postwar period soon made it evident that the success of American policymakers in adapting to a dynamic environment was far less than total. Senator Vandenberg's lament in early 1947 was typical of the anguish felt by vast numbers of fellow Americans. "In a sense we are a tragic generation, despite our blessings and our place in the sun," he reflected, in a speech in the Senate supporting military and economic aid to Greece and Turkey. "We have been drawn into two World Wars. We finally won them both, and yet we still confront a restless and precarious peace. Something has been wrong. It is our supreme task to face these present realities, no matter how we hate them. . . ."[6]

By 1947 the Cold War was well under way. We need not speculate here on the causes of the Cold War nor on the question of whether it was avoidable.[7] Suffice it to note that, having embraced the assumptions about the sources of Soviet conduct articulated by George Kennan in his celebrated 8,000-word cable from Moscow, the Truman administration implemented a policy of "containment of communism" with an ideological fervor that Kennan himself regarded as excessive.[8]

Edwin Fedder's essay in this volume challenges not only the premises that underlay American policies in the heyday of "containment," but also those underlying the seemingly bold departures represented by the Nixon-Kissinger policies. As Fedder observes, the Truman-Acheson policies were pragmatically determined but ideologically articulated. With the transition to the Eisenhower-Dulles policies (a transition effected in the heated atmosphere of McCarthyism), ideology became not only the rhetorical justification of policy but also the operational basis for formulating policy options. As Fedder aptly puts it, anticommunism had become a Frankenstein monster which policy-makers had once used to rally support for policies but now found themselves unable to control.

From the Cold War to Vietnam

The Bay of Pigs invasion, a tragicomic opera staged in the name of anticommunism, launched the Kennedy administration on the same ideological course as its predecessors. Yet in disposition and pronouncement, the Kennedy administration seemed ready to break away from the heady moralism of the Dulles years. As Sorensen observed of the "team" that Kennedy assembled:

> They were, like him, dedicated but unemotional. . . . There were no crusaders, fanatics or extremists from any camp; all were nearer the center than either left or right. All spoke with the same low-keyed restraint that marked their chief, yet all shared his deep conviction that they could change America's drift.[9]

To some observers (this one included), the peaceful resolution of the Cuban missile crisis in 1962 seemed to herald an end to the Cold War; the inspiring appeal by the President in his speech at American University in June 1963 and the Test Ban Agreement of the same year seemed to indicate dramatically

that policy-makers had come to realize that the old slogans provided inadequate guidelines for policy.

Yet policies, actions and rhetoric of American policy-makers
in ensuing years showed few signs of fulfilling the dramatic
promise of the early 1960s. Instead, a prolonged involvement in
Southeast Asia provided a blatant case of institutional inertia
and of the perpetuation of new myths in a futile effort to explain away old realities.

It is instructive, although depressing, to observe that my-
opic perspectives and inflexibility can be characteristic not only
of men like John Foster Dulles, who are given to moralisms,
but also of men who pride themselves as being hardheaded
realists. While purporting to cast aside the ideological blinders
of the Eisenhower-Dulles years, the Kennedy-Johnson men created slogans and myths of their own that proved equally insidious. The so-called axioms of counterinsurgency that spewed
forth from Washington in the 1960s, for example, made up in
zeal what they lacked in empirical accuracy and sensitivity to
the nuances and complexity of revolutionary change.

Year after year, policy-makers continued to indulge not
only in the deception of the public regarding the failure of their
policies, but also to indulge in astounding feats of self-deception.
John F. Kennedy described the Vietnamese problem as one to
be resolved by the Vietnamese themselves, but nevertheless increased from a few hundred to over 16,000 men the contingent
of Americans providing military advisory support to the corrupt
Diem regime. The same administration later exerted pressures
that directly contributed to Diem's downfall and assassination.
Lyndon Johnson, lending support to a series of regimes in
Saigon in the turbulent period that followed the overthrow of
the Diem government, was returned to office in the 1964 elections as the candidate of "restraint" and "moderation," in contrast to Barry Goldwater, a "hawk" whose policy views seemed
to many voters to pose the danger of a larger war. Yet within
months of the election, the bombing of North Vietnam had
begun; American ground troops had been committed; and a
policy of escalation was in effect. Like compulsive gamblers,
President Johnson and his close advisors—civilian and military

—kept upping the ante in hopes that each new hand would bring the dramatic success that would justify the succession of earlier losses. However, the lack of candor not only in preparing the public for the costs of the involvement in Southeast Asia but also in explaining the reasons for being there at all reflected a low regard for the intelligence of the public; in time, such an attitude backfired.

The Growth of Antiwar Sentiment

As Carl Oglesby, one of the organizers of Students for a Democratic Society (SDS), observed in 1967: "One might ponder the official reasons Washington gives for our fighting in Vietnam, and think: These reasons are so bad that we must have fallen into the hands of fools. But one might also think: These reasons are so bad that there must be *other* reasons. The second thought is better." [10] On most major campuses, SDS was one of several relatively small dissident groups at the beginning of the escalation during the Johnson administration. However, disillusionment and alienation gradually spread not only among students and faculty but among the public at large.

The Tet offensive of early 1968 was the catalyst that transformed growing doubts into outright dissent on the part of vast numbers of Americans. Support for antiwar candidates Eugene McCarthy and Robert Kennedy was symptomatic of the decline of public support for the Johnson war policies. As Townsend Hoopes's account reveals, Tet also led to a crystallization of opposition within the government to further escalation.[11] President Johnson's announcement of a partial halt to the bombing of North Vietnam and of his decision not to run for reelection were a response to the sharp decline in his support inside and outside the administration.

Bruce M. Russett points out in Chapter 3 that from the early post-World War II period to the mid-sixties, the majority of Americans had indicated either satisfaction with existing levels of defense expenditures or a readiness to support even higher levels of military spending. During that period, the number of persons favoring defense cuts remained a relatively small minority of the adult population. However, beginning in 1968, opposition to military commitments and military spending mounted sharply—opposition that permeated all sectors of the society, as Russett's data reveal, and that became especially strong in the portion of the public that is most well informed and most active in politics (the "attentive public"). The significance of the shift, as Russett notes, is that, *"for the first time in more than 30 years a majority of the population has come to advocate reduction in military expenditures,* becoming, as never before, a serious potential constraint on national security policy" [emphasis in original].

Russett is sensitive to historical perspectives from which the current level of antimilitary sentiment might be interpreted as merely a periodic fluctuation in popular attitudes. (Some American military professionals console themselves in the present period of antimilitary sentiment with Rudyard Kipling's commentary on the fickle tendency of civilians to regard soldiers as scum in peacetime, but as heroes with the first hint of war.) Russett cites Gabriel Almond's classic study of American opinion, with its emphasis on the shifting "moods" in the public; and Frank Klingberg's 1952 prediction, on the basis of previous cycles of popular support in the United States for intervention or withdrawal, that by the late 1960s the United States would move into a new withdrawal phase.

On balance, however, Russett suggests that present antimilitary attitudes, although not necessarily stable in intensity and direction, represent a shift in popular views that is more than a mere swing of the pendulum. Vince Davis, in his essay in Chapter 4 on the attitudes of young American males toward military service, is even more emphatic.

Davis observes that resistance to military service has been prevalent in American society throughout the history of the republic. In the past, however, an incident that represented a dramatic insult or threat to the nation-state (or which *appeared* to do so, as in the sinking of the battleship *Maine*) could precipitate the mobilization of large numbers of otherwise reluctant persons to serve in the armed forces—especially if the

President were skillful at using the occasion to arouse public opinion. However, the trend seems to be one in which "the required magnitude of the provocative event has grown steadily larger." Indeed, neither in the case of the conflict in Korea nor in that of the involvement in Vietnam did the provocation prove sufficient to galvanize sustained public support and large-scale voluntary enlistment into the armed forces. The prospect, therefore, is that nothing less than "a dire immediate threat to the homeland" would be sufficient to mobilize large numbers of volunteers for the armed forces in the foreseeable future.

Davis notes that his analysis applies primarily to service in ground combat forces, as contrasted with air and naval forces. Industrialization not only made machine-intensive as contrasted with labor-intensive warfare practicable under many circumstances (greater reliance on aerial and naval bombardment rather than deployment of ground troops, for instance); it also made such emphasis more palatable to members of industrial societies. It is because of this trend, Davis suggests, and because the Army more than the other services has been stigmatized by the Vietnam experience, that the Army will be the service most sharply reduced in size during the 1970s.

CIVIL-MILITARY RELATIONS AT THE
COMMUNITY AND OPERATIONAL LEVEL

Peter Karsten's analysis of anti-ROTC sentiments on campuses, which sets recent anti-ROTC outbursts in historical perspective, tends to complement and to reinforce the Davis thesis. Karsten points out that "ROTC was in trouble long before the anti-ROTC movement of the late 1960s." Thus, although opposition to American involvement in Vietnam clearly intensified opposition to ROTC, Karsten suggests that "ROTC drop-outs have rejected the military and what it represents rather than the war per se."

The ROTC issue has its impact especially at what might be termed the civilian community and military operational

level. More than many of the other issues discussed in this book,
the issue falls within the domain of what traditionally has been
described as civil-military relations. That is, the traditional concern for civilian control and supervision of military organizations provides a basic reference point from which to assess the
problem. But reference points other than the traditional one of
"civil control" may be identified as well—for instance, concern
for social and geographic representativeness of recruitment into
government in general; concern for the contribution and relationship of any program in a college or university to the purposes and integrity of the university; concern for the values
and beliefs of young Americans in general, and their sense of
commitment or lack of commitment to governmental service.

Analysis of the closely related topic of the reserves and
National Guard also illustrates the limits of the "civil-military"
dichotomy. Are reservists and National Guardsmen military
personnel or civilians? Obviously, as individuals they are both,
occupying civilian and military roles at various times, the
identification with either role varying from individual to individual. In his essay in Chapter 6, John Probert makes an interesting observation regarding the policy implications of the
boundary-spanning character of the reserves and the guard.
Probert points out that the reserves and the National Guard
potentially provide an institutional link between the regular
armed forces and the civilian sector. If policy-makers recognize
this potential, the link can be used to inform the civilian public
of military requirements and policies, and to test the sentiment
of the public regarding military commitments. Under some
circumstances, feedback through the link can serve as a restraint
against military ventures that are, or would become, contrary
to public sentiment.

Probert advances the hypothesis that if President Johnson
had issued a general call-up of the reserves in 1965 (on the eve
of the major escalation), an immediate and realistic test of how
far the public was willing to go in the involvement in Vietnam
would have been provided. With this visible sign of how serious
the situation in Vietnam had become in the eyes of the Johnson
administration, the public either would have rallied in support,

bracing itself for the costly military campaigns to follow, or there would have been an outcry sufficient to dissuade the administration from such a course of action, thereby terminating the involvement at a much earlier stage.

Racial Tensions in the Military

The reserves and National Guard, and especially the regular armed forces, have been plagued in recent years by problems of discipline, morale, racial tension and drug abuse. When one turns to issues such as race and drugs, which like the ROTC and reserves issues have their effects especially at the community and operational level, reference points other than that of "maintaining civil control" become even more necessary to an adequate assessment of the problems and prospects.

Although in some respects, the armed services of the United States had led the way in the post-World War II period in establishing policies designed to promote equality of treatment and opportunity regardless of race, by the late 1960s the military, like the rest of American society, was experiencing severe racial problems. The involvement in Vietnam, which was increasingly depicted by its critics as neocolonialism and a "white man's war" for which nonwhites were being asked to make the sacrifices in disproportionate numbers, exacerbated racial tensions. In Vietnam, in Germany, at other overseas locations and within the continental United States, coping with latent if not manifest racial conflict became a top priority task for military unit commanders.

Clearly, racial tensions within the military and within the society are interrelated. To recognize the interrelationship, however, should not blind one to distinctive policies or structural characteristics of military organizations which may affect the race problem—for better or worse—in distinctive ways. Richard McGonigal identifies some of the distinctive features of recruitment, regulations, discipline, housing and informal social mores that reflect or aggravate racism within the military establishment. Especially within the past two to three years, the Defense

Department and all component arms of service have adopted
programs designed to reduce if not eliminate the inequities and
conditions that have contributed to racial tensions and conflict.
However, as many black GIs, Chicanos and others from ethnic
minorities have complained, the most serious and pervasive
racism tends to be subtle and within "the letter of the law,"
rather than blatant injustice. As McGonigal suggests, the subtle
forms of racism reflect deeply institutionalized prejudices that
are unlikely to be eradicated merely by Pentagon directives.
Such change is especially unlikely if the programs or directives
fail to provide bridges across the deep cultural chasms between
races. The "heterophily problem," which McGonigal describes
as at the core of the race issue, is one in which anxiety and
hostility are generated by exposure to a culture or subculture
fundamentally different from one's own—a problem that is aggravated, we might add, when interaction includes a phase
during which one subculture has been subordinated to the
other. Although McGonigal offers a number of specific suggestions for reform, on balance he is deeply pessimistic. Racism is
a cancer within the military, and the condition is likely to
deteriorate rather than improve in the remainder of the 1970s.

Just as racism is a societal problem with distinctive manifestations within the armed forces, so drug addiction is a problem which plagues the society as a whole, but with which the
military must cope in ways which best utilize its own resources
and which accommodate its special needs and performance
standards. The optimistic tone with which M. Scott Peck
describes the strides that the military has been making in coping
with a severe drug problem stands in sharp contrast to Mc-
Gonigal's pessimism regarding racism. Peck contends that at
the beginning of the 1970s, the drug problem within the military was considered the cause of the widespread drug problem
that plagued civilian communities and tended to detract attention from the failure of communities and the civilian sector of
government to cope effectively with their own problem. He
argues that the military's bold actions to cope with the drug
problem (including compulsory testing of servicemen for the

use of drugs with the proviso that test results should be used for treatment and cure rather than for criminal prosecution) made the military program for combatting drug abuse a model laboratory, the results of which have been of interest and benefit to other sectors of the society. Some may give the military a less complimentary scorecard than Peck does for its program to combat drug abuse, but the essay provides a discussion of the dynamics of scapegoating that has important implications for contemporary civil-military relations. Moreover, Peck's provocative suggestion that a revolutionary transformation to a better future society may be accelerated by efforts to cope with the drug problem appropriately places the problem in a broader social perspective, and takes the question of lasting cure from the medical-clinical level to that of social and political policy.

Although the agonizing clash of values in a time of intense social change is most vividly revealed by analysis of politics at the community and operational level, one must have a view of national security politics at top policy levels in order to assess the capabilities of the nation-state as a whole to adapt to changing demands.

NATIONAL SECURITY POLITICS AT TOP POLICY LEVELS

Robert Krone's discussion of policy-making in the Nuclear Planning Group (NPG) of NATO serves as a useful reminder that before, during and after the intensive American involvement in Vietnam, the issues that relate to the development and use of nuclear weapons have been central to American national security policy. Such issues include (1) the question of whether nuclear weapons in NATO are primarily for the purpose of deterrence, for defense, or merely for prestige and influence; (2) the question of whether the nuclear arsenal should be composed of "clean" or of "dirty" weapons, and of large-yield or small-yield warheads; (3) the question of what kind of provocation by an adversary would be sufficient to warrant the use of nuclear weapons; and (4) the fundamental issue of how much influence and control each member-nation should have over nuclear weapons policy.

The NPG, within which these issues are now being debated, is, Krone points out, a unique experiment in multilateral planning. It is also a fascinating political forum in which military professionals and civilian policy-makers confer, bargain and plan within and between national delegations. At all levels of NATO, complex patterns of civil-military interaction are observable both intranationally and internationally.

Secretary of Defense Robert McNamara was one of the key American policy-makers who took the initiative both in moving the United States away from the primary emphasis on a massive retaliation strategy in the direction of "flexible response" and in promoting broader participation by European allies in nuclear planning. Indeed, the genesis of the NPG can be traced to McNamara's proposal in Paris in mid-1965.

McNamara's behavior and outlook regarding NATO can be compared and contrasted to the concurrent evolution of his plans and actions regarding Vietnam. James N. Roherty provides a basis for fitting some of the seemingly disparate components of McNamara's attitudes into a coherent whole. Roherty argues that McNamara's policy outlook toward Vietnam as well as toward NATO stemmed from a rather explicit set of assumptions about the nature of the "real world" and about what means could be utilized to achieve policy effectiveness in coping with the world environment. In contrast to NATO, Vietnam was an ever-increasing source of frustration and confusion for McNamara, Roherty argues, because of the admixture of political and military ingredients that defied reduction to a simple calculus or programmed response.

In contrasting McNamara's actions and outlook with those of Melvin Laird, Roherty highlights the importance of the personality variable in national security policy-making, and the related variable that he describes as the "style" of a policy-maker. Roherty describes in detail the differences between Laird's and McNamara's managerial styles. Laird's essential pragmatism and preference for experience to abstract models as

a guide to action contrast with McNamara's quest for predictability and rationality in coping with a turbulent environment.
Likewise, Laird sought to implement a practice of "participatory management," which involved a considerable decentralization of decision-making in the department, with the Secretary
acting as a coordinator and integrator of judgments and actions
made in various specialized components of the organization.
McNamara, in contrast, sought a high degree of centralization,
in an effort to attain more control over and more standardization of procedures throughout the department.

Roherty's focus on the influence of "style" in the Department of Defense, and Krone's focus on the processes of bargaining and compromise that occur among national delegations
and within delegations in making nuclear policies for NATO,
demonstrate that national security policy emerges not from
abstract deduction of the "logical requisites" of particular situations, nor from a simple merger of "civil" and "military" considerations, but rather from a complex and highly political
process.

Samuel Huntington made a similar point several years ago.
In an in-depth study of the formulation of strategic programs
by the American government during the post-World War II
period, he noted that although strategic programs are formulated in the executive branch of government, the process of
policy formulation "bears striking resemblance to the process
in Congress." [12] That is, strategies are not designed by the application of strict rationality to an assessment of military requirements; on the contrary, strategies, like other major policies,
emerge as the result of a political process involving competing
groups and coalitions of groups, reflecting varying interests and
perspectives. As Huntington notes, failure to recognize that
the latter rather than the former description of the formulation
of strategic programs is the accurate one has led many persons to
criticize civilian and military participants (for example, the
National Security Council and the Joint Chiefs of Staff [JCS])
for acting precisely as participants in a political process typically
act.[13]

Lawrence Korb's discussion of the political behavior of the

Joint Chiefs in the budgetary process, and of the conflict between the JCS and the Secretary of Defense, reaffirms the
accuracy of Huntington's insight. From 1947, when the modern defense establishment was created, until 1965, each of the
Joint Chiefs tended to undermine the budgetary rationale that
armed services other than his own had developed, as a means
of enhancing support for his own service. As Korb notes, "The
Army constantly challenged the rationale for a large Navy; the
Air Force considered infantry troops outmoded; and the Navy
ridiculed the big slow bombers of the Air Force." In the early
years of his tenure as Secretary of Defense, Robert McNamara
was able to capitalize on these parochial differences in order
to impose his own vision of what the defense budget required.
However, Korb points out that under the leadership of General Earl Wheeler, the Joint Chiefs learned from past political
failures, and took advantage of McNamara's waning influence
with President Johnson, to present a unified front in arguing
their budget requests. In dealing with McNamara's successor,
Melvin Laird, a man generally sympathetic to the view that
military professionals should be accorded a stronger voice in the
formulation of military policies than they were granted under
McNamara, the JCS proved to be somewhat more successful
in achieving their budgetary goals than they had been in the
initial encounters with McNamara.

On the other hand, as Korb is careful to emphasize, the
picture since the appointment of Laird as Secretary of Defense
is *not* accurately describable as that of "loss of civilian control"
nor of military dominance of the budgetary process. On the
contrary, defense spending as a percentage of the total budget
and as a percentage of the gross national product has dropped
in recent years. Moreover, the pattern of interaction between
the Joint Chiefs and the Secretary of Defense is strikingly similar
to that of earlier administrations. Similar frictions are generated
by the interaction; similar budgetary procedures are utilized;
even similar types of individuals (in terms of prior career experiences and qualifications for the jobs) occupy the key roles.

Thus, to focus narrowly on the issue of the maintenance
of "civil control of the military" (as in the traditional view) is

to obscure the complex pattern of national security politics, and perhaps to miss the larger issue of the maintenance of popular control of government, whether government is dominated by civilian or military policy-makers. As Paul Schratz points out, the policies of the McNamara era and numerous other key defense-policy decisions in recent decades demonstrate that concentration of power in the hands of a *civilian* official may be equally as contrary to democratic norms as concentration of power in the hands of the military.

Schratz reminds us of the useful distinction that Alfred Vagts made, in his classic study of the history of militarism, between "militarism" and "the military way." The latter term simply referred to those techniques and practices which military organizations used to perform their assigned tasks efficiently. The former, however, referred to institutions and attitudes which glorify war or which romanticize or perpetuate military practices, customs or attributes beyond the purpose of contributing to combat efficiency. Militarism, Vagts emphasized, could be found among civilians as well as among military men.[14]

Schratz draws upon Vagts's distinction to discuss a paradox that he has observed in recent American foreign policy, most notably and with disastrous effects in Vietnam: American policies have been militaristic, in the sense of exaggerating military considerations and neglecting political ones, *not because policy was too much in the hands of military leaders but rather because the military participated too little* in contributing to the development of policy! Schratz contends that American military leaders long have isolated themselves from social, political and economic considerations of policy—justifying such isolation to themselves in lofty terms of "subordination of the military" to civilian supremacy in the policy process. Civilian leaders, in turn, when they have deferred to the judgment of military men on issues seemingly falling in the latter's domain, often have accepted uncritically advice in which political considerations were neglected in favor of military ones, narrowly defined. Or at the opposite extreme, civilian officials sometimes have ignored military leaders, preferring instead to act as their own military strategists. As an example of the latter behavior, Schratz cites McNamara's perfunctory response to military advice during the early stages of escalation in Vietnam.

Many persons will disagree with Schratz's assertion that military leaders did not participate in a major way in the formulation of U.S. policies in Vietnam. The influence of General Maxwell Taylor on particular decisions could be cited, for instance, or that of Taylor's protegée, General William Westmoreland, or of Westmoreland's West Point classmate, General Creighton Abrams. However, to argue about the relative influence of particular civilian or military officials on the selection of a particular course of action at a particular point in time may be to miss a more fundamental set of questions that becomes apparent when American involvement in Vietnam is viewed from a broader level of analysis.

When one takes as the object of analysis not a single decision or set of closely interrelated decisions, but rather a pattern of behavior over a relatively broad span of time, the key questions are no longer that of Who made the decision? and Who influenced the decision? but rather that of What factors best explain regularities in behavior over time? and What values, beliefs and structures determined the policy options that were perceived as available and the priorities that influenced choices among options? The influence of the American military and the "military-industrial complex" are among the factors that must be considered when answering these questions in terms of the Vietnamese experience; but imprecision about what is meant by "the military" and "the military-industrial complex" often hinders the analytical judgments that are made.

As suggested earlier, the broad pattern of American involvement in Southeast Asia—and indeed of much of American foreign policy in the decade of the 1960s—was a pursuit of goals that continually proved to be elusive, if not ill-formulated in the first place—a pattern of pouring "good money after bad." If one explains the pattern of escalation as essentially conspiratorial, depicting "the military" or "the military-industrial complex" as groups who willfully manipulated policy for their own self-interest, then one has to explain away the now-abundant evidence of opposition to the policies by some high-ranking military men (and by many lower ranking ones) and among major elements of the defense industry and the "corporate rich."

We feel that a more subtle and more accurate explanation of the pattern is provided if one views "the military" and "the military-industrial complex" not as groups of supposedly powerful men allegedly harboring warlike and imperialistic goals, but as terms to describe *structural components* of the American political system. Existing structures (patterns of roles) in turn tend to be associated with patterns of values and beliefs—with organizational "subcultures," to use a shorthand description. From a structural perspective, the mere fact that a vast civil-military bureaucracy had been created in the 1940s and 1950s as the instrument of Cold War policies (with defense commitments to 43 military allies, U.S. military aid to more than twice that number of nation-states, deployment of more than a million U.S. military personnel in more than 300 installations abroad), helps to explain why no sharp reorientation of U.S. policies away from the Cold War occurred in the 1960s. Moreover, what is salient about the linkages between the defense bureaucracy, defense industry, various members of Congress and sectors of the scientific and academic communities is not that they plotted joint action in the policy arena, but rather that their relationships tended to be symbiotic in the direction of maintaining or expanding existing policies and programs, rather than of assuming the risks inherent in radical departures from existing policies.[15] Moreover, such linkages rendered rigorous cost-accounting of policies and programs impossible because the accounts were maintained largely by those who stood to lose if candid and accurate assessments of the programs were made.

The mythology of anticommunism that had been created as the handmaiden of the massive complex of governmental and quasi-governmental bureaucracy also contributed to policy inertia. No doubt the late Charles Lerche was at least partially correct in suggesting that the leaders of the United States as well as those of the Soviet Union found it useful in terms of maintaining power positions at home and abroad to perpetuate

Cold War rhetoric even after the two sides had found ways of coexisting peaceably.[16] As James Thomson has observed, "the legacy of the 1950s" pervaded the State Department and other governmental institutions subsequently, with paralyzing consequences for American policies in Vietnam.[17]

To discuss structural features and patterns of values and beliefs that impinge upon or influence national security policies is to move well beyond the limits of traditional descriptions of "civil-military relations." In lieu of a view that postulates a neat dichotomy between "civil" and "military" sectors, we have moved to one which focuses on the politics of national security, a process in which various structures compete on behalf of differing value preferences, and in which tradeoffs are made between defense-related and other values.

In his essay Davis Bobrow identifies several of the tradeoffs that ought to be made, and several that probably will be made, between national security and other values in the years ahead. His analysis challenges the underlying assumptions and the narrow definition of national security in the past, and offers a provocative but rigorous framework for formulating national security policies for the future.

In important respects, as noted above in reference to the Russett essay, the altered climate of public opinion that has emerged since 1968 has constrained policy development. However, it is also important to recognize that in other respects the shift in opinion has had a liberating effect on policy-makers, enabling them at last to discard (or at any rate to tone down) the rhetoric of the Cold War and to reexamine many of the assumptions underlying post-World War II policies. Bobrow identifies a number of premises on which American national security policy throughout most of the Cold War period was based. As he notes, policies and actions such as the Nixon doctrine, the SALT agreements, and the negotiations with China and with the Soviet Union represent a movement away from the earlier premises in favor of some sharply contrasting assumptions.

Yet, as Bobrow suggests, even the relatively bold policy departures taken during the Nixon administration may not be sufficient to cope with the changing international and domestic realities of the 1970s. His analysis is designed to push policy analysis and debate not only beyond the outmoded concepts and assumptions of the Cold War era, but also beyond discussion of how future Vietnams might be avoided. As he notes, "Simply because a particular security posture avoids the last war does not necessarily make it good." The intellectual requirement that confronts us in trying to formulate national security policies appropriate to the post-Vietnam era is not only that of recognizing the limitations and inadequacies of prior policies and policy assumptions. Rather, as Bobrow warns, the challenge of the present era also requires a perspective in which national security policies have merit not simply when war is avoided but according to a more complex criterion, including responsiveness to domestic needs and popular control in our own society, and recognition of the desirability of such responsiveness by other regimes to their societies.

The warning by Philip Kronenberg, in the concluding essay, complements that issued by Bobrow. Kronenberg contends that it is the "security-democracy dilemma"—the challenge of reconciling security needs with democratic values—rather than such an unlikely contingency as a military coup d'etat that ought to occupy the attention of those concerned with civil-military relations in America. However, deficiencies in national security structures and perceptual distortions by policy elites impede resolution of the dilemma. Structural deficiencies produce or perpetuate policy error. Moreover, the failure to recognize the complexity of the organizational network involved in national security leads to the imposition of monolithic solutions on a highly differentiated set of structures, with disastrous possibilities.

Military and civilian members of the defense establishment differ as to what adjustments of policy, program and organization are needed in the aftermath of Vietnam and in response to other problems. Estimates range from "none" to "total." As a result, most of the policy and program changes initiated in recent years have had their impassioned internal critics as well as their enthusiastic proponents. The All-Volunteer Army, for

instance, has been bitterly opposed by many military professionals (some on the grounds that it will further isolate the
military from the society), whereas others regard the move to
total voluntarism as thoroughly desirable, a means of getting
rid of malcontents and of thereby improving morale and discipline.

An "identity crisis" plagues civilian as well as military
members of the national security establishment. Ambivalence
and doubt among military professionals, in particular, extend
not only to their self-image but also to the image held by military professionals about the rest of the society. Subjected to a
loss of popular esteem and to heated criticism for their part in
an unpopular war, some military professionals see themselves as
victimized, and society as having been corrupted and led astray
by traitorous critics or weak-kneed politicians.[18] Others take a
sharply different view, arguing that events and actions of recent
years have demonstrated important deficiencies within the
military, and that the military must undertake profound self-
evaluation and reform.[19]

Although differing points of view regarding professionalism
and the relation of the military to the rest of the society are
found within every arm of service and within every grade level,
probably the most persistent rift is that between younger military men (officers, non-coms and enlisted men) and older military professionals.[20] The "generation gap" which separates the
views of many older officers and noncoms from young officers
and enlisted men is of course found among civilian members of
the national security establishment as well. Moreover, the
structural characteristics of military organizations which aggravate the gap and impede communication between those
occupying roles of differing status are also found in civilian
bureaucracy. Layers of bureaucracy and the inhibitions of
subordinate roles in the compliance structure make it difficult
for the young GI, the young officer or the young civil servant
to communicate his feelings accurately to those farther up the
hierarchy. The young subordinate often has had more formal
education than those who supervise him, thereby aggravating

the resentment felt by the subordinate and the anxieties experienced by the supervisor.[21] As Kronenberg notes, these and
other structural characteristics of the defense bureaucracy are
too often ignored by policy-makers, who prefer to apply simplistic principles of management and policy-making to what is,
in reality, a complex of many organizations, each with its own
distinctive technology, recruitment base, traditions and needs.

Civilian and military leaders often are insulated not only
from their subordinates but also from other sectors of society.[22]
To the extent that top civil and military leaders are insulated
from their subordinates and from the society of which they are
a part (not all leaders are significantly insulated, fortunately),
the danger lies not only in a probable failure to detect problems
and changes to which they ought to respond, but (perhaps more
serious) also in a tendency to work vigorously at providing
solutions that are inappropriate.

To cite the dangers and the structural impediments to
reform is not to say that no constructive changes are occurring
nor that the prospect is necessarily bleak. (Like the reports of
Mark Twain's death, those proclaiming the demise of the Army
or of the other armed services have been greatly exaggerated.[23])
Indeed, the current period is one of ferment and innovation
within the professional military establishment and within
civilian agencies concerned with national security policies. One
might point not only to the SALT talks, the negotiations with
China and the Soviet Union, and the Nixon Doctrine, but also
to such changes as experimentation with assignment of destroyer
commands to especially able young naval officers (in the so-called
"Mod Squad"), positions traditionally reserved for more senior
officers; tolerance of beards and mustaches in the Navy; beer in
Army mess halls; "Today's Army Wants to Join You" recruitment themes; encouragement of servicemen on drugs to seek
treatment without fear of punishment; "rap sessions" and encounter groups between black and white servicemen, and utilization of black enlisted men as advisors to post commanders on
race problems; efforts to make ROTC programs more aca-
demically respectable; and increased concern with the status of

women in the armed forces. Some of the changes are merely cosmetic, to be sure; but many reflect creative efforts to adapt to changing times and changing needs.

Encouraging as some of the signs of ferment are, however, it is by no means certain that the military profession, or the national security establishment of which it is a part, will emerge from the aftermath of Vietnam a more vigorous and vital institution than before. General Michael Davison, recently Commanding General of the U.S. 7th Army in Germany, identified both the difficulties and the opportunities of the times when he described "this as the toughest period that we've ever faced. And yet I retain my confidence. I think it is a tremendous challenge . . . that ought to motivate all of us to do our damnedest, because if we're successful in restoring the worth and value of the Army then we've done the country a great service." [24]

It is clear that Vietnam and other sources of turbulence in the domestic and world environments have had an agonizing effect upon the institutions that are involved in the politics of American national security. It is *not* clear that the "lessons" that policy-makers (and all of us) are actively attempting to wrench from the Vietnam experience to apply as presuppositions for future action will be accurate ones. That the lessons are being debated, however, and that current policy assumptions and priorities are being challenged from within the government as well as from without, improve the chances for the evolution of policies that are both knowledgeably based and broadly responsive to the needs and desires of the nation.

A REVISED FRAMEWORK FOR ANALYSIS

At several points in the preceding discussion, limitations and inaccuracies of the traditional concept of "civil-military relations" as applied to contemporary problems have been identified. From such discussion, an alternative to the traditional conceptualization has been introduced—implicitly if not explicitly. In the concluding pages of this introductory essay, the alternative conceptualization will be made more explicit.

In lieu of traditional descriptions, we find it useful to con-ceive of civil-military relations broadly as an issue area within the turbulent context of politics and policy-making, acknowledging the complexity of American civil and military institutions and the blurring of boundaries between the two sectors. In effect, our concern is with U.S. national security policies and politics, and especially with the consequences or implications for such policies and politics of the vast changes that have swept the world and American society in recent decades. The terms "national security policy" and "foreign policy" are used almost interchangeably in the volume because throughout the Cold War era and in such important areas of concern as Southeast Asia, American foreign policy has been dominated by military-security considerations.

Viewed in the broadest perspective, foreign policy is the primary means by which policy-makers attempt, on behalf of a national political system, to adapt to the geopolitical world environment, and by which they attempt to impose a measure of control over the environment in order to achieve their goals. The relationship between system and environment is dynamic; both are constantly changing, thereby posing one another with changing demands and opportunities.

Following David Easton's definition (which in turn draws upon the pioneering work of Arthur Bentley), politics may be viewed as the process by which values are authoritatively allocated in a political system. National security politics are those in which choices are made among values identified with the goal of "national security," or believed to be instrumental to national security, and competing values. The choices, of course, are rarely of the either-or variety, but rather are made in terms of emphasis—in terms of the amounts and kinds of resources that should be committed on behalf of various policy objectives over various periods of time. The nature of politics, involving as it does a struggle over the allocation of scarce resources, is that tradeoffs must be made—a major commitment to one set of goal-values (for example, victory in war) often involves a compromise of other values (for example, individual freedom). The choices sometimes are agonizing, pitting groups against one

another who differ intensely in their views of the kinds of tradeoffs that are appropriate or even legitimate.

The politics of American national security in the present
era are troublesome and frustrating in part because rapid
changes have called into question most of the assumptions
underlying long-standing policies and programs, and have led
many groups within the political system to argue that priorities need to be revised. Moreover, changes in the environment diminish the salience of some kinds of political resources
and increase the salience of others, thereby changing the relative influence of competing groups in the political arena. Any
attempt to depict the present political process conceptually
necessarily involves gross simplifications. Nonetheless, as an
introduction to more detailed discussion that follows in this
and subsequent chapters it may be helpful to attempt such a
conceptual sketch. In Exhibit 1, the relationship etween the
changing geopolitical world and domestic environment and that
portion of the American political system that is concerned with
national security policies is depicted as a cybernetic process.

Changing demands and supports from the external and
domestic environments stimulate changes in the priorities that
groups and individuals have regarding political goal-values,
and changes in the salience of various kin of political resources. From such changes come changes in power structure,
leading to changes in policy; policy change in turn impacts
upon the environment (depicted by the feedback loop), serving
as a stimulant to further change.

The dynamics of the process become more apparent as one
moves from an abstract description to a specifi ation of the kinds
of changes that are occurring in the environment currently,
and to a consideration of the implications of such changes for
national security politics (Exhibit 2). We need not attempt to
describe in detail the examples included in Exhibit 2; the
essays that follow provide elaboration of significant changes
that are occurring in the external and domestic environments,
and suggest implications of such changes for national security
politics. Some of the structural and semantic distinctions that

**Exhibit 1: CHANGING ENVIRONMENT
AND CHANGING NATIONAL SECURITY POLICIES:
A CYBERNETIC PROCESS**

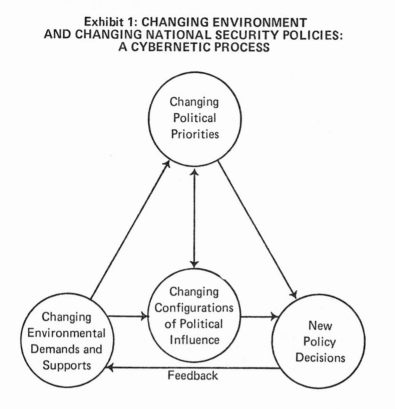

are made in Exhibit 2 need to be mentioned, however, for purposes of clarification and emphasis.

In the second column of Exhibit 2, a number of values are listed (not necessarily in order of importance) that frequently are described as objectives of national security policy, or as instrumental to the maintenance of national security. In the third column, a number of other values are listed—some (for example, accountability of policy-makers to the public) related to preferences for democratic institutions; some (for example, economic prosperity) representing desires that most Americans feel on behalf of themselves and their families; some (for example, arms control) reflecting the widespread yearning for international peace. Many other values might have been added. However, those listed in columns two and three are illustrative

Exhibit 2: THE DYNAMICS OF CHANGE OF PRIORITIES AND ISSUES IN NATIONAL SECURITY POLITICS

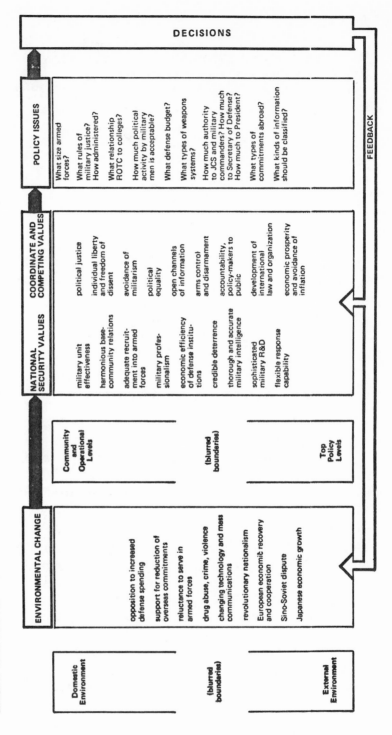

of the kinds of values that often compete in national security policy-making.

Unfortunately, discussions of national security policy often focus exclusively on the values in column two to the neglect of those in column three, thereby presenting a distorted picture of what is at stake for a society in considering a given issue. As suggested in Exhibit 2, the issues of national security politics are ones which involve potential gains or costs not only in terms of the values listed under the "national security" heading, but also in terms of values such as those in column three. In considering the question of what size armed forces the society should maintain, for example, one appropriately might make an assessment not only of force levels deemed necessary to provide support for diplomatic objectives, deterrence, a mobile striking force or other goal-values suggested in column two, but an assessment also of the probable responsiveness of a military establishment at various force levels to popular needs and desires, of the likelihood of maintaining individual liberty with a military establishment of various sizes, and of similar values indicated in column three. In short, national security policy decisions, like all policy decisions, involve tradeoffs among competing values.

The present era of change (including changes such as those in column one of Exhibit 2) challenges existing policy assumptions and the priorities that have been accorded to various values in national security policy making. The issues suggested in column four are among the central ones that have arisen as a consequence of the challenges to assumptions and priorities. How any one of us would want to have the various issues resolved will, of course, depend upon the preferences that we have in terms of competing values, our judgment about the nature and magnitude of current and future threats to national security, and our assessment of available resources. Apart from our normative preferences, the empirical questions of how the issues will in fact be resolved is contingent upon the existing power configurations, which also are susceptible to change in response to changing environment (as suggested in Exhibit 1, but not in Exhibit 2, because of limitations of space). The policy decisions that are made in response to each of the various issues in turn affect subsequent opportunities and challenges in the domestic and world environments (as the feedback loops in Exhibits 1 and 2 suggest).

An analytical distinction is made in Exhibit 2, and in the organization of the volume, between adaptation to change at the community and operational level (efforts by military post commanders and civilian community leaders, for instance, to work out mutually amicable guidelines to cope with a growing drug traffic) and adaptation at top governmental levels (such as weapons systems decisions made in DOD). Obviously the distinction is somewhat artificial. Guidelines are established in Washington for coping with such problems as drugs, racism and antiwar protest, although the successful implementation of the guidelines hinges upon the skill and sensitivity of leaders at the community and operational level. Nevertheless, the distinction may have the usefulness of highlighting the fact that significant issues of civil-military relations (that is, issues of national security politics) impinge upon the individual citizen and the individual member of the armed forces, and their respective communities and units, as well as upon the top-level organizations that are usually the focus of attention in discussions of national security affairs.

To develop fully the analysis suggested by the framework provided in Exhibits 1 and 2 would require several volumes rather than one. We cannot attempt here to consider all of the pertinent questions, nor to analyze all of the potentially interesting implications of the dynamic process of interaction sugges ed. However, a number of important concepts are examined he essays that follow; a number of critical policy decisions a d pro ams are analyzed; and a number of important questions are raised if not definitively answered. The common theme is that we are entering—however painfully and awkwardly—a new era in American foreign relations. The challenges of this new era require not only a bold and critical reassessment of existing national security policies, but also an adaptation and revision of the traditional concepts and perspectives that have been our guidelines for policy.

NOTES

1. Erich Maria Remarque, *All Quiet on the Western Front,* trans. A. W. Wheen (Boston: Little, Brown, 1928) pp. 289-290.

2. Like all historical analogies, this one can be overdrawn, of course. Nonetheless, the elements of similarity of the two situations are worthy of serious contemplation. For example, in comparison to Remarque's description of the anguish and doubt experienced by the post-World War I German soldier, consider the plight and emotions of the American veteran of the war in Vietnam described in a recent study, "Wasted Men," Veterans World Project, mimeographed, (Edwardsville, Ill.: Southern Illinois University, 1972).

3. See Albert K. Weinberg, "The Historical Meaning of the American Doctrine of Isolation," *American Political Science Review,* 34 (June 1940):539-547. For a refutation of the thesis that American policies in the 1920s and 1930s were "isolationist," see William A. Williams, "The Legend of Isolationism," *Science and Society,* 18 (Winter 1954): 1-20.

4. Lippmann, as quoted by Arthur H. Vandenberg, Jr., ed., with Joe Alex Morris, *The Private Papers of Senator Vandenberg* (Boston: Houghton Mifflin, 1952) p. xxi.

5. For a glowing appraisal by a participant in policy-making at the time, see Joseph Marion Jones, *The Fifteen Weeks: An Inside Account of the Genesis of the Marshall Plan* (New York: Harcourt, Brace and World, 1955).

6. Vandenberg, *Private Papers of Senator Vandenberg,* p. 348.

7. For three contrasting interpretations, see Lloyd C. Gardner, Arthur Schlesinger, Jr. and Hans J. Morgenthau, *The Origins of the Cold War* (Waltham, Mass.: Ginn-Blaisdell, 1970).

8. George F. Kennan, *Memoirs: 1900-1950* (Boston: Little, Brown, 1967). Kennan discusses the Truman Doctrine and his views of it in Chapter 13. The cable is discussed in Chapter 11 and is reproduced in an appendix.

9. Theodore C. Sorensen, *Kennedy* (New York: Bantam Books, 1966) p. 287.

10. Carl Oglesby, "Vietnamese Crucible," in Carl Oglesby and Richard Shaull, *Containment and Change* (New York: Macmillan, 1967) p. 7.

11. Townsend Hoopes, *The Limits of Intervention* (New York: McKay, 1969).

12. Samuel P. Huntington, *The Common Defense: Strategic Programs*

in National Politics (New York: Columbia University Press, 1961) p. 146.

13. Ibid., pp. 166-174.

14. Alfred Vagts, *A History of Militarism: Civilian and Military*, rev. ed. (New York: Meridian Books, 1959) pp. 13-17.

15. The point is well documented in Bruce M. Russett, *What Price Vigilance? The Burdens of National Defense* (New Haven: Yale University Press, 1970).

16. Charles O. Lerche, Jr., *The Cold War . . . And After* (Englewood Cliffs, N.J.: Prentice-Hall, 1965) pp. 29-34.

17. James C. Thomson, Jr., "How Could Vietnam Happen? An Autopsy," *The Atlantic Monthly*, 22 (April 1968): 47-53. Reprinted in *The Politics of U.S. Foreign Policy Making*, ed. Douglas M. Fox (Pacific Palisades, Calif.: Goodyear, 1971) pp. 299-309. Also reprinted in slightly abbreviated form in *No More Vietnams? The War and The Future of American Foreign Policy*, ed. Richard M. Pfeffer (New York: Harper and Row, 1968) pp. 44-50.

18. For example, see Captain Robert J. Hanks, USN (ret.), "Against All Enemies," *U.S. Naval Institute Proceedings*, 96 (March 1970): 23-29. The Hanks article was selected as the 1970 Prize Essay in the *Proceedings*.

19. See Col. Robert G. Gard, Jr., USA, "The Military and American Society," *Foreign Affairs*, 49 (July 1971): 698-710. Also Col. Richard F. Rosser, USAF, "American Civil-Military Relations in the 1980's," *Naval War College Review*, 24 (June 1972): 6-23.

20. For example, see Commander James A. Barber, Jr., USN, "Is There a Generation Gap in the Naval Officer Corps?", *Naval War College Review*, 22 (May 1970): 24-33; also, a study conducted by the U.S. Army War College, *Leadership for the 1970's* (Carlisle Barracks, Pa.: Army War College, July 1971); and a poll of 29,000 airmen and 12,000 Air Force officers described in "AF Poll on U.S. Problems Identifies Age, Ethnic Gaps," *Navy Times*, Nov. 3, 1971.

21. The Moskos study of the enlisted subculture in the Army provides the shrewd insight that egalitarian as well as authoritarian aspects of the military have tended to be important sources of irritation for college-educated enlisted men. Such individuals typically come from middle-class or upper-class backgrounds, and resent being on equal status with, or in subordinate status to, men who have had less formal education and who tend to come from working-class backgrounds. Charles C. Moskos, Jr., *The American Enlisted Man* (New York: Russell Sage, 1970) Chap. 3.

22. For example, see the discussion by Lewis H. Lapham, "Military Theology," *Harper's* (July 1971) p. 76.

23. For example, see Edward L. King, *The Death of the Army: A Pre-Mortem* (New York: Saturday Review Press, 1972).

24. Quoted by Haynes Johnson and George C. Wilson in the first of a series of reports on the Army that appeared in the *Washington Post* in September 1971, collected and reprinted as *Army in Anguish* (New York: Pocket Books, 1972) p. 28.

THE CHANGING
POLICY ENVIRONMENT

2

U.S. COMMITMENTS AND ALLIANCES: SOME IMPLICATIONS OF THE CHANGING INTERNATIONAL ENVIRONMENT

Edwin H. Fedder

THE PATTERN OF COMMITMENT

Since 1947, the United States has constructed a global network of "interlocking" alliances designed to extend an American guarantee to any "free" nation that might come under the threat of or an actual attack by a "communist" nation. The alliance policy of the United States, best exemplified by NATO, established a U.S. role different from those which preceded America's entrance into big-power politics after World War II, a role that encouraged American decision-makers to reject notions of national separation, nonalignment, neutrality and noninvolvement not only for the United States but for others as well. The result has been a very rapid expansion of the number of alliances involving the United States; by 1955 we were allied with 42 nations.

Although they hardly seemed so at the time, our early post-war steps were rather halting and hesitant when compared to some of our more recent adventures. The Truman Doctrine asserted a guarantee and implemented limited technical, military and economic assistance programs to Greece and Turkey. The Marshall Plan was little more than a concept until it was put into operation by the "users," the Organization for European Economic Cooperation. And NATO was developed at least as much in response to European demands as to American initiative.

In other parts of the world, our profile was considerably lower. The Rio Pact of 1947 was designed to put into practice the multilateral Monroe Doctrine that had been articulated in the charter of the Organization of American States. By and large, we were virtually nonparticipant observers of developments in the Middle East, South-Southeast Asia and Africa. We occupied Japan, offered some aid and comfort to Chiang-Kai-shek and were content with the division of Korea.

At that time our foreign policy was pragmatically determined. The Soviet Union alone was capable of doing us great harm. Since capability was widely held to be father of the deed, diminishing that capability would reduce the likelihood of the deed, and there were two ways to effect that reduction: the adversary could reduce its advantages unilaterally; or one of the adversaries could increase its capability disproportionately vis-à-vis the other. Since the United States could not assume that the Soviet Union would diminish its capability of its own accord, such diminution, it was felt, would have to be imposed upon the Russians externally, if at all.

In essence, the assorted steps taken by the Truman administration from 1947 to 1949 added up to a foreign policy which was designed to prevent Soviet power and influence from spreading in Europe. The underlying assumptions of that foreign policy begged the question of Soviet intentions to expand; nor did it suggest any significant self-analytical preoccupation with notions of grand designs or even predetermined sets of preferred future behaviors on the part of American decision-makers. No ideological traumas were induced by accommodation to fascist governments in Portugal and Spain or to the communist government of Yugoslavia. The decision to diminish the Soviet threat was based upon assessment of Soviet capability, not Soviet ideology.

But Truman's foreign policy was articulated in ideological, not pragmatic terms. The *coup de Prague,* the Berlin blockade, Russian policy regarding the Baltic states were all presented as evidence of the depravity and essentially limitless ambitions of Stalin to extend his domain. Such articulation catered to popular and congressional emotions and was pragmatically calculated to marshal sufficient support for the Truman programs. Such articulation also inadvertently reinforced the development of often-virulent anticommunist movements, exemplified by the career of the late Senator Joseph McCarthy of Wisconsin. At the risk of straining the analogy, anticommunism became for the Truman administration a Frankenstein monster bent upon the destruction of its creator.

As the Truman-Acheson foreign policy was pragmatically determined, the Eisenhower-Dulles foreign policy was ideologically determined. Dulles viewed communism as monolithic and predatory. Communist states, including China, were viewed as extensions of Soviet power and as instruments for achieving Soviet designs for global domination. To meet this threat, the Secretary sought to ring the Soviet bloc with multilateral alliances designed to accomplish for the Middle East (through the Baghdad Pact) and South-Southeast Asia (through SEATO) what NATO was presumed to have achieved for Europe. This structure was to be buttressed by a variety of "commitments," patterned after the Truman Doctrine, and by bilateral alliances with Taiwan and Japan. Indeed, in a very few years, the United States was making alliances and commitments with virtually any country that proclaimed itself anticommunist and indicated interest in such an alliance or commitment.

The NATO and Truman Doctrine models proved to be very seductive to Dulles despite the fact that the necessary and sufficient conditions for NATO did not hold elsewhere and despite the fact that the culprit in Greece (the *raison d'etre* of the doctrine) was not Soviet expansionism but Yugoslav meddling in troubled waters. The Baghdad Pact did not arise out of the Arab states' perceptions of imminent Soviet threat, nor was its structure and organization based upon Middle Eastern precedents. Indeed, although the pact was intended to link Arab states, only Iraq joined, and that move precipitated a revolution and subsequent withdrawal. Although the coalition's name was changed to Central Treaty Organization (CENTO), Arab rejection remained total. SEATO's experience was parallel: it was not organized in response to indigenous demand; it did not represent indigenous perceptions of threat; and only one principal local state, Pakistan, joined. Pakistan has since entered into alliance with China (the principal target of SEATO) against India, while retaining membership in SEATO.

Apparently, CENTO and SEATO have been counterproductive in terms of greater increments of security for the United States. Both CENTO and SEATO were viewed as thinly veiled attempts to perpetuate or reintroduce colonialism and imperialism into their respective regions. As such, their behavior was perceived as far more threatening than Soviet activity.

Dulles' convictions about the depravity of Soviet ambitions led him to insist that nations that did not support the United States were *ipso facto* aiding and abetting the Soviet Union. Nations that were willing to place themselves on the firing line were entitled to the strongest possible levels of American support. Fence-straddlers discovered rather quickly that they could virtually guarantee American support by threatening to turn to the Russians if the United States balked.

By the end of Dulles' tenure, every state that perceived or claimed to perceive a communist threat or threatened to go over to the other side was embraced in a commitment that was nurtured by U.S. technical, economic and military assistance. Receiving American assistance became a major industry for many national economies. While it would be difficult to determine the motives of government officials in receiving countries, it certainly seems clear that the production of side-benefits far exceeded any additional increments of security.

The Dulles alliance ring served as a sort of Berlin wall

separating hostile camps. Two global spheres of influence were separated by the ring, with each of the superpowers tacitly agreeing not to intrude in the other's sphere. It was essentially a rather passive arrangement in which discordances occurred infrequently and usually on our side. Many critics argued that we had adopted a largely defensive posture designed to react to communist initiatives, thereby according to the enemy the advantages of selecting the timing and location of probing maneuvers.

In addition, we adopted a policy of massive retaliation that was either inconsistent with global containment or sufficiently nonrational to be unfeasible. Massive retaliation required, by definition, raising the stakes of responding to communist challenges so high that had such challenges occurred, the threatened response would have been unlikely or catastrophically excessive. Other than adding significantly to U.S. defense costs and to the rhetoric of the Cold War, the concept of commitments was neither particularly viable nor operationally significant.

Upon coming into office, the Kennedy administration shifted to a policy of flexible response which was designed to increase American capabilities for fighting limited conventional and nuclear wars. The concept of commitment was thereby made viable and operationally feasible. The increased mobility and striking power of U.S. forces was capable of flexible initiative as well as response. The new administration was convinced that responding to challenge was inherently too limiting and uncharacteristically too passive for American foreign policy.

A new scenario emerged that indicated that communism was spreading too easily and too rapidly in the underdeveloped world because it operated in a void left by the passivity of democracy. Were the forces of freedom to enter the struggle and provide an alternative, communism could be placed on the defensive. Thus, we begat nation-building and counterinsurgency, as if we knew what we were about regarding either of those elusive notions.

Dulles' conceptualization of commitment as rewarding those who chose our side in a bipolarized global alignment was not terribly threatening since it did not suggest efforts at rolling back the perimeters of communist domain. In contrast, the Kennedy and Johnson administrations redefined commitment as an active, aggressive concept. We articulated a commitment to resist by force attempts at forcible conquest. But we also asserted a commitment, particularly in Vietnam, to create conditions that would alter the status quo by substituting positive change in lieu of passive acceptance. This was dramatically evidenced in pressuring Diem, and in the Tonkin Gulf and other incidents.

THE NIXON POLICIES

The Nixon administration's vaunted lower profile is still taking shape; however, some preliminary observations concerning commitments and alliances may be suggested. First, bilateral or multilateral alliances assume significantly lower priority than in the four previous postwar administrations. While preferring negotiation to confrontation with our declared adversaries, we have preferred confrontation to negotiation with our principal allies. The failure to consult with Japan or, less significantly, Taiwan about the opening to China signaled a major devaluation of our bilateral alliances with each. The Japan-U.S. Security Pact can no longer be looked upon as the keystone to our security policy in Asia. The first Kissinger mission communicated a sense of urgency to Japan to begin making its own arrangements for accommodating China. Any possible interference in such signals was taken care of by floating the dollar and imposing the 10 per cent surcharge on imports without notice, much less consultation or prior attempts at negotiating differences.

The keystone to our European security policy, West Germany, was the other prime target of the new economic policy. Certainly Germany's *Ostpolitik*—initiatives toward detente with the East—was reinforced if not given added impetus by American unilateralism. It should be recalled that Brandt's first articulation of the *Ostpolitik* was met by sharply hostile reactions from the Nixon administration on the grounds that it would inherently weaken NATO. The alliance, then, was to be preferred to detente, which was an elusive target at best. Today, it would seem that detente is a higher order of priority than is the alliance.

A related item should be noted, although full discussion would carry far beyond the limits of this essay. The Nixon administration demonstrates little concern for the nuances of multilateral diplomacy so vigorously championed by its predecessors. The new economic policy was invoked in a fashion more reminiscent of de Gaulle's unilateral demands upon the Common Market than of the Kennedy Round tariff negotiations. Cynical grandstanding on the Chinese representation question at the UN was not calculated to protect and defend UN interests while promoting our own—yet they were not incompatible. The United States wants less emphasis on the UN, not more. Similarly, it seeks less emphasis on the various alliances. It apparently exalts the American national role, rejecting the binding ties of internationalism, wispy and limp as they are.

The Nixon-Kissinger conceptualization of commitment is essentially passive, reminiscent of Dulles' usage. But there is an important difference. Dulles' passivity was rooted in a conceptualized international system that was bipolarized in two implacably hostile camps. The ring of commitments and alliances represented the frontier of American concern—the outer perimeter whose breach might invoke retaliation upon a massive scale directed against the opposite pole. The Nixon-Kissinger commitment is rooted in an essentially nonpolarized international system comprising national units, states, that interact according to agreed-upon rules of behavior based upon long-standing custom and usage. States base their activities upon national interests; i.e., national values are more significant than are international values.

Comparing Nixon-Kissinger policy regarding Taiwan to that of Eisenhower-Dulles illustrates the contrast very well. During the Korean War, the United States stationed some forces on Taiwan and mounted a naval patrol off the Taiwan Straits.

The devices were continued after the war to underscore our commitment to defend Taiwan from an invasion by the Communist Chinese that was neither imminent nor likely to become imminent. At the same time, it "guaranteed" that Chiang Kaishek would not attempt to launch an invasion of the mainland. The U.S. presence assured that a Chinese solution would not be promoted, that the conflict between Taiwan and the mainland would be frozen indefinitely.

The Nixon administration is apparently promoting conditions that might be favorable to a Chinese solution to the Taiwan issue once Chiang Kai-shek departs the scene. While remaining committed to aid Taiwan in the event of invasion, we no longer accord credibility to that threat. Consequently, in the fall of 1969, we decided to withdraw the destroyer patrol from the Taiwan Straits for budgetary reasons. Since China had long demanded such removal, along with trade and travel relaxations, as a precondition to "normalizing" relations, conditions were ripe for a diplomatic move. As Robert Kleiman reported:

> In these circumstances, Secretary of State Rogers on November 7, 1969, secretly cabled the American Embassies in Tokyo, Seoul and Taipei to notify those Governments that the regular Taiwan Straits Patrol would be discontinued for budget reasons on November 15. Taipei complained bitterly in private.

> But within days after the unannounced suspension of the destroyer patrol, Peking's representatives in Hong Kong were asking whether the move had any significance. They were assured that it had.[1]

There can be no doubt that the present administration attaches little significance to perpetuating commitments to states which it considers to be peripheral actors in the international system. Our concerns vis-à-vis the lesser actors are minimal except as they affect relations among the primary actors. U.S. interests in Vietnam, for example, are secondary to U.S. relations with China. Viewed this way, U.S.-Vietnam policy should not determine U.S.-Chinese policy; indeed, our position in Vietnam is probably expendable in terms of our interests with China.

As set forth in these pages, a pattern emerges that traces shifts in American concepts of alliances and commitments through five postwar administrations. We noted first, under Truman-Marshall-Acheson, the development of a pragmatic, limited policy of "containing" the Soviet Union in Europe by means of NATO and the Truman Doctrine. Second, we noted under Eisenhower-Dulles the assertion of bipolarity accompanied by proliferating alliances and commitments built upon the NATO and Truman Doctrine models and designed to contain the spread of monolithic communism anywhere on the globe. Under Kennedy-Rusk, we began the search for detente in Europe while activating our Asian commitments by embarking upon nation-building and counterinsurgency warfare in Indochina. Under Johnson-Rusk, while continuing the pursuit of detente with the Soviet Union, our escalation of the war in Vietnam was accompanied by increasingly rigid articulations of commitment. Finally, under Nixon-Kissinger, we noted significant devaluation of alliances and commitments, as well as of international organizations, as instruments for achieving U.S. national foreign policy objectives.

POLICY PREMISES APPRAISED

Obviously, the concepts upon which our policies have been based have changed. What effects have such changes had on policies and ultimately on outcomes? If the concepts underlying a policy are false, the policy is likely to be nonefficacious or even dysfunctional. Even if the concept is true, the policy may still be nonefficacious or dysfunctional, for the effects of policies upon outcomes are rarely direct. Especially in dealing with foreign policies, we often have difficulty identifying intervening variables, much less accounting for them. Yet the concept employed determines the premise upon which a given policy may be based. If the premise is fallacious, so too must be the policy. If desired ends are still achieved, the achievement must be attributable to unprogrammed intervening variables or to something other than the stated policy.

Virtually any policy decision effectively narrows the range of options available to a decision-maker. Frequently, the range of options that had been available prior to decision was so imperfectly understood that changes in the range are difficult to perceive. Consequently policy-makers (and critics) often disregard the changing circumstances, as if to ignore what is uncertain will remove ambiguity.

When the United States enters into an alliance or undertakes a commitment with a nation, such an act alters U.S. relations with that nation and others. Probably the most important effect is the impact of such ties upon reduced flexibility. The reduction in flexibility, however, may be virtually imperceptible despite the numerous references to the strength and viability of commitments made by policy-makers and scholars.

No alliance or commitment, for example, acts as or stimulates an automatic *or even* predictable response. All that the parties "guarantee" is to undertake appropriate response according to each party's constitutional procedures. Article V of the North Atlantic Treaty includes a statement that is typical of the most specific undertaking. It reads, in part:

> The parties agree that an armed attack against one or more of them in Europe or North America shall be considered an attack against them all, and consequently they agree that, if such an armed attack occurs, each of them . . . will assist the Party or Parties so attacked by taking forthwith, individually and in concert with the other Parties, such action *as it deems necessary,* including the use of armed force, to restore and maintain the security of the North Atlantic area [italics added].

What is appropriate or necessary may range from verbal support to the direct entry of military forces into combat. Neither alliances nor commitments transform the decision-making processes of the parties to the extent that the decision to take specific action no longer remains discretionary to each of the parties. Indeed, much of the history of NATO has encompassed discussions of the ways by which the American commitment to provide physical military support to the European allies can be made credible. The American military presence is hostage to the credibility of the guarantee.

Short of an attack by the Soviet Union against a European ally, the American response remains speculative. Specific contingency plans may be put into effect or, in the context of the crisis, new decisions may be reached. As is well known, searching for information, including breaking our old contingency plans, diminishes with the intensity and urgency of a crisis. A Soviet attack would change the whole ball game and necessitate a revaluation of the elements that go into making the critical decisions. There is a tendency in the literature to gloss over such considerations by assuming that the range of options has in fact been significantly narrowed. But, a cursory glance at history will demonstrate that anticipated predictable and obvious responses are not necessarily made. Even during an invasion, the target country has a choice of responses. In 1968, Czechoslovakia chose to submit rather than resist invasion by Warsaw Pact forces.

Decision-makers will frequently justify their decisions as having been forced upon them by circumstances; however, such justifications are patently false. This is not to state that decision-makers may not be victims of self-deception, although instances of such self-deception are probably far less frequent than are lapses of memory and poor judgment. In point of fact, he who makes a decision cannot evade the responsibility for it by passing the buck to alliance requirements or to prior commitments.

James L. Payne's *The American Threat* illustrates quite vividly how far some observers carry the notion of environmental limitations on decision latitude. He asserts that ousting Castro from Cuba in 1960 or 1961 would have created a "credible deterrent threat" to "future communist thrusts—in Laos, Vietnam. . . ." [2] The author argues that not only are American policy-makers bound by numerous (unstated) commitments, but that such commitments have been thrust upon them because the United States is "a nation following an ongoing deterrence policy."

Obligations or commitments are, to a large extent, thrust

upon it [the United States]. It has values which are challenged by opponents; it has set precedents in defending them. These values and precedents create expectations about a nation's future behavior. And that is, analytically, what threats or commitments are: the expectations of others. Leaders can, of course, refuse to meet these expectations and suffer a corresponding loss of reputation. But it is not in their power to eliminate, without cost, a specific threat.

To understand this conclusion, it is helpful to examine the nature of the most general threat we project: to defend any free world country against outright communist attack—should our assistance be necessary to defeat the attack.[3]

Payne is seized by the germ of an idea that was nurtured in a hybrid culture of official propaganda, establishmentarian scholarship and ahistoricism. The germ is to be found in the fact that commitments and alliances generate legitimate demands upon the parties. As a function of an alliance or commitment, each party may reasonably expect the other party or parties to take some appropriate action. Payne, among others, carries such commitments to the point of inferring that the obligation extends to the dispatch of American troops upon the demand of a second party. Were this the case, the most critical decisions involving American strategy would be made by a host of foreign officials for their own purposes.

The nature of a commitment may be quite different from its articulation in official statements. U.S. policy in Vietnam cannot be explained as living up to our commitments to defend the territorial integrity and political independence of South Vietnam. Quite the opposite is the case. In 1954, we accepted the terms arrived at in Geneva providing for reunification of Vietnam following a plebiscite to be held in 1956, and prohibiting the introduction of foreign military personnel or material. Eventually we opposed holding the elections and pressed military assistance, including personnel, upon a reluctant Ngo Dinh Diem.

Our adventures in the 1960s were not a function of mili-

tary commitments to sundry regimes, but resulted from pre-
occupations with notions of strategic policy which could only
be implemented militarily. It was thought that carefully developed strategic policy could produce measured effects upon
target actors. Yet the effects of discrete decisions upon the
choice patterns of others are usually indeterminate except in
simulated environments. Step-level increments of escalation designed to "compel" the other side to acquiesce or submit may
make good sense in terms of simulated experience but are not
the product of historical research. One defense strategist predicted, in 1965, that North Vietnam would relatively quickly
be brought into line by bombing because Ho Chi Minh was
no longer a guerrilla and would not chance having his newly
industralized economy destroyed.

Defining situations and posing solutions for vexing problems is a difficult process even when perfect information is
available. In the arena of foreign policy, information is usually
scarce and largely unreliable. Situations are defined on the basis
of scanty information that is likely to be erroneous. The margin
of error tends to be high in the best of conditions; and the
margin tends to increase exponentially as conditions deteriorate.
But the opportunities for refuting such definitions of situations
are equally hampered by scarcity of reliable information. And
the burden of evidence generally rests upon those who reject
definitions of situations and posed solutions.

Because of information scarcity, the foreign policy community tends to respond to hypotheses and theories that purport
to make sense out of otherwise unmanageable or unintelligible
data. Such hypotheses and theories offer keys which promise to
unlock the secrets of international behavior. Notions such as the
"balance of power" and "domino theory" are advanced as if
they were accurate descriptors even though little agreement has
been reached as to the components of power and the mechanisms of balance, and even though nations and dominoes share
no logical or analogical properties.

Under such circumstances, it should come as no surprise
that plausible arguments often substitute for logical arguments.
Nor should it be too surprising that decisions of war and peace

are often based upon plausible, not logical, arguments. Contending theories and arguments are frequently selected on esthetic grounds rather than on the basis of their intrinsic efficacy. If a theory or argument sounds convincing, decision-makers and others may be convinced.

Plausible arguments or theories find particular acceptability when tied to predictions of dire consequences if prescribed action is not taken. Thus, failure to position elements of the Seventh Fleet in the Taiwan Straits would have resulted in the "loss" of Taiwan to mainland China; failure to intervene in the Dominican Republic would have resulted in the accession of a Castro-like government; failure to defend South Vietnam would have resulted in the fall of Cambodia, Laos, Thailand, etc. Each of these statements is a non sequitur because the conclusion does not follow the stated premise.

By definition, a non sequitur is an invalid statement even though the premise or the conclusion, taken separately, may be valid. When a non sequitur is stated as a premise for decision, we are presented with serious difficulties. An invalid statement cannot serve as a rational premise for making decisions on policy issues. The practice of statesmen articulating non sequiturs is widespread and may be condoned as an attribute of political license. The use of non sequiturs by scholars is also widespread and should not be condoned because the product of such non sequiturs is and can only be nonsense. When policy-makers turn to scholars for advice and counsel, they should be better served.

In the new introduction to *A World Restored,* Henry Kissinger asserts that: "Whenever peace—conceived of as the avoidance of war—has been the primary objective of a power or a group of powers, the international system has been at the mercy of the most ruthless member of the international community." [4] This is presented as axiomatic, as an unassailable proposition. Yet, it cannot be axiomatic since the avoidance of war by a power or a group of powers is not logically related to the mercy of the ruthless. Two unstated assumptions may be gleaned from the statement: first, that war is a function of the avoidance of war; and second, that the quest for peace rather than stability results in disequilibrium which will likely lead to war.

In discussing stability and other concepts, Kissinger illustrates another logical fallacy which permeates the literature, tautological reasoning. He states that "whenever the international order has acknowledged that certain principles could not be compromised even for the sake of peace, stability based on an equilibrium of forces was at least conceivable." "International order" is not defined but may be contextually derived as a function of "legitimacy" which "means no more than an international agreement about the nature of workable arrangements and about the permissible aims and methods of foreign policy." And stability is a function of legitimacy, "having resulted not from a quest for peace but from a generally accepted legitimacy. Thus, international order = legitimacy = stability = order. And the notion is reduced to a tautology incapable of explanation or of description.

Any power "which considers the international order or the manner of legitimizing it oppressive" is a revolutionary power and all "relations between it and other powers will be revolutionary." Adjustment of differences will be "tactical maneuvers to consolidate positions for the inevitable showdown, or as tools to undermine the morale of the antagonist." Diplomacy ("the adjustment of differences through negotiation" or "the art of restraining the exercise of power") is impossible in relations with a revolutionary power; it "is replaced either by war or by an armaments race." [5]

Kissinger suggests that the pursuit of peace with a revolutionary power jeopardizes stability because it places the international system at the mercy of the "most ruthless" power. In arriving at this conclusion, he reifies concepts so that: "ages . . . search," "international order has acknowledged" and "states may die. . . ."

The lesson of *A World Restored* is clear: we must confront revolutionary powers with sufficient force to compel their acceptance of legitimate international order. Measures short of a threat or use of force will endanger stability. So long as the disputants accept the principles of international order (as in the Middle East), stability may be maintained by means of equilibrated forces. If a disputant is revolutionary (such as North Vietnam), entering into negotiations would jeopardize the stability of the international system. But revolutionary powers may always avail themselves of the option of accepting the rules, thereby becoming nonrevolutionary. Thus, the government of North Vietnam could make negotiations at Paris possible by agreeing to (1) refrain from using force; (2) release of prisoners; and (3) recognize (de facto) the legitimacy of the government of the Republic of Vietnam.

THE KISSINGER THEORY OF WORLD ORDER

In the context of Kissinger's "theory" of international relations, the Nixon-Kissinger conceptualization of alliances and commitments appears to contain obvious doctrinaire elements which are quite dissimilar to Dulles' ideological constructs. Kissinger apparently finds differentiating between communist and noncommunist states essentially uninteresting from the standpoint of classifying state behaviors. To Kissinger, the critical question is whether or not a given state is revolutionary; i.e., whether it may or may not be threatening. To Dulles, the threat posed to noncommunist states by communist states was inherently functional to communist ideology. Revolutionary regimes were threatening, therefore, if and only if they were communist.

Examined out of the context of Kissinger's theory, the policies adopted by the Nixon administration appear to bear more resemblance to the pragmatism of Truman-Acheson than to the foreign policies of the other postwar administrations. But, examined in context, the dissimilarities are striking.

The principal contrast between Kissinger and Acheson arises in their views of the international system. Kissinger posits a closed system comprising national actors, each of which does its own thing according to implicitly codified rules of behavior.

States that reject the rules threaten the stability of the system; therefore, they must become legitimate or be suppressed. Kissinger argues that dysfunctional behavior by one state or a group of states threatens the maintenance of the delicate equilibrium established by international order.

Acheson's approach was sharply different. He tended to reject *all* notions of an international system as the plain or fancied gibberish of social scientists and poets. Acheson's pragmatism insisted that "solutions" may only be devised for concrete problems. He was not interested in such abstract concepts as international order, stability, equilibrium or legitimacy. Neither was he concerned with reinforcing proper international etiquette. Finally, Acheson did not accord much significance to adjectival descriptors such as revolutionary, communist, legitimate, peace-loving or democratic.

To Kissinger the means employed by the United States are designed to achieve an end which is a more orderly world system. To Dulles the means were designed to achieve the end of preventing monolithic communism from engulfing the world. To Rusk, the means were often ambivalently designed to achieve rather ambiguous ends, such as rapprochement with the Soviet Union while reversing the tide of communist advances in Southeast Asia particularly and the Third World generally. To Acheson, the means of foreign policy was what it was all about. Separating means from ends is not as easy as might be inferred from this discussion. When the means are belligerent and conflictual (as with NATO, the Truman Doctrine, German currency reform, German rearmament and so on), the ends are likely to be belligerency (or "quasi-belligerency") and conflict. Acheson's means helped achieve more than two decades of turmoil, hostility and war.

NOTES

1. *The New York Times,* November 1, 1971, p. 41.

2. James L. Payne, *The American Threat* (Chicago: Markham, 1971) p. 126.

3. Ibid., pp. 127-128.

4. Henry A. Kissinger, *A World Restored* (New York: Grosset and Dunlap, 1964) p. 1.

5. Ibid., pp. 1-3.

3

THE REVOLT OF THE MASSES: PUBLIC OPINION ON MILITARY EXPENDITURES

Bruce M. Russett

MYTHS ABOUT POPULAR CONCERN

Many theories about the sources of national security and foreign policy stress the limiting, and occasionally the initiating, effect of public opinion. Explanations solely in terms of external stimuli are definitely inadequate, even for such phenomena as

This is an extended and updated version of a chapter appearing in Bruce M. Russett, ed., *Peace, War, and Numbers* (Beverly Hills, Cal.: Sage, 1972). The initial version was written while the author was visiting professor at the University of Brussels on Fulbright-Hays and Guggenheim awards, and the research was supported in part by Grant No. 2635 from the National Science Foundation. The author is indebted to Philip K. Hastings of the Roper Public Opinion Research Center, Williams College, for providing most of the survey material cited here, and to Alfred O. Hero for bringing some of it to his attention. Philip Converse made available material from an SRC survey carried out under his direction. H. W. Moyer provided valuable assistance in a seminar paper at Yale. Moyer, James Clotfelter, Arnold Kanter, Michael Sullivan and H. Bradford Westerfield offered useful comments, but all opinions expressed here are the sole responsibility of the author.

military expenditures and arms races.[1] A search for determinants within a nation's domestic political system may concentrate upon governmental or interest elites, as is done in the variants of theories about a "military-industrial complex," or it may probe deeper to include mass attitudes. Among analysts who have considered the question, there are a number of conflicting views. Some formerly well-regarded beliefs have been shown to belong largely in the category of mythology; others were probably correct in their time but need sharp revision under conditions of the new politics of the 1970s.

Political leaders have sometimes assumed that mass opinion constituted a major constraint on the choice of military policy, and have hesitated, for fear of popular reaction, to pursue policies they thought desirable. But in the past, public opposition to military spending really was not widespread. At the beginning of World War II President Roosevelt moved very cautiously toward intervention because he thought the majority of the people were not ready to support a large defense program and aid to the Allies. Yet most citizens of the United States actually did desire a program of rearmament in the late 1930s. In other periods differing arms policies have been pursued within the context of fairly stable mass opinion. For example, during the entire Cold War period from 1946 to 1960 national surveys repeatedly found a substantial majority of the population in favor of a large army and navy. Despite this relative constancy of preference on the mass level, national policy varied from initial disarmament, through the beginnings of a cautious buildup, the exertions of the Korean War, and the cutbacks associated with the "new look" of the Eisenhower administration, to the makings of a new buildup at the beginning of the Kennedy years. The pattern of mass preference on military spending has changed drastically, however, very recently. *For the first time in more than 30 years a majority of the population has come to advocate reduction in military expenditures,* becoming, as never before, a serious potential constraint on national security policy. This chapter examines relevant data on several assertions concerning the state of public opinion toward defense spending over the last four decades.

The myth of public constraint was expressed clearly by Walter Lippmann:

> At critical junctures, when the stakes are high, the prevailing mass opinion will impose what amounts to a veto upon changing the course on which a government is at the time proceeding. Prepare for war in time of peace? No. It is bad to raise taxes, to unbalance the budget, to take men away from their schools or their jobs, to provoke the enemy.[2]

Two specific propositions are embedded here. First, government decisions, including military policy, are shaped and limited by public opinion. Second, at most times ("time of peace") public opinion serves to restrict and reduce the level of defense spending. The public is allegedly insensitive to the requirements of national security and requires that the defense budget be curtailed in favor of tax reductions or popular domestic programs.

Senator J. William Fulbright, on the other hand, more recently typified the view that mass opinion serves as a primary impetus to military spending and a barrier to its reduction. In 1964 he castigated

> the readiness with which the American people have consented to defer programs for their welfare and happiness in favor of costly military and space programs. Indeed, if the Congress accurately reflects the temper of the country, then the American people are not only willing, they are eager to sacrifice education and urban renewal and public health programs—to say nothing of foreign aid—to the requirements of the armed forces and the space agency.[3]

Although there is some ambiguity about whether popular opinion is correctly perceived ("if the Congress accurately reflects the temper of the country") this is nevertheless a fairly clear statement of a widely held view. Moreover, while the systematic literature on arms races considers various sorts of possible restraints on expenditures, mass attitudes are seldom among them.

EARLY PERMISSIVENESS AND PRO-PREPAREDNESS

The first careful study of the survey data on this matter very firmly and convincingly rejected the proposition that public opinion restricts military spending. According to Samuel P. Huntington, Lippmann and others of like mind attributed to the mass public "a view which it did not possess and an attitude it did not hold." [4] Huntington found in the surveys that on military programs and the defense budget the public tended to follow the lead of the Administration when the Administration took a definite position. In situations where the Administration did not take a strong stand public opinion was, at the least, passive and permissive and, at the most, very favorably disposed to stronger defense. In a recent review Alfred O. Hero advanced a similar view, but stressed the general preference for a large defense establishment.[5]

The general public acquiescence in heavy defense spending up to the late 1960s, with occasional but not common very heavy pressures for increases, is documented clearly in Exhibits 1, 2, 3 and 4. Only the percentages favoring a reduction in defense effort are given in the exhibits since that will be our primary interest, but those favoring an increase are shown in Exhibit 2.[6] The solid lines in both exhibits show responses over time to somewhat differing questions in a variety of AIPO, NORC and Roper national surveys from Exhibit 3; the dashed lines separate questions asked more than four years apart. The dotted lines between December 1950 and June 1953 indicate, from Exhibit 4, responses to an identical question asked in ten NORC surveys.

Exhibit 1 shows, first and most obviously, that except for the most recent years mass opinion certainly never really constituted a constraint on the level of military spending or the size of the armed forces. Save in the responses to a couple of questions seriously biased against military spending, in Exhibit 1 we see that those in favor of reducing the resources going to

EXHIBIT 1
PERCENTAGE OF RESPONDENTS FAVORING *LESS* DEFENSE SPENDING

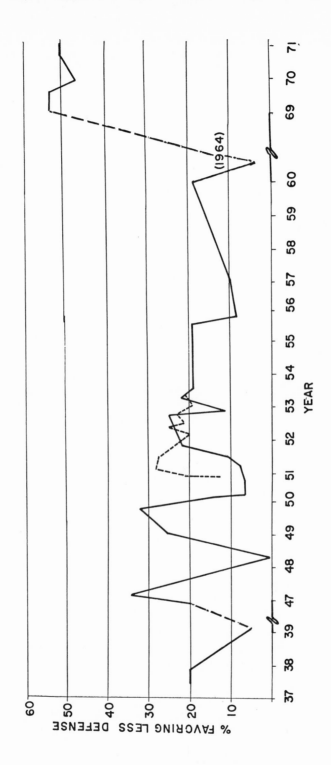

defense always numbered less than 30 percent of the population, with the remainder wishing an increase, expressing satisfaction with current levels, or indifferent and uninvolved (don't know). At times the percentage wanting less military spending fell very low indeed, below 10 percent—and this was usually precisely at times when the political leadership considered external threats to be especially serious and the need for a military buildup to be greatest; e.g., 1939, the beginning of the Cold War in 1948, and the first year of the Korean War. (The 1939 case is especially poignant, given President Roosevelt's difficulties with Congress in pushing Selective Service and rearmament. Similarly, the lack of actual constraint in March 1950, before the Korean War, is noteworthy. About that time NSC-68 was produced, many in the government were convinced that American defense forces should be dramatically expanded, and the fear was expressed that the people would be unwilling to bear the burden. For many of these leaders the Korean War, despite its costs and dangers, at least had the virtue of providing an occasion for the buildup they wanted and hesitated—probably unnecessarily—to embark upon.)

Exhibit 2 shows the proportion of the population favoring an increase in the military establishment. This percentage was always, again except for the late 1960s, higher than the corresponding percentage who wished for a reduction, but still it normally held at a level of well under half the population. The only exceptions to this last statement occurred during external crises: 1939, March 1948 (immediately after the communist coup in Czechoslovakia and at the time of increasing threat to Berlin—but before the blockade); and, more surprisingly, March 1950 before the Korean War.

This characterization is further supported by the only available series of identical questions asked over a number of surveys to the same kind of sample: the NORC material from Exhibit 4. Again the proportions favoring a change in the status quo, either for an increase or a decrease in defense spending, remain well under half—typically about 20 percent for each. The only serious exceptions are the number in the first two surveys (45 percent and 36 percent) who favored more defense in the first

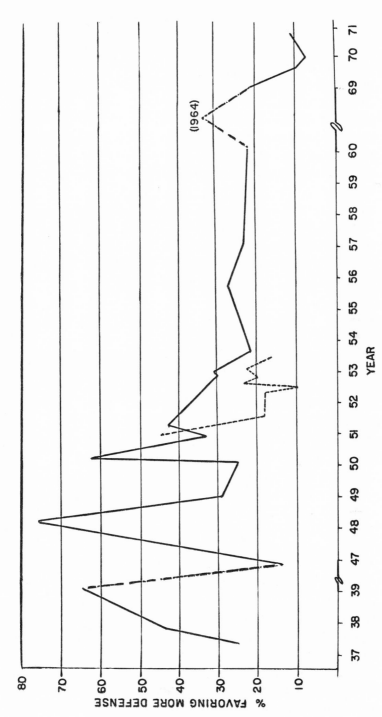

EXHIBIT 2
PERCENTAGE OF RESPONDENTS FAVORING *MORE* DEFENSE SPENDING

months of the Korean War. After 1951 the figures fluctuate within a very narrow range, and the differences from one survey to the next are usually not statistically significant.[7]

Regardless of political leaders' perceptions, we have a picture of a public that was generally ready to rely on the judgment of the political leadership, to acquiesce in existing or planned levels of military strength. Only a minority favored change in either direction. This is true generally across the population by income and educational levels. On education, for example, the college-educated and those with only grammar school education differed at most only about 15 percent in the percent who wished defense spending to be cut, with the better-educated almost always more favorable toward the military.[8] (That is, 20 percent of the college-educated might favor a reduction where 35 percent of those with grade school education held that opinion.) To the degree popular dissatisfaction with arms levels existed, pressures for increase were more widespread than for decrease. *Hence, when spending did go up there was greater resistance to cutting it back to its original level than there had been to the initial boost.*

There is other evidence supporting an image of public permissiveness:

1. When asked generally whether they were "satisfied with the way" America's military strength was being handled, the overwhelming majority usually expressed substantial contentment. For example, in an AIPO survey as late as May 1966, during the Vietnam War, 88 percent declared themselves "extremely well," "considerably well," "considerably well" or "somewhat" satisfied.

2. The low emphasis on the defense spending issue is shown in the response to open-ended questions asking whether, without suggesting items, there was any category of government spending that the respondent thought ought to be increased or decreased. Military expenditures were rarely mentioned. For instance, in AIPO surveys in January 1959, April 1963, and October 1963 neither the percentage for increase nor for decrease in defense ever reached as high as 7 percent. By contrast, typically one-

third of the respondents volunteered foreign aid as a candidate for the axe, and in April 1963 15 percent of the sample wanted public spending for education to be increased.

3. Over the years, congressmen have reported relatively little correspondence from their constituents on the issue of military expenditures.[9]

4. There is substantial, if perhaps shallow, support for mutual disarmament. In response to repeated AIPO and NORC questions between 1946 and 1963 asking whether the United States should agree to reduce its armed forces if other countries (or specifically the Russians) cut down theirs, typically about half the sample, and almost always a majority of those with opinions, approved. The level was almost entirely independent of changes in opinion about the desirability of building or reducing the American armed forces, and was particularly strong even in 1951 and 1952, when our data in Exhibit 2 showed more than 30 per cent of the respondents in favor of greater American military spending. This state of affairs gave political leaders a good deal of freedom to promote disarmament, perhaps even at the same time they advocated increased military expenditures.

POSSIBLE CAUSES OF VARIATION

A second important element in these data concerns the wide swings in attitudes toward military spending in the early years, followed by the evening out of fluctuations and the stabilization of opinion during the 1950s. For the entire 1947-1960 period both the highs and the deepest lows in both graphs come before 1951; after that the entire range of fluctuation is only about 20 percent despite substantial variation in the form of the question. And the only later fluctuations even that big involve the lows of December 1952 and October 1955, each of which has an unbiased question preceded and/or followed by biased ones. This is what we would expect with an issue that is new, or at least seen in a new context—the emerging Cold War —but later becomes embedded in a structured set of attitudes toward the new situation. The early oscillations in attitude toward military spending perhaps reflect the great swings in mood and emphasis on foreign policy noted in Gabriel Almond's classic study. Like opinion on foreign policy, attitudes toward military spending also seem to have settled down and respond less to dramatic external events.[10]

Much of the variation that does exist is probably due to substantial changes in the way the question about military spending or preparedness is phrased. I have noted with asterisks or double asterisks those questions in Exhibit 3 which seem to me to be seriously biased—nearly always, incidentally, against high levels of military spending. Types of biases include:

1. In question wording, offering only the option of an increase or decrease in spending, not retaining the current level. ("Remain the same" is always coded, even if not offered explicitly.) This tends to inflate answers in both the increase and decrease categories, perhaps by about 5 percent in each. Two AIPO surveys in January 1939 asked otherwise quite similar questions, except that one did not offer "remain the same" explicitly. The one offering only change produced percentages of 8 for decrease and 67 for increase; where the status quo was offered the percentages were 3 and 62 for change respectively.

2. Offering only a choice of a decrease or the status quo, and not offering or coding increase. With "increase" not offered, "keep about the same" may lose some of the attractiveness it would have as a middle course, and some people may then choose "decrease" instead.

3. Explicit reference to the possibility of reducing taxes, or to the desirability of "cutting down on expenses," can be expected to prejudice many answers against high spending levels.

4. One survey, that by AIPO in February 1947, asked a two-part question in which the attitude portion was

Exhibit 3: NATIONAL SURVEYS ON DEFENSE SPENDING, 1937-1971

May 1937 AIPO No. 82
>"Do you think the amount of money we are now spending on the Army and Navy is too much, too little, or about right?"
>
>Too much: 20%

*October 1937 AIPO No. 101
>"Do you think government expenditures should be increased or decreased for the Army and Navy?" ("Remain same" not offered, but coded)
>
>Decreased: 20%

*January 1939 AIPO No. 143
>"Do you think government spending should be increased or decreased for national Defense?" ("Remain same" not offered, but coded)
>
>Decreased: 8%

January 1939 AIPO No. 145
>"Should government spending for national defense be increased, decreased, or remain about the same?"
>
>Decreased: 3%

*November 1946 AIPO No. 385
>"About half the cost of our government today goes to support the Army and Navy. Which of these do you think should be done—
>
>"Reduce taxes by cutting down our Army and Navy? Keep our Army and Navy as they are for another 3 years?" ("Increase" not offered or coded)
>
>Reduce taxes by cutting: 20%

November 1946 NORC No. 146
>"This year the United States is spending about thirteen billion dollars on our armed forces. Which of these things do you think Congress should do *next* year—
>
>Reduce the size of our armed forces, in order to save money.
>
>Keep them at their present size, *or Increase* the size of our armed forces, regardless of cost?"
>
>Reduce: 21%

**February 1947 AIPO No. 391
>"Have you followed the arguments in Congress for and against cutting down on the money for the Army and Navy?"
>
>*If yes.* "Do you think Congress should reduce the amount of

money which the Army and Navy have asked for?" (Increase not offered or coded)

Yes: 35%

Note: This response is very unusual, because the respondents with college education are much more likely (by about 13%) to favor reduction than are those with only grammar school education. Ordinarily there is a slight negative relationship between education and favoring reductions. Since those with higher education are more likely to answer yes to the first part of the question, it is clear there is in this formulation a bias toward reduction.

March 1948 Roper Fortune No. 64

"Do you think our military strength should be increased at the present time, left about the same as it is now, or do you think it should be cut down?"

Cut down: 1%

January 1949 NORC No. 163

"Last year the United States spent about thirteen billion dollars on our armed forces. During the coming year, do you think we should spend more than this amount, or less, on our armed forces?"

Less: 26%

**September 1949 AIPO No. 447

"Do you think it is a good idea or a poor idea to cut down on expenses in the U.S. military defense setup at this time?" (Increase not offered or coded)

Good: 33%

February 1950 AIPO No. 453

"Do you think the amount of money we are now spending on the Army, Navy, and Air Force is too much, too little, or about right?"

Too much: 15%

March 1950 AIPO No. 454

"Do you think U.S. Government spending should be increased, decreased, or remain about the same on the following:
National Defense?"

Decreased: 7%

*November 1950 AIPO No. 467

"When the Korean war began, the United States had about one and a half million men in the armed forces. It has been decided to increase this number to three million men. Do you think this number is too high or too low?" (About right not offered, but coded)

Too high: 7%

April 1951 NORC No. 303

"During the coming year, do you think we should cut down the amount we are spending on our rearmament program, keep it about the same, or spend even more on our armed forces?"

Cut down: 8%

*July 1951 AIPO No. 447

"If the Korean war is brought to an end soon, do you think the United States should continue our defense program as planned, or do you think the defense program should be reduced?" (Increase not offered or coded)

Reduced: 11%

*December 1951 NORC No. 315

"Do you think our government should keep on building up our defenses and helping our allies, even if it means continued high taxes for you?" ("Keep on building" is ambiguous.)

No: 22%

*November 1952 AIPO No. 508

"Do you think the government should spend more money or less money for the defense purposes?" (Same not offered, but coded. Includes qualified less)

Less: 25%

December 1952 NORC No. 334
As in April 1951

Cut down: 11%

*April 1953 AIPO No. 514

"At present there are about 3½ million men in our Armed Forces, both in the U.S. and overseas. If a truce is reached in Korea, do you think we should cut down the size of our Armed Forces, or not?" (Increase not offered or coded. Includes qualified should)

Should: 22%

*August 1953 AIPO No. 519

"Do you think too much of the taxes you pay is being spent for defense, or is too little being spent for defense?" (About right not offered, but coded)

Too much: 19%

*September 1955 AIPO No. 553

"Do you think we should keep on spending as much as we do now for our defense program, or should we cut down on the amount we spend for defense?" (Increase not offered or coded)

Cut down: 19%

October 1955 NORC No. 378

"During the coming year, do you think we should cut down the amount we are spending on our arms program, keep it about the same, or spend even more on our armed forces?"

Cut down: 8%

February 1957 AIPO No. 579

"The biggest part of government spending goes for defense. Do you think this sum should be increased, decreased or kept ahout the same as it was last year?"

Decreased: 9%

February 1960 AIPO No. 625

"There is much discussion as to the amount this country should spend for national defense. How do you feel about this—do you think we are spending too little, too much, or about the right amount?"

Too much: 18%

October 1964 AIPO
(Reported in Free and Cantril [1967], p. 90)

"Is it your impression that the strength of United States defense is about right at present, or do you feel that it should be either increased or decreased?"

Decreased: 4%

December 1968 AIPO No. 773

"More than half of the money spent by the U.S. government goes for military defense. Looking ahead the next two or three years, would you like to see this amount increased or decreased?" (Same not offered, but coded)

Decreased: 53%

July 1969 AIPO No. 784

"There is much discussion as to the amount of money the government in Washington should spend for national defense and military purposes. How do you feel about this: do you think we are spending too little, too much, or about the right amount?"

Too much: 53%

November 1969 AIPO No. 793
As in July 1969

Too much: 46%

September 1970 AIPO

"Congress is currently debating how much money should be spent for military purposes. Would you like to have your congressman vote to keep spending for military purposes at the present level, increase the amount, or reduce the amount?"

Reduce: 49%

March 1971 AIPO
As in July 1969

Too Much: 50%

Reported in Lloyd A. Free and Hadley Cantril, *The Political Beliefs of Americans* (New Brunswick, N.J.: Rutgers University Press, 1967) p. 90.

*I have noted with either single or double asterisks those questions which seem to be seriously biased.

addressed only to those who acknowledged paying attention to the congressional debate about defense spending. This survey, and another (AIPO in September 1949), both of which failed to offer "increase" and asked simply whether the respondent thought it a good idea "to cut down on expenses in the U.S. defense setup," mark the pre-1968 highpoints of opposition to military spending. It is very possible that the bias there is so serious that the responses should be removed from the trend study, though I have left them in with cautions.

5. Explicit reference to the current or planned size of the armed forces or military spending might, at least relative to the stripped-down question, impress the respondent particularly with the burden at issue. Relevant phrasing includes references to "about half the cost of our government today," "thirteen billion dollars," "the biggest part of government spending," "and 3 and one-half million men." This seems, however, not to be a notable biasing factor if adjacent surveys November 1950–April 1951, October 1955–February 1957–February 1960 and December 1968–July 1969 are compared. Hence such phrasing alone does not suffice to award an asterisk.[11]

6. A few surveys asked about the level of American military "strength" rather than spending; in such cases there may

have been some small relative bias toward *increases*.

Because of the relatively few data points available, and much more importantly because of the variation in question wording, it is impossible to apply any very sophisticated trend analysis.[12] Some hypotheses about the possible effects of war occur. One is that at the inception of war or severe external crisis, the popular response is one of patriotic rallying round the flag, with an immediate *jump* in opinion very *favorable toward expanding the military* to deal with the threat, and drop in the number of people wishing to curtail defense spending. While we must be very careful about post hoc attribution of the label "severe crisis" to those events corresponding to increased public sentiment ,for military spending, some of this phenomenon seems to be present in 1939 and at the time of the Czechoslovak coup in 1948.

The effect of the Korean War is harder to pin down. As manifested by both the February and March 1950 surveys in Exhibit 1, and the March survey in Exhibit 2, opposition to military spending had *already* dropped very sharply just before the onset of the war, perhaps in reaction to announcement of the first Russian atom bomb test in late 1949, and then remained low for more than a year thereafter. The war probably helped retain a climate of opinion very favorable toward greatly expanding the military, but preceding lows are more puzzling. Here, however, it is essential to pay close attention to the questions' wording. The February and March 1950 questions are essentially unbiased, and again are preceded and followed by surveys using queries which tend to exaggerate opposition to the military. The preceding survey, of September 1949, is a particularly grave offender. Thus the immediately pre-Korean lows are probably deceptive, and it is likely that the war really did create a substantial change in opinion—that the November 1950 low, on a question that might be expected to inflate the proportion favoring a smaller army by perhaps 5 percent, is a true low in large part induced by early wartime conditions. This would be predicted by most of what we now know about popular response to international crises. A similar situation seems to have arisen in the enormous—and short-lived—up-surge in preparedness sentiment early in 1948.

A second war-related hypothesis, especially reflecting the apparent building of public distrust and hostility toward the military over the course of the long U.S. involvement in Indo-china, is that *as any war* (in this case the Korean conflict) *drags on, public opposition to the military will mount.* The evidence supporting this hypothesis is nevertheless extremely slim. Anti-military sentiments did seem to build up over the course of the latter half of 1951, but there is no apparent change thereafter. Even the rise in antimilitary feeling in 1951 is dubious, because much of the shift in the solid line in Exhibit 1 may be ac-counted for by the insertion of important bias in all but one of the questions from July 1951 through September 1955. The one unbiased question in this set appears in December 1952, and the percentage then expressing a desire for a smaller army is very markedly lower than before and after. About all that is clear is that in Exhibit 2, measuring the proportion who want a larger army, there is indeed a substantial and rather steady drop that cannot be attributed to question bias.

Exhibit 4: NORC SURVEYS
ON DEFENSE SPENDING, 1950-1953

"Do you think the people in this country have been asked to make too many sacrifices to support the defense program, not enough sacrifices, or about the right amount?"

Too many

No. 295	December 1950	13%
No. 298	January 1951	22
No. 300	March 1951	29
No. 312	August 1951	28
No. 323	April 1952	20
No. 327	June 1952	25
No. 329	August 1952	21
No. 333	November 1952	23
No. 337	February 1953	19
No. 341	June 1953	21

END RUSSETT Ex. 4

Thus, the effect of the war was to produce a popular frame of mind that neither supported further expansion in the armed forces nor generated important sentiments for reducing the army. And the latter cannot be simply attributed to wartime patriotism ("Don't cry out against the armed forces while a war is going on") either, since no new antimilitary sentiments surfaced after the war despite the efforts of the Eisenhower administration to cut the military budget and reduce military manpower.

The failure of opposition to the military to emerge in mass opinion is especially striking since presidential popularity is generally considered to be a victim of extended wars. Harry Truman's popularity rating dropped from over 40 percent at the beginning of the Korean War to 23 percent in early 1952 (though it then rose again into the low 30s), and Lyndon Johnson's fell from about 70 percent just after his election to under 40 percent in 1968. This last should not be taken too seriously, however, because domestic events and a "normal" decline in a president's esteem greatly compound and confuse the effects of war. Our impressions that long wars severely damage leaders' popularity are actually very hard to document convincingly.[13]

Another plausible set of hypotheses concerns the relation of actual levels of military spending to the publicly desired level. One might suppose either that there is a close positive association between actual and desired levels, probably because mass opinion perceives and responds to the same external events that cause political decision-makers to raise or lower the military budget, or that actual and desired levels are negatively related, as mass opinion holds a fairly stable image of a desirable level of military spending and reacts against sharp changes in either direction. Furthermore, the above hypotheses might apply to a more or less simultaneous association, or to one that lags either way. Mass opinion might follow after the elite's changes in response to threat, or in a political system very sensitive to mass opinion it might first be necessary to have change in mass opinion before the political leadership would be willing to vary military spending significantly.

Exhibit 5 shows the level of military spending as a per-

EXHIBIT 5
DEFENSE AS A PERCENTAGE OF GNP, 1946-71*

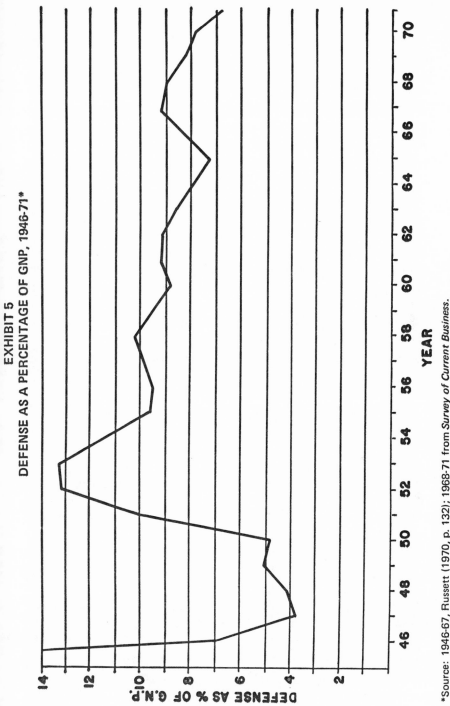

*Source: 1946-67, Russett (1970, p. 132); 1968-71 from *Survey of Current Business.*

centage of gross national product (GNP) over the period 1946–
1971. Precise tests of the above hypotheses are impossible because of variation in the questions and the incomparability of
data points for the two variables—survey responses perhaps two
or three times a year, expenditure data on an annual basis. But
even on inspection it is apparent that there is little support
for any of the above hypotheses. A simple sign test for a concurrent relationship in the direction, up or down, of annual
changes in each variable (correlation of the magnitudes of
changes would be too powerful for these data) also shows no
relationship. For 12 years where one can match changes in the
two variables, they are positively related in five and vary in
opposite directions in the other seven. Introduction of a one-
year lag either way does little better. Nor does it improve
matters to use the total military budget, or the military proportion of government spending, instead of the military share of
GNP. No simple explanation of public attitudes toward defense expenditures is adequate, and the puzzle becomes even
more perplexing as we look at more recent events.

THE SLEEPER AWAKES

The general image we have now built up—of a public
usually rather indifferent to the size of the armed forces and the
level of military spending, uninvolved and basically prepared to
follow its political leadership, if anything more disposed toward
building a larger army than toward reducing it—makes very
strange reading in light of the data for mass opinion since 1968.
Recent antimilitary feeling is absolutely unprecedented from
the beginning of scientific opinion-sampling. What had been a
less than 20 percent minority who wanted to reduce the defense
budget has become approximately half the populace; whereas
two decades ago nearly one-fourth of the population could
always be counted on to support increased military spending,
those ranks have shrunk to only one American in ten. The
recent questions are essentially "perfectly straight" without any

notable biases. It is also remarkable that this happened at a time when military expenditures were decreasing; even though these expenditures were higher than they had been since the early 1960s, they were far below the expenses characteristic of the Korean War and even lower than those of 1954–1959 (see Exhibit 5). And opposition has remained at a *stable* high level through five surveys over more than two years—a striking difference from earlier patterns.

Moreover, popular disenchantment with the military currently permeates all sections and levels. In the AIPO survey of July 1969, for instance, none of the standard major population categories—sex, race, education, occupation, age, religion, politics, region, income or community size—shows less than 45 percent of its members responding that too much government money goes to national defense, and none more than 60 percent. This is a remarkably even distribution. The widest differential is for education, with 60 percent of the college-educated group declaring that too much money goes to defense, as compared with only 46 percent of the population with only a grade school education holding that opinion. This spread increased in September 1970 to 60 percent among college-educated individuals and 40 percent among those with only elementary schooling.

Such a clear association of education with opposition to defense spending is also new; it suggests that *antimilitarism is now strongest in the attentive public.* In other words, it is concentrated precisely in that part of the population most likely to vote, to express its opinions, to make campaign contributions and to participate in some form of organized political activity. Such attitudes are thus especially likely to be politically effective, and military spending as a political issue has become very potent.[14]

Supporting evidence can be found in a Survey Research Center (SRC) study of October 1968. Respondents were asked to indicate their generalized sentiments toward "the military" on a 0 to 100 scale called a "feeling thermometer." Of those with only a grade school or high school education, 39 percent placed their sentiments in the "warmest" or most favorable

decile of the scale, but only 18 percent of those with some
college education did so. Similarly, favorable attitudes toward
the military were negatively associated with information on the
extent of military spending. Another question on the SRC
survey asked respondents what proportion of the national government's budget they thought went to defense. The correct
answer was just under 40 percent; the median answer was 50
percent. Of those who thought less than 20 percent of the budget
was devoted to defense, a full 40 percent scored themselves in
the warmest decile of the feeling scale toward the military. Even
those who thought defense took between 80 and 99 percent of
the budget tended to have favorable attitudes toward the military—37 percent of those put themselves into the top decile.
But only 29 percent of respondents with a remotely accurate
image of the military establishment's true size (placing it from
20 to 79 percent of the budget) were in the most approving
decile.

Furthermore, other research has shown strong associations
between both class and media attention and a shift in attitudes
against the Indochina War. Those high on the first two variables were most favorable toward the war in 1964, but showed
the sharpest shift by 1968. More than half of the middle-class
respondents who read heavily and who initially favored a strong
stand in Vietnam had turned away from that stance, as compared with less than 15 percent of working-class respondents
(whether or not they read the media often) who had turned
against the war. At the elite level, a survey in mid-1969 of more
than 300 chief executives from the 500 largest industrial corporations and 50 largest commercial firms declared, "Almost
two-thirds think the nation's defense expenditures are unduly high because of waste and inefficiency." And a survey of
500 top business, labor, governmental and media leaders in late
1971 through early 1972 found 64 percent wanted to see military spending cut, against just 17 percent who thought it should
be increased.[15]

These astonishing shifts both against military spending and
against the Indochina War, especially among the attentive
public, are closely associated. They may also have occurred at

much the same time. The regrettable near-absence of survey material on attitudes toward military spending for the early and middle 1960s greatly handicaps any attempt to fit the two together confidently, but we have some evidence. First, there is the one survey between 1960 and 1968, taken in October 1964, with a relevant question. It registers a 16-year low of only four percent who felt that "the strength of United States defense" should be decreased. While this may in part reflect a question bias (presumably "defense strength" would be more popular than "defense spending"), it suggests that the shift had not yet come in 1964.[16]

Second, we can match evidence on shifts in attitude toward both war and defense spending during the Korean War, and try to infer from that, in addition to evidence on attitudes toward war only during the Indochina War, how the missing component might have behaved. As Mueller's data reveal, popular approval of the Korean War dropped sharply immediately after the Chinese intervention at the end of 1950, but then remained essentially stable, at a lower level, for the remainder of that conflict. This pattern is remarkably similar to the data shown in Exhibits 1, 2 and 3 concerning support for defense spending. Furthermore, Mueller shows that erosion of popular approval of the Indochina War began in earnest in mid-summer 1965, it had fallen off sharply by May 1966 (from 61 percent to 49 percent), it declined rather steadily until about August 1968 (to 35 percent), and thereafter remained pretty stable.[17] If antimilitary attitudes paralleled those toward the war, as they did for Korea, then the period 1965-1968 really would mark the big change. But the growth in antimilitary feeling was much greater in the later conflict than in the earlier one.

The association between attitudes toward war and toward the military should not be overstated, nor interpreted as necessarily causal. There is also some reason to suspect that the roots of antimilitary sentiment have been growing for a long time. The 18 percent preference for less military spending in February 1960 marked an 11-year high for an unbiased question. President Eisenhower's farewell warning about the "military-industrial complex" came in the context of growing, if still

Exhibit 6: HIGHEST SENATE VOTES FOR
CUTTING DOD EXPENDITURES, 1946-1971

Items:

1946-1947 No negative votes.

1948- Supplemental Defense appropriation. Adopted 74-2.

1949-1950 No negative votes.

1951- Flanders motion to recommit DOD appropriation with instructions to cut total to $55 billion. Rejected 29-49.

1952- Morse amendment to reduce Air Force appropriation by $200 million. Rejected 33-43.

1953- No negative votes.

1954- Long amendment to reduce by $45 million funds for the barracks program. Rejected 12-63.

1955-1956 No negative votes.

1957- Dworshak amendment reducing DOD funds by $182 million. Rejected 24-49.

1958- No negative votes.

1959- Young motion that the Senate recede from its amendment to increase by $15 million House approved funds for civil defense. Rejected 12-72. Senate increase merely restored House cut, did not exceed original executive request.

1960- Appropriate $40 billion to DOD for fiscal 1961. Adopted 83-3.

1961- No negative votes.

1962- Young amendment to delete $94 million appropriated for civil defense. Rejected 14-68.

1963- Saltonstall amendment to cut DOD procurement appropriation by 1%. Rejected 43-45.

1964- Nelson amendment to reduce DOD appropriation by 2%. Rejected 11-62.

1965- Young amendment to reduce civil defense funds by $35 million. Rejected 13-72.

1966- Young amendment to reduce by $15 million appropriation for civil defense. Rejected 27-59.

1967- Young amendment to reduce civil defense allotment by $20 million. Rejected 32-55.

1968- Williams amendment to reduce defense authorization by $700 million. Adopted 45-13.

1969- Smith amendment to delete funds for Safeguard while allowing development of other ABM systems. Rejected 50-50.

1970- Hart-Cooper amendment deleting $322 million for deployment of Safeguard ABM system in Missouri and Wyoming. Rejected 47-52.

1971- Nelson amendment reducing by $2 million authorization for research and development on submarine communication system Project Sanguine. Accepted 44-42.

Notes

1959-   Did not consider Thurmond motion to reduce MATS funds by
         $20 million since Thurmond's primary motivation was not a
         reduction in defense spending. Rather, he was against spending
         the money in the civilian sector, which he felt would impair
         the development of military air transport capabilities. See
         Congressional Record July 13, 1959, pp. 13202-13208 and
         July 14, 1959, pp. 13291-13316; particularly p. 13202 and p.
         13315.
1963-   Another motion to show fairly strong anti-defense feelings was
         Young's motion to reduce civil defense funds by $47 million.
         Rejected 28-48.

modest, public concern. By the end of the 1950s and the 1960s
the Cold War had become less important to many Americans;
particularly after the Cuban missile crisis of 1962 images of
stability, parity and low threat became widely accepted. The
lower emphasis on the Cold War may well have made possible
a reexamination of its assumptions, providing the basis for very
different opinions at the end of the 1960s when, under the
impact of Vietnam, military and foreign policy questions once
more seemed pressing.

It might be hypothesized either that popular sentiment produces, or that it follows high-level political antimilitarism. Exhibit 6 graphs the ups and downs of one measure of legislative
opposition to defense spending over the period 1946-1971. It
shows the highest percentage of the Senate recorded in favor of
any reduction in military authorizations or appropriations
below the level requested by the executive branch, as manifested in each session of Congress.[18]

As with the graph of actual military spending, there is no
consistent relationship between year-to-year changes in congressional resistance to defense spending and such resistance in the
mass public. An increase in Senate votes to cut the defense
budget was about as likely to coincide with a decline in popular
preference for such a move as with a similar increase. The
search for a lagged relationship, however, turns up something a
bit more promising. In six out of eight cases where one can
match an increase or decrease in Senate antimilitarism with sub-

sequent popular changes, the two correspond. Nevertheless, the number of cases is too small to allow us to take the finding very seriously.

More impressive is the overall similarity in pattern between Exhibit 6 and the relevant portions of Exhibit 1. Both mass and political elite showed some opposition (stronger in the latter case) as the Korean War continued, and both reached their peak at the end of the 1960s as the Indochina War dragged on. Whereas in the initial post-World War II decade it often happened that not a single senator was recorded in favor of reducing the defense budget, from 1966 onward more than one-fourth of the senators took such a position. Ignoring the wide fluctuations in mass opinion as registered in the polls of the 1940s (due in substantial measure to changes in question wording), the only important divergence between the elite and popular patterns probably occurred in 1963, when considerable sentiment emerged in Congress for reducing military spending. Even here we cannot be sure that such a divergence occurred, because we lack proper measures of popular sentiment for that period. But the fact that Senate opposition quickly fell off again until several years later suggests that the legislative doves failed to strike an immediate chord of popular resistance.

Yet by the end of the 1960s opposition to defense expenditures had become widespread at all levels of the political system, and it is by no means obvious who was leading whom. It seems quite likely that in the recent phase congressional antimilitarists were responding to public opinion as much as they were molding it. While the senatorial doves doubtless made opposition to the military respectable in a number of less-exalted quarters, it is also true that many of those solons either took up an already popular issue or used the new sentiment as an opportunity to express some latent feelings about defense spending that they previously feared to speak about. The precise mechanism triggered by this mass sentiment is unclear and doubtless varies for different politicians.

If the new attitude toward the military cannot be attributed solely to political leadership from the top, nor to simple fatigue with war or opposition to extraordinarily high military budgets (compared with past budgets either as a share of total government spending or of GNP those of 1968-1971 are not extraordinary), where does it come from? Here one can only speculate. We should not forget that the Korean War was an unpopular conflict which produced a good deal of skepticism at home about American political leaders. But the Indochina War almost certainly reached much lower depths of public esteem. It dragged on over twice as long, brought more casualties, and resulted in a much less favorable gain/loss balance for American foreign policy than did the Korean conflict. Despite some ambiguities and hopes for reunifying Korea, the war of the 1950s did achieve the minimal goals of the government and of most Americans—communist aggression was repelled. The same cannot be said for the 1960s war in Indochina; whatever the ultimate outcome the communists almost certainly will play a major role in the government or in much of the territory of each of the three Indochinese states, and the avowed aim of the American government—establishment of a democratic regime in South Vietnam—seems very distant. The Indochina War is the clearest failure of American foreign and military policy in 150 years. A special casualty has been popular respect and awe for the efficiency of the American professional military, which has resulted in a new willingness to cut military funds. The McNamara years of new-style civilian analysis of military budget proposals may also have contributed somewhat to a general skepticism of military demands.

Furthermore, disillusionment with the military arises at a time of domestic crisis and new needs for government spending. The 1950s in large part constituted a period of reaction against big public expenditure programs, of fears of big civilian government. Thus, at least on the public expenditure level, there were few popular competitors to the defense budget. But with current requirements for better health, better cities, pollution control and a fight against hunger, new demands, widely considered legitimate, are being made for public funds. Some programs initiated or expanded in the Eisenhower administration, for example the great post-Sputnik inputs into education and research, are now contributing to this climate.

Another probable contributing factor is the presence in the electorate of a whole generation with no adult memory of intervention in World War II or even of the beginnings of the Cold War. This new cohort of voters is thus less ready to accept the standard arguments for an interventionist foreign policy or the need for large armed forces.[19] In the September 1970 survey 60 percent of voters under 30 wanted to reduce military spending, whereas only 46 percent of those 30 and over gave such an answer. Similarly, Moyer has found that congressmen born after 1920 are more skeptical of military spending than are their older colleagues.[20] In an article published two decades ago Frank Klingberg presented some fascinating evidence for generation-long cycles of involvement-withdrawal in American foreign affairs—a cycle which he predicted to move into its withdrawal phase in the late 1960s.[21]

Political dissent, as measured by thinking the war "a mistake," or by disapproval of the President's performance in general, rose during both the Korean and Indochina wars. This had not happened during World War II.[22] Both recent wars, the latter surely more than the former, contributed to a general disaffection with the entire political system. Very possibly the strong antimilitarism fed especially by the Indochina failure will bring the United States back in a lasting way toward the widespread suspicion of the military so typical of the country before World War II. Those who would welcome such a decline in approval of the military may not necessarily, if they value stability of the entire political system, so heartily welcome its general delegitimization.

In any case, what is clear is that the former popular permissiveness toward military spending is gone. Should the new climate of mass opinion be politically influential we will have to revise our conceptions about the determinants of military and foreign policy. Implications for the likelihood of violent international conflict are also apparent. Research is increasingly establishing a causal link from high arms levels to war.[23] If politically effective, mass resistance to military spending may therefore help prevent not just wasteful arms races, but war itself.

NOTES

1. This argument is developed at much greater length in Bruce M. Russett, *What Price Vigilance? The Burdens of National Defense* (New Haven, Conn.: Yale University Press, 1970).

2. Walter Lippmann, *The Public Philosophy* (Boston: Little, Brown, 1955).

3. Quoted in Julius Duscha, *Arms, Money, and Politics* (New York: Ives Washburn, 1965).

4. Samuel P. Huntington, *The Common Defense* (New York: Columbia University Press, 1961) p. 235.

5. Alfred O. Hero, "Public Reaction to Government Policy," in *Measures of Political Attitudes*, ed. John P. Robinson, Jerrold Rusk and Kendra Head, (Ann Arbor, Mich.: University of Michigan Institute of Social Research, 1968) pp. 29-31. Caspary shows evidence that in the 1950s a conviction that the United States had made "too many sacrifices for defense" was frequently associated with opposition to foreign military and economic assistance, and to international commitments more generally. William R. Caspary, "Dimensions of Attitudes on International Conflict: Internationalism and Military Offensive Action," *Peace Research Society (International) Papers,* 13 (1970): 1-10.

6. Not all the data points represented in Exhibit 1 (favoring reductions) are found in Exhibit 2, since some questions did not offer an increase in spending as an option. Relevant questions were not asked during World War II nor, with one exception, between 1960 and the end of 1968.

7. For these sample sizes, the typical marginals we are dealing with and the sampling methods used during most of the period, it seems appropriate to consider differences of less than 5 percent from one survey to another (that is, for example, 23 percent giving one answer in one survey and 19 percent giving the same answer in another) as not statistically significant at the .05 level, and hence perhaps due to sampling variation. Where the questions vary, as in Exhibit 3, of course even 5 percent difference will not be significant. On these problems see the discussion in Norval Glenn, "Problems of Comparability in Trend Studies with Opinion Poll Data," *Public Opinion Quarterly,* 21 no. 1 (Spring 1970): 82-91.

8. This bias is not great enough to affect the trend analysis except

perhaps to undervalue by no more than 1 percent the extent of antimilitary feeling in the earlier surveys when better-educated people were
oversampled. See Glenn, "Problems of Comparability."

9. Huntington, *The Common Defense*, p. 249.

10. Gabriel A. Almond, *The American People and Foreign Policy* rev.
ed. (New York: Praeger, 1960). See also Karl W. Deutsch and Richard
L. Merritt, "Effects of Events on National and International Images," in
International Behavior: A Social-Psychological Analysis, ed. Herbert
Kelman (New York: Holt, Rinehart and Winston, 1965). For some evi-
dence that Almond's description of swings in mood is exaggerated, see
William R. Caspary, "The Mood Theory: A Study of Public Opinion and
Foreign Policy," *American Political Science Review*, vol. 64 no. 2 (June
1970): 536-547.

11. This also suggests that merely "knowing the facts" does not itself
produce any particular attitude for or against military spending. Note
also below that while education is associated with approval of military
spending in the early Cold War years, this relationship has reversed in
the very different context of 1968-1972.

12. For an excellent example of what can be done with many data-
points and fully comparable questions, see John E. Mueller, "Presidential
Popularity from Truman to Johnson," *American Political Science Review*, vol. 64 no. 1 (March 1970):18-34.

13. See Mueller, "Presidential Popularity."

14. On the basis of limited evidence it would appear that a similar
decline in enthusiasm for military spending occurred rather earlier in
other countries. During the Korean War in September 1952 the United
States Information Agency surveyed citizens of five Western European
countries on the question, "Do you favor (name of country) building up
its military forces at this time, or are you against it?" The responses
ranged from 45 percent in favor in West Germany to 79 percent in
Britain. United States, Office of the High Commissioner for Germany,
A Survey of Public Opinion in Western Europe (Paris: Research Analysis
Staff, HICOG, 1953). As late as November 1962, 41 percent of Canadians
felt that defense forces should be larger and only 4 percent wanted
them smaller. John Paul and Jerome Laulicht, *In Your Opinion: Leaders' and Voters' Attitudes on Defense and Disarmament* (Clarkson, On-
tario: Canadian Peace Research Institute, 1963). The shift in opinion
against military spending in Britain seems to have begun as early as
1955, when the defense option was chosen by 32 percent of respondents
in a nationwide survey asking, "If the government wants to cut down
its spending, which of these would you put first?" Samuel P. Huntington,
The Common Defense (New York: Columbia University Press, 1961)
p. 243. In March 1966, 55 percent of Britishers expressed approval of
"the Government's decision to limit spending on defense" in a National

Opinion Poll. Similarly, over the winter of 1964-1965 in France, Norway and Poland, a proportion ranging from nearly half to over two-thirds of those with opinions preferred to cut defense spending rather than leave it at current levels or raise it. Johan Galtung, "Public Opinion on the Economic Effects of Disarmament," in *Disarmament and World Economic Interdependence,* ed. Emile Benoit (Oslo: Universitetsforlaget, 1967) p. 173.

15. For these three pieces of evidence see respectively, James D. Wright, "Life, Time, and the Fortunes of War," *trans*action (now *Society*) vol. 9 no. 3 (Jan. 1972): 47-52; Arthur M. Louis, "What Business Thinks," *Fortune,* vol. 80 no. 4 (Sept. 1969): p. 207; and Allen Barton, "The Limits of Consensus Among American Leaders," mimeographed (New York: Bureau of Applied Social Research, Columbia University, 1972).

16. The modest rise from 1957 to 1960 in antimilitary sentiments, followed by a decline in 1964, is very similar to trends that were going on in public willingness to see Communist China seated in the United Nations. After a significant increase over 1957-1961 in the proportion of the population so willing, the trend reversed, and popular hostility to Peking increased during the Kennedy years. Thus the beginning of the Kennedy administration may well represent a modest but aborted opportunity for a relatively early emergence of public attitudes less conditioned by the Cold War. See Gerry Ruth Sack Tyler, "A Contextual Analysis of Public Opinion Polls: The Question of the Admission of Communist China to the United Nations" (Ph.D. diss., Yale University, 1972).

17. John E. Mueller, "Trends in Popular Support for the Wars in Korea and Vietnam," *American Political Science Review,* 65 no. 2 (June 1971): 358-75.

18. Thus votes merely in *opposition* to *increases* volunteered by Congress are not shown. I use percentage of the Senate, rather than total votes, to allow for the expansion of the Senate with the admission of Alaska and Hawaii. Also, I use only the number of senators so recorded on a roll-call vote, omitting pairs and later announcements of position, on the grounds that on those roll-calls that are deemed really important and politically salient (e.g., in 1969 and 1970) most senators will appear. Inclusion of pairs and announcements would somewhat raise the more-than-zero levels of opposition that appear in most of the earlier years, but not greatly change the pattern.

19. A good systematic analysis of the effect of different life-experiences on opinion can be found in Davis Bobrow and Neal E. Cutler, "Time-Oriented Explanation of National Security Beliefs: Cohort, Life Stage, and Situation," *Peace Research Society (International) Papers,* 8 (1967): 31-57.

20. H. Wayne Moyer, "House Voting on Defense: An Ideological Explanation," in Bruce M. Russett and Alfred C. Stepan eds, *Military Force and American Society* (New York: Harper and Row, 1973).

21. Frank Klingberg, "The Historical Alternation of Moods in American Foreign Policy," *World Politics*, vol. 4 no. 2 (Jan. 1952).

22. Robert B. Smith, "Disaffection, Delegitimization, and Consequences: Aggregate Trends for World War II, Korea, and Vietnam," in *Public Opinion and the Military Establishment*, ed. Charles C. Moskos (Beverly Hills, Cal.: Sage, 1971).

23. For example, see the contributions by Nazli Choucri, Jeffrey Milstein, and Michael Wallace in Russett, ed., *Peace, War and Numbers*.

4

LEVEE EN MASSE, C'EST FINI: THE DETERIORATION OF POPULAR WILLINGNESS TO SERVE

Vincent Davis

In the past, Americans have often passionately, sometimes even violently, resisted personal participation in combat, and have used various means, including political influence, to avoid circumstances that could require such participation. But before Vietnam, American political leaders were able to recruit enough soldiers to fill the combat ranks by using one or more techniques of mass mobilization. The Vietnam experience suggests that such techniques are decreasingly effective; it now appears that nothing short of a dire immediate threat to national survival will arouse popular commitment to serve in the ground combat forces.

The historical pattern

The major evidence supporting this assertion is to be found in a review of American wars. American historical experience reveals the following persistent patterns: [1]

—reluctance by American political leaders, in response to public opinion, to involve the nation in war in the first place.

—reluctance by political leaders to force Americans to serve in a war once the nation is involved.

—persistent efforts to utilize machines in lieu of manpower in American military forces.

—the ineffectiveness of many if not most techniques to coax substantial numbers of Americans to serve in the military in general, in wars in particular and in ground force combat most particularly.

—great effort by many if not most Americans, once they find themselves at war and especially in ground combat, to get out as quickly as possible regardless of the consequences for the war itself.

—the massive unpopularity of most American wars that last for more than a year or two, even if they appear headed toward something that looks like "victory."

—rapid demobilization of military forces, often cutting the Army back to skeletal proportions, after American wars.

American military leaders have sometimes been left with virtually no troops at key points in several wars. It happened to General George Washington at Valley Forge and to other colonial officers at various times during the American Revolution, as the Continental Congress and other authorities experienced great difficulties in raising and maintaining ground forces. Similar situations occurred during the War of 1812. In 1847 in the Mexican War, General Winfield Scott was poised for the final triumphant attack on Mexico City when his troops simply walked away and straggled back toward the U.S. border as their enlistments expired, resulting in a suspension of the war and great loss of life. Calls for volunteers were never fulfilled in the Civil War, and the Congress, after many unsuccessful efforts, finally passed a conscription bill because the "dwindling response to the calls for volunteers was extremely alarming." [2] But this legislation led to major draft riots, especially in New York City. The Spanish-American War was the only U.S. conflict in which more than enough volunteers enthusiastically signed up, but this brief war lasted only three months in the summer of 1898. Even so, there was great discontent and a desire among the troops to go home before the battle's end.

The late eighteenth and the entire nineteenth centuries in American military history thus witnessed a continuing dilemma between efforts to raise military forces by volunteer methods, which were successful only in the early summer of 1898, and conscription methods, which were always highly unpopular and sometimes bitterly resisted. The same dilemma, with approximately the same results, has persisted throughout the twentieth century to the present day.

In some respects, however, there appears to have been a subtle but significant shift in the personal values that sustained Americans when ultimately they did find themselves in combat in twentieth century wars (in contrast to those of the eighteenth and nineteenth centuries), as suggested by a reading of novels, poetry, plays and private memoirs pertaining to the various military conflicts over the entire scope of American history.[3] Prior to 1900, the American fighting man generally tended to believe he was superior to his enemy in one—and usually more than one—of the following ways: the feeling that he was part of a superior civilization, a superior race, certainly a superior nation, advantaged by a superior technology and a superior military organization, while representing a superior set of religious convictions. But around the turn of the twentieth century, these senses of superiority gradually began to erode. There was a steady shrinkage in the size of the primary group or basic unit of social cohesion with whom the American soldier identified and for whom he thought he was fighting, to the point where he was fighting almost entirely for his own private individual survival in the Vietnam War in the 1960s.[4] Larger values and loyalties had for the most part seemed to disappear.

CAVEATS

Before moving from a quick sketch of the historical trend in American attitudes toward military service to a tentative explanation of the trend, it is important to stress two conclusions that are *not* implied or suggested in this essay.

First, the contentions here must not be confused with arguments suggesting that Americans have gradually become more and more opposed to war. On the contrary, there is no great outcry or even subtle opposition against wars in which the United States is not involved and does not seem likely to become involved—such as the military actions in Czechoslovakia and Nigeria in the 1960s and the situation in Pakistan in the early 1970s. Even American pacifists and peace societies seldom seem greatly agitated about military developments where U.S. involvement appears remote. The assertions here pertain only to trends in American attitudes with respect to personal participation in combat and therefore, by extension and inference, to wars in which the United States is involved or seems likely to become involved actively. Indeed, even pertaining to wars of this kind, there is often little American opposition as long as circumstances allow most Americans to think there is little likelihood of their personal involvement in combat. This has sometimes led to a kind of curious public schizophrenia in which Americans seem on the one hand to favor their nation's active involvement in a war but, on the other hand, believe and trust that this will require no significant sacrifices from them. More will be said later here about some implications of this national ambivalence.

Second, the assertions here must not be confused with arguments suggesting that the United States is a "decadent society" which is perhaps participating in "the decline of the West." An eminently distinguished professor of international relations at Princeton University voiced support for this particular proposition in a conversation with the author in June 1971, and one can hear and read various versions of this theme in numerous places. President Nixon in early July 1971 apparently told a group of media executives in Kansas City, according to widespread press reports, that he felt this kind of decline into decadence could well be the fate of the United States unless appropriate remedies were promptly implemented.[5] But this essay is not designed to support contentions within this "America is growing soft" school of thought. Indeed, no such normative implications are intended one way or another. Depending on one's more general predictions for the future of international relations, and perhaps on one's particular value preferences, a growing American reluctance to participate personally in combat could be viewed either as "a good thing" or "a bad thing." This essay is not designed to be either optimistic or pessimistic on such future possibilities.

A TENTATIVE EXPLANATION OF THE TREND

But, then, if the trends and tendencies suggested here are at all accurate, how can they be explained? It is difficult—and risky—enough to hazard these sweeping descriptive generalizations inferred from almost two centuries of American history, and it is even more difficult and speculative to posit explanations. Historians tend to look at each war and to offer idiosyncratic explanations pertinent only to each, which is doubtless a prudent scholarly procedure. But idiosyncratic explanations fail to account adequately for what appear to have been trends and tendencies persisting over 200 years of U.S. history in widely varying circumstances.

Gary L. Wamsley has suggested that Americans' longstanding resistance to military conscription—and, by extension, resistance to military service and especially combat duty—is explained by a continuing "antimilitarism" within the nation's "political culture" which was originally transmitted to North America by the early colonists.[6] This explanation is at least partially satisfying insofar as it pertains to those beliefs, attitudes and pervasive values which can be described as *public* perspectives often institutionally articulated and enshrined in the national society's laws, declarations, policies and official rhetoric. To this extent the present author tends to agree with Wamsley, especially for the period of national history prior to 1900.

The Wamsley explanation, however, is less satisfying—perhaps not even relevant—with respect to those essentially individual, *private* and personal values tending to sustain a man in combat which, it was suggested a few paragraphs earlier, began to show substantial erosion starting with the turn of the twentieth century. On the other hand, Wamsley's contention that the public values of antimilitarism were communicated from Western Europe to America by the early colonists is an idea suggesting some comparisons between Western Europe and America. A casual reading of novels, poetry, plays and private memoirs written by Europeans pertaining to their nations' involvement in wars reveals essentially the same trends evident from the counterpart American literature. Indeed, in many respects the erosion and shrinkage of private personal combat-sustaining values were even more pronounced in Western Europe than in the United States after 1900. With Germany as the primary (occasional) exception, Western European nations appeared as reluctant to go to war as the United States and were generally as ill prepared for war when they did ultimately become involved. Even before 1900, for much if not most of the nineteenth century, most Western European nations seemed as relatively unenthusiastic about going to war as did the United States.

Historians have tended to use familiar arguments such as the "Pax Britannica" idea, the "concert of nations" and the "balance-of-power system" to explain the relative absence of major war in Europe in the nineteenth century. Similarly, it has been said that the United States escaped involvement in military conflicts outside North America because it was the chief beneficiary of the preoccupation of European powers with each other, including the allegedly free protection provided by the British fleet, the protection afforded by the wide oceans and the accompanying American policy of "isolationism." As for the twentieth century, the great violence of World Wars I and II may have blinded scholars to the fact that most Western European nations as well as the United States avidly sought to avoid involvement in both.

One conceivable conclusion, therefore, is that common elements in the Western European and American value systems as well as common elements in their experiences in the nineteenth and twentieth centuries must be looked for as components of an explanation for their popular reluctance to become involved in war. As for common values, both areas were committed to economic growth through private endeavor encouraged and supported by governments. The increasingly secularized "Protestant work ethic" was by no means confined to Protestants, in that Catholics and Jews were in many respects equally caught up in the individualistic search for material gain and prosperity. Rationalistic and scientific procedures were the common heritage from the Renaissance and the Enlightenment, and science and technology became the servants of the quest for economic growth. The Industrial Revolution was the result, and this in turn generated its own requirements in terms of daily values-in-practice and life styles regardless of residual rhetorical commitments to more transcendental and metaphysical values.

In simpler terms, the industrialization of Western Europe and North America was accompanied by the ever more vigorous and successful pursuit of materialistic comforts, to the point where high consumer demand was necessary for economic stability and further growth. (In 1958, when President Eisenhower was asked at a press conference what could be done to break the then-current recession, he replied simply, "Buy, buy, buy.") The spiralling commitment to private gain and economic growth was part of the industrialization process, and required life styles for the average man that were increasingly at odds with the life styles required in military organizations and starkly

at odds with the life styles in combat. Western European and
North American nations were accordingly compelled increasingly to seek their military manpower—most especially their
volunteer recruits for the ground forces—from the least industrialized (i.e., the rural traditional agricultural) sectors of their
societies. But, by the 1960s and early 1970s in the United States
and to some extent in Western Europe as well, even agriculture
had become increasingly mechanized and industrialized. The
last remaining source of readily willing and able recruits for
military careers or even short-range military service began to
dry up. Increasingly, modernized countries have found that the
only popular, and therefore politically viable, forms of military
force were those machine-intensive mechanized forms requiring
limited personnel whose skills were quite similar to the skills
called for in a modern plant or factory.

Take the case of the rural peasant in most traditional agricultural societies among the less-developed countries. For this
individual, service in his nation's military is not likely to result
in a net decrease in his standard of living and may very well
represent an increase. The peasant serving as a soldier is likely
to wear better clothes, eat better food, live in more sanitary
conditions, receive better medical care—indeed, to have a
longer life expectancy, even allowing for occasional combat in
wars—than his peasant counterpart trying to scratch out a
living on, for example, the banks of the Nile. But then take the
case of all but poverty-level rural workers in the United States.
Even if such an individual could improve his standard of living
by enlisting in the Army, he has been socialized from birth in
terms of prevailing social values which are not likely to make
him think of the military as an appealing career. Moreover,
even if taxes *could* be increased to provide a higher level of
comfort within a military career, those above the poverty level
would probably think that they could "do better on the outside" in civilian life. For a citizen of the modern industrial society, no amount of creature comfort which could be provided
in a military career would offset the reduced life expectancy in
combat, and wars have come along often enough in the twentieth century that the average citizen would have to conclude

that a military career might well include occasional combat. If this average citizen inquired about the premiums for life insurance if work in a combat zone was foreseen, he would confirm his hunches about reduced life expectancy.

Granted that these explanations here are speculative as to the reasons for the alleged steady shrinkage in the values tending to sustain Americans and Western Europeans in combat, and therefore the steady shrinkage in the number of people willing to serve in the military, particularly in ground forces, and therefore the growing unpopularity of involvement in war, a major question remains: Why, then, have the Western European nations and the United States become so frequently involved in such violent wars in the twentieth century? Social scientists still have very little reliable knowledge on which to base answers, but guesses can be suggested. Regarding the frequency of wars, our guess is that the same processes of industrialization which have made Western Europeans and Americans less willing to participate in wars have at the same time tended to reinforce international interdependence and thus tended to encourage international conflicts. As for the violence of modern wars, the same processes of industrialization—and therefore the mechanization of warfare—have led to the increasing use of remotely launched weapons of mass destruction (long-range artillery, aerial bombardment, missiles and rockets and so on).

MOBILIZING THE RELUCTANT WARRIORS

If it is necessary to be highly speculative about reasons for the frequency and violence of twentieth century wars involving Western European nations and the United States in the face of steadily growing popular unwillingness to serve in combat, it is possible to be somewhat less speculative in suggesting some of the circumstances that have succeeded in mobilizing large numbers of otherwise reluctant Americans to serve. Historically, the most efficient short-run circumstance offsetting the long-run trend against American willingness to serve in the military has been some shocking catalytic event which at least temporarily outrages other American values and provokes or galvanizes the American public into support for national military responses. But, in accordance with the long-run trend, the required magnitude of the provocative event has grown steadily larger. In 1898 the sinking of a single American warship in Havana harbor was largely sufficient. In the 1914-1917 period the sinking of several ships by an adversary's submarines was required. By 1941 the sinking of the larger part of the Navy's fleet was the requisite catalyst. In view of this history, adversaries after World War II tended to avoid any such provocations. No such catalytic event of single dramatic proportions was provided by adversaries in the cases of the Korean and Vietnam wars, and both wars were highly unpopular almost from the beginning (in part, of course, because it was rather quickly discovered that each of these wars could not be successfully managed with mechanized mass-destruction weaponry alone but required substantial ground forces; public opposition, although sometimes accompanied by thick layers of moralizing and legalizing, tended to correlate directly with casualty figures).

Parenthetically at this point, and with an eye toward the future, it might be noted that Americans have historically been more easily provoked into military responses by events at sea or involving ships than by events on the land, for reasons that are not understood by this author. The unpopular Korean and Vietnam wars were responses by the United States largely to events on the land. But, interestingly, when President Johnson concluded that a provocative event was needed to generate public support for greater American involvement in Vietnam, he chose an asserted event at sea (in the Gulf of Tonkin) rather than any number of events involving comparable or greater threats to American lives and equipment on the land. As for the future, it may be worth noting that a provocative event at sea is at least more conceivable in the 1970s and subsequent decades in view of the dramatic surge of Soviet naval capabilities alongside smaller anticipated reductions in American naval forces than in other forms of U.S. military capability. Nevertheless, in view of the long-run trend, the basic expectation here still remains that a provocative event—even one at sea—would have to be of sufficient magnitude to be widely perceived as a direct and dire threat to national survival before it could trigger large public support for U.S. military involvement on a sustained large scale.

A second efficient short-run circumstance occasionally off-setting the long-run trend against American willingness to serve in the military, is the typical American tendency to give the President the benefit of the doubt and to rally enthusiastically behind him for at least a few months after the outbreak of hostilities. But this kind of fervent unquestioning patriotism tends to be an emotional jag which seldom produces public support for much more than a year or two at the very most, and clearly for less time as casualties rise if "victory" appears distant.

A third technique that American political leaders have tended to use to maintain public support when the leaders concluded that military involvement was in the national interest, has involved a range of methods for manipulating or deceiving public opinion. For example, several successful presidential candidates ran for office on platforms promising no or very limited American involvement in existing or prospective wars but then broke those promises shortly after winning elections. Cases in point would include Woodrow Wilson in 1916, Franklin Roosevelt in 1940 and Lyndon Johnson in 1964, with less clear-cut examples provided by Harry Truman in 1948 (his January 1950 declarations that Korea was outside the U.S. defense perimeter) and John Kennedy in 1960. Richard Nixon, somewhat similarly, suggested in 1968 that he would promptly extricate the United States from Vietnam if elected.

Another version of public opinion manipulation once widely used was official government encouragement and assistance to the entertainment and journalistic media in producing plays, movies, newsreels and publications designed to villify adversaries while stressing the righteousness of the American cause. This positive form of manipulation was widely used in World War II, less so in the Korean War and less yet again in the Vietnam War, perhaps because of the inherent difficulties in controlling the television media. But there appeared to be a gradual increase in using negative forms of manipulation. The negative side generally included various techniques of direct or subtle media censorship, such as the Roosevelt administration prohibitions against showing or publishing any photographs of American war dead (a prohibition that began to break down in mid-1943) and various efforts by the Kennedy and Johnson administrations to discourage media publication of "bad news" from Vietnam (as was widely reported by David Halberstam and other journalists).

Political manipulation of public opinion seems to be effective only for a limited time, perhaps for not more than a year, unless the official "good news" is reinforced from separate sources (such as reports by non-American but nonhostile media). If the other evidence does not exist or does not reinforce the "good news"—worst of all, if the other evidence moves in the opposite direction—the political management of the problem leads quckily to what has more recently been called a "credibility gap." For example, by the time in mid-1943 that U.S. political censorship against publishing photographs of American war dead began to break down, separate evidence suggested to the American public that military success was in sight. Yet, even though all evidence by late 1944 indicated that the United States was well on the way to winning a decisive military victory in a generally popular cause, public support began to wane sharply and people such as Secretary of the Navy Forrestal worried along with President Roosevelt about premature "psychological demobilization." [7] This suggests that there is some finite time limit on American public support even for successful or victorious wars in popular causes, especially when high casualty levels are sustained.

The fourth circumstance or technique used in the United States to offset popular unwillingness to serve in wars has been a more or less direct acknowledgement of the previously suggested consequences of industrialization, which ultimately requires a large literate consumer society (i.e., values, attitudes, beliefs, life styles and standards of living) increasingly differentiated from the demands of a military society. There were occasional grudging accommodations in the form of some relaxation of traditional military requirements, but these could scarcely bridge much of the growing gap between the life of an infantryman in combat and even average expectations in civilian life.[8] The solution was thus twofold: first, to recruit military personnel largely from those rural and agricultural areas where the gap between civilian and military lives was least pronounced,[9] and second, to emphasize those mechanized forms of military service which minimized the gap from the other end.

In other words, American political leadership has been increasingly compelled to deemphasize combat ground forces (which are labor or manpower-intensive) and to stress naval and air forces (which are machine-intensive). As Wamsley indicated, the long-standing myth of an armed and trained civilian militia or reserve helped to persuade Americans that, in case ground forces were ultimately required, they could be obtained from this source and everybody else could avoid this kind of participation.[10] But the Korean War demonstrated that reservists were no more enthusiastic than conscripts to fight a war, and in the Vietnam War President Johnson decided that he faced less domestic political risk in raising conscription levels than in calling up reserves. Meanwhile, during the protracted periods of the twentieth century when the United States was not actively involved in military encounters, the implied public demand for lightly manned or mechanized military systems produced a need for military strategies which could rely on such mechanized systems and could thus promise quick success without much damage to American lives or property. Such a strategic solution was offered by the Navy from the 1890s to World War II, and the Navy was accordingly the politically preferred service (i.e., received the larger appropriations) during that period. The Air Force was most persuasive in offering a quite similar strategic solution from 1945 into the mid-1960s, and thus became the politically preferred service during this period.[11]

Implications for the 1970s

From all of the arguments and evidence suggested here, it is possible to offer some crude predictions for the immediate future and then to speculate more generally in anticipation of the longer-range future.

First, the U.S. Army, as the primary ground force service, will be more severely reduced in the 1970s than the other American military organizations, largely for the basic reason that it *is* the primary ground service, and this is the form of military service (and implied combat roles) that Americans like least of all. The Army has been sharply cut if not demobilized after every American war, but it will be all the more severe in the 1970s because it was more seriously stigmatized by publicity surrounding Vietnam operations than the other services. However, to the extent that the Army remains in existence, it will become increasingly mechanized in the effort once again to reconcile the irreconcilable dilemma between the conviction that the nation somehow needs a ground force service and the fact that Americans strongly resist participating in the combat elements of such forces.[12]

The Air Force will also be significantly reduced in the 1970s, partly because technology has been almost *too* successful in devising new hardware-intensive (mainly missile) systems to substitute for manpower in performing many traditional Air Force roles (generally associated with manned aircraft), and because the Air Force was also to some extent stigmatized by publicity surrounding Vietnam operations. There may be a limit to which American values will tolerate impersonal mechanized forms of mass destruction. The Air Force of the future is likely to have somewhat more diversified long-range missile systems, perhaps somewhat more manned aircraft in the smaller tactical plane category, but far fewer of the large manned bombers which General Billy Mitchell taught the Air Force to believe was the prime weapon of air warfare.

The U.S. Navy will be reduced, too, after the Vietnam War, but less severely than the Army or the Air Force, partly because it remains highly machine-intensive (although still requiring substantial manpower to operate the machines and equipment), partly because it enjoys more inherent strategic and tactical flexibility than either the Army or the Air Force in an organic sense, and partly because it suffered the least degree of stigma in Vietnam publicity. Finally, the one most significant form of growth in Soviet military capability is the surge in naval forces, which will add to the U.S. Navy's political appeal in the 1970s. The Navy will therefore become once again—more by default than design, and not because of its own efforts or any new strategic thinking in the Navy—the nation's "first line of defense." [13]

Aside from the levels and categories of American military forces maintained in the 1970s and beyond, probably nothing short of a dire immediate threat to national survival could produce public support for actually using these forces, i.e., for American military involvement in a war or warlike situation, if significant casualty levels (perhaps 250 fatalities per month) were sustained for more than a few months or a year at the most. None of the old circumstances that were previously able to mobilize public support is likely to be successful in the future. Public opinion manipulation is harder and harder if not absolutely impossible to manage with a more sophisticated and better-educated citizenry enjoying access to an ever-wider range of international information sources. Any future moods of jingoistic enthusiasm for military engagement are likely to be very short indeed, perhaps a week or two in duration, as the price of engagement becomes more quickly apparent and better publicized than in the past.

Some short-run circumstances, such as a temporary shortage of jobs in the civilian economy, could make somewhat larger numbers of Americans willing to serve in the military. This was the case in the 1930s when the military forces were used for relief and rehabilitation purposes. Similarly, nonmilitary crises and disasters—such as widespread floods or other natural catastrophes in the United States or elsewhere—might make some reservists willing to participate in call-ups for short periods. But the point is that no such circumstance will be effective if it appears that combat service is the likely result. The troops would remain unwilling to serve in combat and therefore ineffective in war, notwithstanding traditional and newer techniques of training, morale-building and motivation.[14]

The explicit consequence is that the government of the United States has been effectively foreclosed for the indefinite future from one traditional form of military involvement: ground force actions. Significant but less strong inhibitions would deter the substantial use of other forms of military capability. Other observers, it might be noted, have reached somewhat similar conclusions. For example, *New York Times* foreign correspondent C. L. Sulzberger, making reference to a work published in France by American political scientist Robert Lawrence, concluded in late 1970 that the United States was effectively deterred or inhibited from using either large-scale nuclear weapons or smaller-scale conventional military forces.[15]

QUESTIONS FOR FUTURE RESEARCH

If the arguments of this essay are accurate, they have profound implications for American foreign and military policy, as well as for the overall structure of international relations in the future. Clearly, of course, the speculative propositions here need to be subjected to rigorous empirical testing before they can provide a legitimate basis for policy change.

The basic contention here, for example, is that the growing range and strength of constraints on the U.S. deployment of forces in combat, most especially ground forces, are now almost ironclad. These constraints should be taken as a constant rather than a variable, since they are relatively impervious to manipulation and external stimuli. But it has also been suggested that many if not all of the same trends are at work in other modern industrialized societies, as indicated in part by the great reluctance of numerous American allies to increase their ground forces regardless of what the United States does or does not do. New research should therefore certainly be comparative, including Britain, France, West Germany, the Scandinavian nations and Japan, all of which may be under similar constraints against the use of sustained levels of ground forces.

Pressing comparisons further, it might be possible to show, for example, that all nations with significant access to the sea tend to shift from ground-oriented and manpower-intensive military forces to a sea-based and machine-intensive force structure at similar or parallel stages in industrial development, in the absence of a large and less developed hostile nation with large ground forces in adjacent territory. A variation on this theme might even partially explain the apparently sudden new Soviet development of naval forces in the 1960s, constrained only or mainly by the Chinese ground force threat, thus suggesting future developments in Soviet strategic thinking and military force commitments under various foreseeable circumstances. The primary foreseeable circumstance would be a reduction in the Chinese ground force threat as perceived from Moscow. This reduction could come about in several ways, including an actual reduction in Chinese ground forces, or a redeployment of those forces away from the Soviet border areas, or growing Soviet confidence in its nuclear strike forces as a deterrent against the Chinese ground threat, or growing Soviet encirclement of China by establishing strong new allies in South and Southeast Asia, or some combination of these possibilities. In any case, if the Soviet leaders in Moscow should perceive a reduction in the Chinese ground force threat for any reason or reasons, it seems likely that Soviet strategic thinking would become increasingly enthusiastic about the advantages of expanding naval forces. These advantages include the relatively lower political costs (compared to ground forces) of operating near other nations' borders on a worldwide basis, the opportunity to counter U.S. naval forces already operating worldwide, the relatively long operational life of naval equipment, and—perhaps most importantly in connection with the main arguments elsewhere in this essay—the increasing compatibility of skills and lifestyles in civilian life and in military service (naval variety) in an increasingly industrialized and urbanized Soviet Union. Thus, within this kind of expectation, the naval elements within the overall mix of Soviet military forces would steadily grow in proportion, and would be increasingly deployed on a worldwide basis as the military component of an ambitious but less overtly threatening Soviet global diplomacy.

Speculative writing about the future nature and frequency of warfare is not rare in modern times; but virtually all such literature, including the present essay, leads to one firm conclusion: None of these efforts will be very persuasive unless and until behavioral scientists are able to support their conclusions with more high-quality and long-range trend data.[16]

NOTES

1. Two useful overall surveys of American military history are Walter Millis, *Arms and Men: A Study in American Military History* (New York: G. P. Putnam's Sons, 1956) and T. Harry Williams, *Americans at War: The Development of the American Military System* (Baton Rouge: Louisiana State University Press, 1960). However, Williams deals almost exclusively with the Army, to the neglect of the other services.

2. Gary L. Wamsley, *Selective Service and a Changing America* (Columbus, Ohio: Charles E. Merrill, 1969) pp. 18-25.

3. For more details, see Vincent Davis, "Trends in Popular Willingness to Serve in Combat: Pre-Hypotheses, Conjectures and Other Impressions" (Paper delivered at the annual convention of the Inter-University Seminar on Armed Forces and Society, in Chicago, Illinois, November 1971). This paper was adapted from a book-length manuscript written by Davis in 1962-1963, which was apparently deemed unpublishable by prospective publishers in part because of some reckless and far-fetched forecasts that, if the United States became involved in war in Southeast Asia, it would be enormously unpopular and militarily inconclusive.

4. Charles C. Moskos, Jr., *The American Enlisted Man: The Rank and File in Today's Military* (New York: Russell Sage, 1970) pp. 144-146. This otherwise superb book is marred only by the fact that—like so many other books on "the American military"—it is based almost ex-

clusively on the U.S. Army, thus ignoring significant differences among the subcultures of the several armed services.

5. For example, see "U.S. Approaches Zenith, Must Avoid Decadence, Says Nixon," a report under the byline of Frank Cormier, Associated Press, in the *Newport* (Rhode Island) *Daily News*, July 7, 1971, p. 11.

6. Wamsley, *Selective Service*, pp. 15-16.

7. Walter Millis with E. S. Duffield, eds., *The Forrestal Diaries* (New York: Viking, 1951) pp. 5-7.

8. This author learned from several authoritative sources in the U.S. Army that the average cost for maintaining each U.S. basic infantryman in the Vietnam War was about $40,000 per year, exclusive of weapons systems and direct military equipment. Most of this money was spent in an effort to transport as much of the American standard of living and life style as it was feasible to transplant into a foreign combat environment—well-constructed barracks and other physical facilities, hot and cold running water, hot meals, radio and television stations and receivers, and the like. The total cost for the annual maintenance of an Army division in Vietnam averaged more than $1 billion, approximately equal to the cost of a large aircraft carrier. The costs of maintaining the ground force soldier do not include such related but separate costs as the expenditures involved in the 12-month rotation system (which also entailed many nonmonetary costs) and periodic "R & R" leave trips outside of Vietnam.

9. See, for example, Morris Janowitz, *The Professional Soldier* (New York: Free Press, 1960) pp. 79-103; the data presented by Janowitz clearly demonstrate the predominance of people from rural and agricultural areas in the armed forces. Other evidence reinforces the point; an article by Ralph Blumenthal in the *New York Times*, May 28, 1971, p. 11, reported on the number of ROTC units that had been discontinued on many university and college campuses, almost all of which were in the industrial East, and the growing number of new ROTC units, almost all of which were located mostly at smaller schools in rural and agricultural areas elsewhere.

10. Wamsley, *Selective Service*, pp. 16-17.

11. Vincent Davis, *The Admirals Lobby* (Chapel Hill: University of North Carolina Press, 1967) p. 113.

12. General William Westmoreland, Chief of Staff, U.S. Army, was quoted in the October 16, 1971 issue of *The New Republic*, p. 17: "Today machines and technology are permitting economy of manpower on the battlefield, as indeed they are in the factory. But the future offers even more possibilities for economy. I am confident the American people expect this country to take full advantage of its technology—to welcome and applaud the developments that will replace wherever possible the

man with the machine." Edwin Newman, in *The New York Times Book Review*, December 20, 1970, p. 12, reported that "Gen. Westmoreland has called [for] 'the automated battlefield,' with warfare a matter of management and technology, and battles . . . in which the infantryman no longer need carry a weapon and in which everything will be done by remote control." Newman was commenting on a book by Ward Just, *Military Men* (New York: Knopf, 1970).

13. This conclusion is supported by substantial trend-type evidence particularly from budget developments in the Department of Defense; for example, see the article under the byline of William Beecher, *New York Times*, November 9, 1971, p. 1.

14. In support of this and other key points in this essay, the following figures are from authoritative sources in the U.S. Army. In early 1971 the Army determined that it needed about 20,000 new recruits per month to maintain prescribed force levels. Approximately 5,000 of these were being raised from "true volunteers" (men with draft lottery numbers so high that they were virtually certain not to be drafted). Of these 5,000, approximately 300 were volunteers for the "combat arms" (armor. artillery and infantry). As of the fall of 1971, various new techniques had been successful in generating approximately a tenfold increase (up to about 3,000 per month) in the volunteers for the combat branches. Army authorities tend to feel that one of the most effective of the new techniques was the various options offered, particularly the choice of unit in which to serve or geographic region in which to spend the initial 16 months of service. Most chose Europe, on the assumption that the war in Vietnam would be terminated before an initial 16 months in Europe would make them conceivably eligible for a Vietnam assignment. In other words, the less likely an actual combat assignment, the easier it is to recruit for the combat arms. Other new recruiting techniques included allowing certain units to engage in their own direct recruiting, but all of these efforts were confined to rural and agricultural areas in the South, Southwest and Rocky Mountain states, again demonstrating the relatively greater ease of recruiting combat forces from these sectors.

For a useful short review and analysis of motivational techniques in earlier and more recent military periods, see Lieutenant Colonel James L. Scovel, "Motivating the US Soldier to Fight in Future Limited Wars" (Thesis, U.S. Army War College, 1970) pp. 12-25.

15. C. L. Sulzberger, "Solving an Ugly Dilemma," *New York Times* November 15, 1970, sec. 4, p. E-11.

16. For an earlier statement of the same position, see Vincent Davis, "The Role of the Military Officer in American Life and Government: A Research Note" (Paper presented at the annual convention of the American Sociological Association, San Francisco, California, August 1967).

CIVIL-MILITARY RELATIONS AT THE COMMUNITY AND OPERATIONAL LEVEL

5

ANTI-ROTC: RESPONSE
TO VIETNAM
OR "CONSCIOUSNESS III"?

Peter Karsten

Originally an elitist *reserve* officer training program designed
to acquaint future national leaders from the "better" colleges
with the art of war, ROTC has, since World War II, become a
major source of *career* officers for the armed services. Along
with the escalation of the war in Indochina, ROTC has come
under criticism on many of the nation's campuses for the dogmatic nature of its curricula, that fact that it is subject to outside control, and its military presence among the community
of scholars.[1] Of course, all of these issues could have been
argued before Vietnam, and it seems clear that reaction to the
war has precipitated much anti-ROTC sentiment.

For a while in 1968 and again in 1970, it looked like
ROTC was "on the ropes" (which is why this chapter was originally supposed to deal with "The Fate of ROTC"). A number
of prestigious colleges, many of them charter members of the
ROTC roster, withdrew credit for ROTC courses or asked

the services to phase out their campus units. Fire-bombs were used against these and other ROTC units. Between 1966 and 1970 the number of campuses requiring male students to take ROTC declined from 106 to 42, and during that same period, 25 colleges that had required Air Force ROTC decided it would no longer be compulsory.

How are we to interpret the effects and significance of this anti-ROTC sentiment? How has the military responded? Where is ROTC going in the 1970s?

The first step necessary in understanding the anti-ROTC explosion is to place it in historical perspective. And once that is done it becomes evident that ROTC was in trouble long before the anti-ROTC movement of the late 1960s. For example, though it was a virile part of the officer procurement program throughout the 1940s and 1950s, compulsory Army ROTC has been on the wane for more than a decade and a half, falling steadily from 170 compulsory units in 1956 (69 percent of all Army ROTC units) to 161 in 1961 (65 percent), 144 in 1963 (58 percent) and 117 in 1965 (47 percent).[2] Concurrently total Army ROTC enrollment fell from 174,718 in 1962 to 157,723 in 1965.[3] For some reason the post-Korea, post-McCarthy generation was not responding to ROTC as enthusiastically as preceding generations.

Congress responded with an ROTC Vitalization Act in 1964, providing among other things 5,500 ROTC scholarships for each service (previously scholarships had been available only to Navy ROTC students) and a two-year alternate ROTC program for incoming junior college transfer students and "delayed-reaction" candidates. Western and southern congressmen expressed the hope that there would be a "good geographical distribution of scholarship recipients."[4] Simultaneously, a Mershon Study Group at Ohio State University proposed an innovative curriculum mix of civilian and military ROTC instructors. In 1966-1967 ROTC enrollments rose for the first time in a decade. Colonel Stephen White, Chief ROTC Public Affairs Officer for the Continental Army Command, told the Army Advisory Panel on ROTC Affairs in January 1967: "Viet-

nam, the threat of the draft . . . have been favorable to our recruiting efforts. It now appears that we shall have little difficulty
in achieving an acceptable level of enrollments for the immediate future." [5]

The next several years must have been frustrating and
disappointing to Colonel White. Overall ROTC enrollment for
all services fell steadily from 260,000 in 1966-1967 to a low of
87,000 in 1971-1972. The decline is largely a function of the
continued demise of compulsory ROTC (the Air Force will
have only three such units left by 1972, two of them at military
colleges), but the services are not expressing undue alarm; the
"elective" programs are now described as "more effective and
economical." [6] Since about half of ROTC students appear to
be draft-motivated,[7] the shift to a random lottery draft system
has caused as many as one-third of the draft-motivated to resign,
but it also has caused a sizable number of low lottery number
sophomores to enroll in the two-year ROTC program, offsetting
much of the loss of those with high lottery numbers. On-campus
opposition to or rejection of the military appears to account
for the rest of the decline, as many officer candidates have become sensitive to antimilitary sentiment—and are resigning.

Why are they resigning? The author of a recent survey of
Air Force ROTC dropouts at the University of Massachusetts,
Captain Michael Duto, found that nearly 50 percent of those
who had resigned indicated that both "appearance requirements (such as length of hair)" and "unwillingness to wear the
uniform on campus" were "significant factor[s]" in their decisions to withdraw from ROTC. As Captain Duto put it: "Our
cadets are not full-time, 24-hours-a-day military men; they are
first of all, students, who must constantly associate with the rest
of the collegiate community." [8]

A recent survey of 42 1967-1969 dropouts from Army
ROTC and Air Force ROTC at the University of Pittsburgh
supports Duto's Massachusetts findings. The dropouts are
"greening," and ROTC symbolized "Consciousness II." [9] Typical comments were: "I dislike the regimentation," or "ROTC
doesn't let you be yourself." The girlfriend of one Pittsburgh

Army ROTC student advised the head of the unit: "Your stupid haircut regulations are going to break up our relationship!"

Opposition to the war surely accelerated the dropout rate, but probably because it drew attention to the extent to which ROTC was symbolic of the "establishment" and its values. A sampling of 177 Army, Air Force and Navy ROTC students at Ohio State and Pittsburgh recently revealed a level of support for the Vietnam War among the ROTC student population that was substantially above that of the rest of the randomly sampled male student population, and at very nearly the same level as that found in a sampling of Annapolis students simultaneously polled. But on virtually every other issue the ROTC students were much closer to their non-ROTC classmates than they were to the Annapolis sample.[10] The point is that while the ROTC student is reasonably secure in his pro-Vietnam position, despite campus criticism of the war, he finds criticism of himself as "a uniformed straight" or a "skinhead" intolerable.[11] Only one student in 49 of Captain Duto's respondents indicated that "campus reaction" to "U.S. military activity in Southeast Asia" had made a significant difference in his decision to withdraw from ROTC, and the Pittsburgh survey confirmed Duto's findings: all resigned for reasons other than opposition to the war in Indochina. It seems quite possible that ROTC dropouts have rejected the military and what it represents rather than the war *per se.*

On the surface it appears that hostility to the Vietnam War has driven ROTC off the campuses of some of the "better" colleges for good—or at least for the foreseeable future. Between 1966 and 1970 ROTC units at 29 colleges were disestablished by one or another of the services. Once again, historical analysis provides interesting perspective. In 1965 the cost accountants in the Defense Department's Management Improvement Program (MIP) required an evaluation of all "uneconomical" ROTC units—that is, units graduating an average of less than 25 officers per year over a four-year stretch. After a probationary period of a year or two, MIP directed, any unit unable or unwilling to take the necessary steps to "improve production" was to be disestablished. Over 50 percent (15) of the 29 campuses losing ROTC units in the late 1960s were deprived of ROTC on the initiative of the military because they were "not major producers of officers and their enrollment projections showed no possibility for improvement." [12] The remaining 14 colleges initiated the disestablishment proceeding themselves, but nearly all were "low producers" who would probably have been phased out within the next few years anyway. Among these "self-destructing" low producers were Harvard, Princeton, Columbia, Stanford, Brown and Dartmouth. Assistant Secretary of Defense for Manpower and Reserve Affairs, Roger Kelley, was "a trifle concerned" about the loss of these prestige institutions, but not enough to cause him sleepless grief, for they represented less than 2 percent of the annual total of ROTC graduates.[13].

All the services have waiting lists of colleges hoping to acquire ROTC programs. Many of these colleges, General B. B. Cassiday recently told the Air Force ROTC Advisory Panel, "have the characteristics generally associated with high production and high rates of retention in the Air Force." [14] That is, they are young, southern, southwestern or Rocky Mountain colleges with student populations more sympathetic to the establishment than is true of the Ivy League and other "prestige" schools [15] (see Exhibits 1 and 2). Thus while ROTC enrollments have been declining on the vast majority of campuses over the past decade, they have been rising recently on campuses like Texas A & M, Baylor, Purdue, Louisiana Tech, San Diego State, San Jose State, Central Washington State, Portland, Lehigh, Fresno State and East Texas State.[16]

The services are moving to curb plummeting ROTC enrollment figures in a number of ways. In 1968 the Army launched an extensive publicity campaign complete with TV spots, high school recruiting teams, letters to the parents of potential ROTC students and brochures with "psychedelic covers," [17] a campaign designed to improve the image of ROTC. The Defense Department's Special Committee on ROTC (the Benson committee) recommended a number of innovations in September 1969 and issued a follow-up progress

Exhibit 1. COLLEGES AND UNIVERSITIES ADDING ARMY ROTC UNITS (1968-1971)

State College of Arkansas, Conway
Arkansas AM & N, Pine Bluff
Western Illinois University, Macomb
Morehead State University, Ky.
Central Missouri State College, Warrensburgh
Rider College Trenton, N.J.
Eastern New Mexico University, Portales
St. John's University, Jamaica, N.Y.
Stephen F. Austin State College, Nacogdoches, Tex.
Brigham Young University, Provo, Utah
Wisconsin State University at Oshkosh and Stevens Point
University of South Alabama, Mobile, Ala.
Southeastern Louisana College, Hammond, La.
Appalachian State University, Boone, N.C.
Rochester Institute of Technology, Rochester, N.Y.
Old Dominion College, Norfolk, Va.
Wisconsin State University, Whitewater
Northern Illinois University, DeKalb
Northern Michigan University, Marquette
Long Island University, Greenvale, N.Y.
Central State College, Edmond, Okla.
Northeast Missouri State College, Kirksville
Francis T. Nichols State College, Thibodaux, La.
Florida Institute of Technology, Melbourne
Southern Colorado State College, Pueblo
Kearney State College, Kearney, Neb.
Jackson State College, Jackson, Miss.
Virginia Commonwealth University, Richmond
Boise College at Boise, Idaho
Alabama A&M College, Normal
Alcorn A&M College, Miss.
Austin Peay State University, Tenn.
Campbell College, N.C.
East Central State College, Okla.
Missouri Western College, Mo.
Southwestern State College, Okla.
University of Tampa, Fla.
Weber State College, Utah
Wisconsin State University at LaCrosse
Wisconsin State University at Platteville

Source: New York Times, February 4, 1969, p. 9, and Colonel Gerald Perselay, USAF, Assistant Secretary of ROTC Programs, to author, February 16, 1972.

Exhibit 2. NEW AFROTC UNITS 1971
INSTITUTIONS SELECTED FOR NEW DETACHMENTS

Angelo State University, Tex.
Arkansas A&M College
College of Santa Fe, N.M.
Mississippi Valley State College, Miss.
Newberry College, S.C.
Norwich University, Vt.
Parsons College, Iowa
Southern Illinois University at Edwardsville
Southern Utah State College
Sul Ross State University, Tex.
Troy State University, Ala.
University of Missouri at Rolla
University of Puerto Rico (Mayaguez Campus)
University of Southern Mississippi
Valdosta State College, Ga.

Source: "Briefing for AFROTC Advisory Panel by Brigadier General B.B. Cassiday," January 18, 1971, mimeo, AFROTC Headquarters, Maxwell AFB, Alabama, Slide 2.

report a year later.[18] The Navy is establishing new units on black campuses, and all three services are increasing their efforts to recruit black officer candidates at existing units.[19] Congress has recently passed legislation that increases the number of ROTC scholarships, raises subsistence pay, and allows for "cost-sharing" payments to host colleges at a rate of more than $500 for each ROTC graduate per year (a move designed to increase the host college's interest in ROTC production levels). At least one service has asked to be allowed to reach down into the lowest decile of its Officer Qualifying Test scores to boost enrollments.[20] Additional "ladies auxiliaries" are appearing on campuses, with the object of "glamorizing" ROTC.[21] Taking its cue from Betty Friedan rather than the *Playboy* centerfold, the Air Force is actively encouraging the enrollment of future WAF officers. Over 500 women were enrolled in Air Force ROTC programs as of late 1970. And finally, the services are looking with some satisfaction to the growth and vitality of the Junior ROTC (JROTC) program.

JROTC, a high school program established for all the

services by the ROTC Vitalization Act of 1964, is steadily moving toward its authorized strength of 1,200 units (650—Army, 275—Air Force, 245—Navy, 30—Marine Corps). The three-year program (tenth through twelfth grades) offers male students a choice of an "academic track," designed to prepare them for college ROTC or a service academy, and a "technical

Exhibit 3. ANTI-ROTC INCIDENTS, SCHOOL YEARS 1968-1969 AND 1969-1970

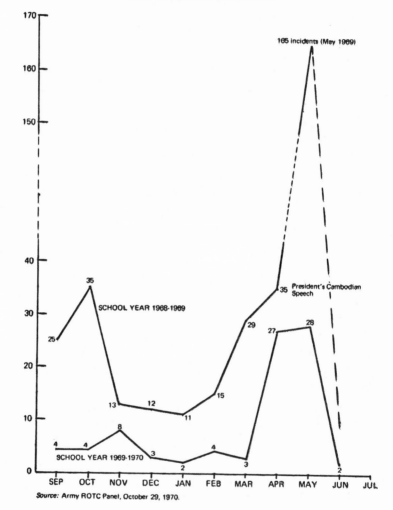

Source: Army ROTC Panel, October 29, 1970.

track," designed to move them into the enlisted ranks with E-2 standing and high motivation. No less than 43 percent of the 1970 crop of Air Force JROTC graduates went on to join college ROTC, obtain a service academy appointment or enlist in one of the services.[22] As General Cassiday recently put it, "The favorable impact of the junior ROTC program on the military services [and coincidentally on "senior" ROTC] seems undeniable." [23]

Just as the Vietnam escalation accelerated anti-ROTC sentiment, so the Nixon administration's "Vietnamization" program appears to have decelerated the anti-ROTC movement. Anti-ROTC activity in the weeks following President Nixon's Cambodia speech in late April 1970 marked the high-water mark of hostility to ROTC on campus (see Exhibit 3). Thereafter, anti-ROTC activity declined as U.S. forces were steadily withdrawn from Southeast Asia and draft pressures slackened (see Exhibits 4 and 5). A number of campuses that were considering disestablishing ROTC in 1969 and 1970 (among them Cornell, MIT and Holy Cross) now appear to have reversed themselves. Princeton, which expelled ROTC, has asked the military to reopen discussions.[24] The cancellation of 25 deferments is expected to boost enrollment in the two-year (junior and senior year) ROTC program offered by the Army and the Air Force, a program popular under the lottery draft system and the reduced credit allowed ROTC on many campuses (see Exhibit 6). ROTC may well be out of the woods in terms of the Vietnam War. And it has come out of the woods with a "lower campus profile," a new image, a better academic program, a potentially fatter wallet and a higher regard for blacks and women.

Nonetheless, despite the new image, despite all of the innovations, and despite the winding down of American involvement in Southeast Asia, ROTC may well be in much the same trouble it was in when it first asked Congress for help in 1964. The war may have simply provided temporary acceleration to an anti-ROTC trend that had been spreading for at least a decade.

Fifty years ago the "better" campuses and their "Platts-

Exhibit 4. ANTI-ROTC INCIDENTS

Category	July 1- October 20, 1969	July 1- October 30, 1970
Demonstration	44	6
Act of Vandalism	5	3
Theft of Arms & Ammunition	0	1
Bodily Assault of ROTC Cadre and Cadets	2	1
Riot, Fire or Bombings	5	6
Bomb Threats	1	12
Total	57	29

Source: Army ROTC Panel, January 1971.

END KARSTEN EX. 4

Exhibit 5. ACTIVITIES AGAINST AFROTC

Category	1969-1970	1970-1971	Percentage of Change
Major Damage/Injury	4	3	−25
Unfavorable Official Host Institution Action	15	2	−87
Minor Damage/Injury	30	21	−30
Disruptive Demonstrations	10	0	−100
Official Host Institution Studies	68	31	−54
Serious Threats of Disruption and/or Violence	26	33	+37
Nonviolent Demonstrations	33	19	−43
Unfavorable Student and/or Faculty Studies or Petitions	25	22	−12
Adverse Literature	117	57	−51

Source: Cassiday, "Briefing," Slide 9.

END KANSTEN EX. 5

burg" predecessors were enthusiastic supporters of ROTC.[25] But at the same time that ROTC was becoming the major source of career officers—in the 1950s and 1960s—the simultaneous "greening" of the upper-middle class was producing Ivy Leaguers who were either disinterested in the military life style or purposefully antagonistic towards it and other formal establishment symbols. It is unlikely to flock to a resurrected "extracurricular" ROTC program. If Cornell has decided to let ROTC remain, the decision is probably academic, since Cornell ROTC units will soon be falling below the required production levels, a function of declining enrollments. A number of Ivy League faculty and administrators hope to save ROTC,[26] either on a city-wide "crosstown" site off campus (or at least on someone else's campus), or as a summer camp program along the lines of the Marine Corps Platoon Leader Program or the various OCS-OTS postgraduate programs. But the former idea has thus far been an expensive, inefficient failure (the handful of students who seek out the off-campus site find it inconvenient, and their schedules do not mesh with those of students from other campuses, which means that they must often be dealt with tutorially).[27] And it is by no means clear that the Platoon Leader, OCS, or OTS programs will attract those who ordinarily passed through the now defunct ROTC units.[28]

A century ago the localistic, agrarian South and West constituted the heartland of "isolationist," anti-"Regular" and anti-ROTC sentiment.[29] Now well integrated into the national system and beginning to enjoy its fruits, these regions are more enthusiastic about ROTC, Old Glory, and the Ten Commandments, while the turned-on "better" campuses are dropping out. It is, of course, not inevitable that the "greening" of Ivy League elites will eventually reach the redneck-bluecollar grassroots.[30] One anonymous (but obviously non-Ivy League) member of the Army's ROTC Advisory Panel recently consid-

Exhibit 6. SENIOR ROTC ENROLLMENT TREND*

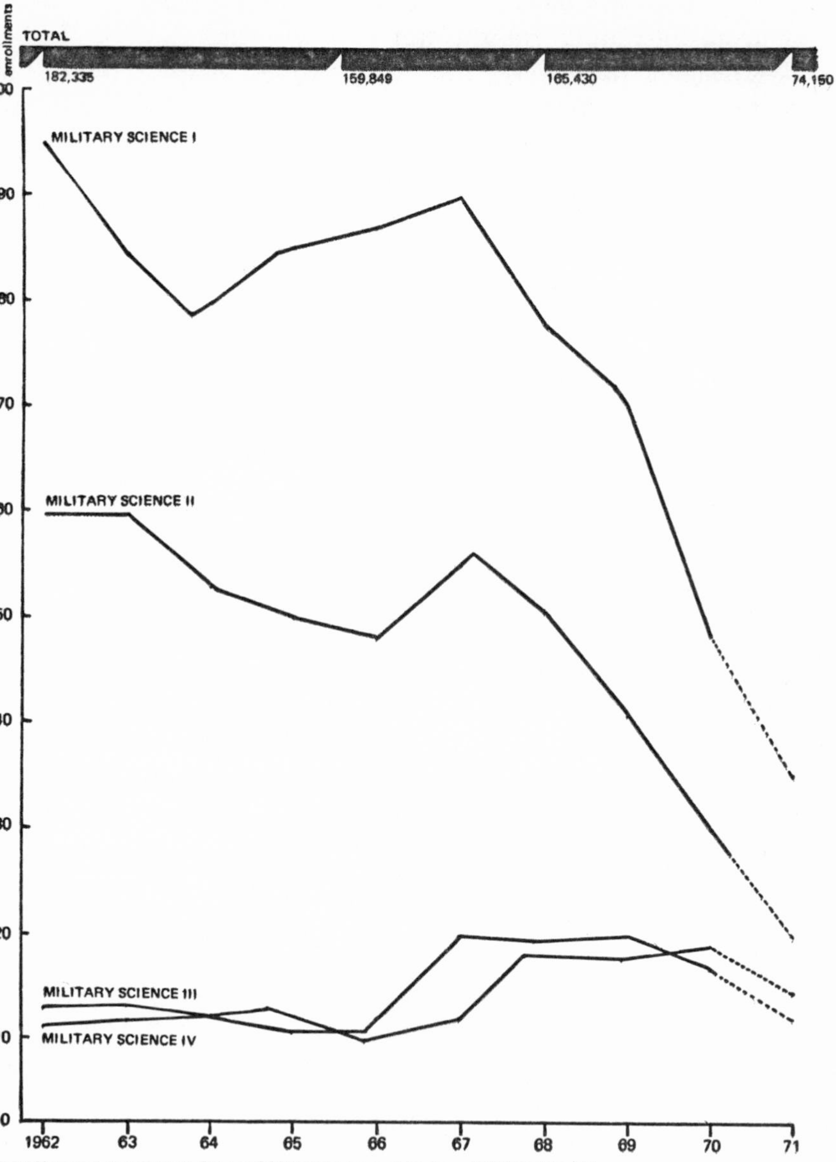

Source: "Meeting of Army Advisory Panel on ROTC," Department of the Army, DCSPER-RUO, 1970

*By beginning of year.

ered such "greening" unlikely: "I may be guilty of heresy when I say this, but what happens at the Ivy League doesn't have as much influence on what happens in our region as it used to." [31]

But other members were not so sure. ROTC may live on quite comfortably in its new setting for some time, but what happens in Boston and Berkeley generally happens in Edwardsville and Mobile too. Time will tell.

Perhaps the question of whether ROTC will survive on U.S. campuses is no longer a very meaningful one. Even if ROTC does survive and thrive in its new environment, the more important point that should be extracted from the story of ROTC's game of campus musical chairs is that the program has managed to survive only by changing its recruitment base, by reaching down into the mainstream of American society, by receding from the well-heeled, humanistic Ivy League elite and drawing from the more technically oriented upwardly mobile, lower-middle-class vital core,[32] a move coincidental with the extension of college opportunities to this segment of American youth. Eventually the social origins and personality traits of ROTC officers and "volunteer" enlisted personnel may overlap, by which time the elite may be pretty thoroughly antimilitary. Unless the "greening" reaches down to those grassroots soon we may be in for some civil-military tensions such as we have been seeing in the cities—increasingly independent, militant police vying with increasingly insulated, suburban, uncompromising ACLU elites. The cancellation of 2S deferments may boost ROTC enrollments, but only on campuses with ROTC units. Unless he joins (and is accepted in) the Marine Corps Platoon Leader program, the low-draft-lottery-number Harvard sophomore who loses his college deferment may end up as a private first class in some future Mylai assigned to a platoon commanded by a lowest-decile-Officer-Qualification-Test lieutenant from a southwestern state.[33]

Terry Robbins recently maintained that "ROTC is a class privilege—available only to those segments of the middle and working classes who can go to college. Ideologically, it strengthens the view that ordinary working people in America are unworthy to guide the nation's destiny." [34]

ROTC clearly *was* a class privilege, but it is becoming less identifiable with class and more identifiable with personality and ideology each year. Claims of the worthiness of ordinary working people to guide the nation's destiny may be based on misconceptions of the military's role. The military follows orders emanating from the civilian policy-makers in Washington, the civilian elites who guide the nation's destiny. Working-class people appear to be less willing to initiate overseas adventures than their more elitist compeers,[35] but they may be more willing to execute such adventures once the Bundys and Rostows have committed the nation to them. The Calleys and Medinas of America are followers, not morally conscious leaders, and we need leaders. Rousseau, Jefferson, Engels and Jaures all sought citizen armies led by citizen officers as a means of combating and preventing autarchy. But *which* citizens? It may make a difference. But for better or worse, there will be few John Kerrys in the U.S. officers corps in 1984.[36]

NOTES

1. There have been many critiques, but among the more cogent that I have seen are Alfred Young, *et al.*, "Do We Dare To Say No?" mimeographed (DeKalb, Illinois: Northern Illinois University, March 11, 1968); Lance Buhl, "The Case Against ROTC," *Harvard Bulletin*, May 25, 1970, p. 25; and Samuel P. Hays, "Military Studies at the University: A Proposal" mimeographed (Pittsburgh: University of Pittsburgh, 1969).

2. "Army ROTC Facts," Dept. of the Army, DCSPER-RUO, Feb. 1, 1971, p. 3.

3. "Meeting of Army Advisory Panel on ROTC [hereafter cited as Army ROTC Panel]," Dept. of Army, DCSPER-RUO, Jan. 26, 1967, Appendix, pp. 2, 4.

4. Army ROTC Panel, p. 10.

5. Ibid., p. 30.

6. Army ROTC Panel, November 21, 1968, p. 9.

7. K. H. Kim, Susan Farrell and Ewan Clague, *The All-Volunteer Army* (New York: Praeger, 1971) p. 87.

8. Captain Michael Duto, "The Problem—Retention," *AFROTC Education Bulletin*, 13 (March, 1971): 6. Cf. Radway's remarks about the resignation of service academy officer candidates in the mid-1960s who were offended by the "Mickey Mouse" they encountered; Laurence I. Radway, "Recent Trends at American Service Academies," in *Public Opinion and the Military Establishment*, ed. Charles C. Moskos, Jr. (Beverly Hills, Calif.: Sage, 1971) p. 24.

9. The "greening" referred to is, of course, that of Charles A. Reich, *The Greening of America* (New York: Random House, 1970).

10. See Ed Berger, *et al.*, "ROTC, Mylai, and the Volunteer Army," *Foreign Policy* (Spring, 1971): 135-160.

11. Cf. Major Archie C. Ringgenberg, "Long Hair vs. Short Hair," *Army ROTC Newsletter* (Oct.-Nov., 1970) pp. 5-6, and letters to the editor from LTC William E. Jones, Jr., and SGM Herman O. Allmendinger, "Two Responses to the Problem of Haircuts," *Army ROTC Newsletter* (May-June, 1971) p. 8A.

12. Brigadier General B. B. Cassiday, "Briefing for AFROTC Advisory Panel," mimeographed (Maxwell Air Force Base, Ala., AFROTC Headquarters, January 18, 1971); Office of the Deputy Assistant Secretary of Defense (Education), "Establishment and Disestablishment of ROTC Units (Washington, D.C.: Department of Defense, n.d.).

13. *Air Force Times*, September 30, 1970.

14. Cassiday, "Briefing," p. 4.

15. Edwin Snee, a University of Pittsburgh undergraduate, recently compared ROTC production in 1957 with the rest of American college graduates for that year and discovered that: the least populated regions graduate the largest percentage of ROTC students per capita; the region with the highest Gourman academic rating (weighted average), the Pacific Coast region with a Gourman rating of 534, had the lowest percentage of graduates receiving ROTC commissions (8.2 percent), whereas the region with the lowest Gourman rating, the South, with a rating of 430, produced the highest percentage of ROTC officers (13.8 percent) of its total graduate population. See also the report for the Carnegie Commission on Higher Education by Richard E. Peterson and John A. Bilorusky, *May 1970: The Campus Aftermath of Cambodia and Kent State* (Berkeley, Calif.: Carnegie Commission on Higher Education, 1971).

16. *Air Force Times*, Dec. 16, 1970, p. 13. On some campuses enrollments in one branch have risen while those of other branches are falling. Thus AFROTC at the University of Pittsburgh is thriving while Army ROTC enrollment at the same institution declines. This appears

to be due to the sustained and aggressive recruitment and public relations program pursued by AFROTC at Pittsburgh.

17. Army ROTC Panel, April 25, 1968, pp. 11-14, Annex D, pp. 1-6; Army ROTC Panel, October 29, 1970, Annex B, p. 4.

18. Office of Assistant Secretary of Defense (Manpower and Reserve Affairs) "Report of the Special Committee on ROTC to the Secretary of Defense" (Washington, D.C.: September 22, 1969); Office of Assistant Secretary of Defense (Manpower and Reserve Affairs) "Implementation of Recommendations Contained in the Report of the Special Committee on ROTC to the Secretary of Defense" (Washington, D.C.: September 15, 1970). The Benson committee appears to have been designed to calm the ire of Congressman Mendel Rivers as much as it was designed to innovate and "liberalize" ROTC. For a good critique of the committee's report see Laurence Radway, "The Future of ROTC," (Paper delivered at the Inter-University Seminar on Armed Forces and Society, Chicago, Illinois, October 1969).

19. The services are finding recruitment of blacks difficult, however, for much the same reason that they have had difficulty on Ivy League campuses; black students are reluctant to join visibly "establishment" institutions on campus.

20. Cassiday, "Briefing," Slide 6.

21. Army ROTC Panel, Annex F, April 16, 1970, p. 16; Cassiday, "Briefing," Slide 18.

22. Commander Ralph Williams, "The Junior NROTC Program," in *U.S. Naval Institute Proceedings* (June 1969): 134-137.

23. Cassiday, "Briefing," p. 23, Slides 22-24.

24. Based on conversations with LTC Charles Hyland, Assistant to Dr. George Benson, Deputy Assistant Secretary of Defense (Education), Major Dewey Johnson, AFROTC Headquarters staff, Maxwell Air Force Base, Alabama, and a scanning of AFROTC Headquarters files.

25. See, for example, John G. Clifford, "The Plattsburg Training Camp Movement, 1913-1917" (Ph.D. diss., Indiana University, 1969); and Gene Lyons and John Masland, *Education & Military Leadership: A Study of ROTC* (Princeton: Princeton University Press, 1959).

26. See, for example, Radway, "Future of ROTC"; and Alfred Fitt, Special Advisor to Yale's President Kingman Brewster, communication to the author, March 31, 1971.

27. Based on conversations with various members of AFROTC Headquarters and Army ROTC Headquarters.

28. I have spoken to OCS and OTS policy and recruitment supervisors of all three services, but it is impossible to say whether or not enrollment of students from campuses which have abolished ROTC is increasing in OCS, since the services have not asked themselves that

question and thus do not have such data readily available to anyone else who might ask the question.

29. See my "Armed Progressives" in *Building the Organizational Society*, ed. Jerry Israel (New York: Free Press, 1972).

30. Peter and Brigitte Berger feel that it will not. See their essay, "The Blueing of America," *New Republic* (April 3, 1971) pp. 20-23. I find their argument very persuasive.

31. Army ROTC Panel, Annex F, April 16, 1970, p. 4.

32. Ed Berger, pp. 139-140. Similarly, the academies have become more open. Compare Peter Karsten, *The Naval Aristocracy* (New York: Free Press, 1972), Chapter 1; Morris Janowitz, *The Professional Soldier* (New York: Free Press, 1960); Ed Lebby, "The Professional Socialization of the Naval Officer" (Ph.D. diss., University of Pennsylvania, 1971).

33. Berger, *et al.*, "ROTC, Mylai, and the Volunteer Army," *passim.* My position here is very similar to that of Harry A. Marmion, "Where Will the Officer Corps Come From?" in *The Case Against a Volunteer Army* (Chicago: Quadrangle, 1971), pp. 49-56.

Simultaneous with the creation of an AFROTC unit on his campus, the President of Sul Ross State College reportedly remarked: "I'd *love* to see my Sul Ross lieutenants commanding Princeton privates!"

34. Terry Robbins, "Time of the Furnace" (Cleveland: Ohio Region of the Students for a Democratic Society, *ca.* 1969) p. 4.

35. See, for example, Richard F. Hamilton, "A Research Note on the Mass Support for 'Tough' Military Initiatives," *American Sociological Review* (June 1968): 439-445.

36. John F. Kerry was a leader of the Vietnam Veterans Against the War during the peace protests in Washington, D.C. in the spring of 1971. Kerry, a former Navy lieutenant junior grade, won a Silver Star, a Bronze Star, and three Purple Hearts while commanding a "swift boat" in Vietnam. He testified in opposition to continued U.S. military involvement in Vietnam before the Senate Foreign Relations Committee. See John F. Kerry, "Let's Try and Glorify the Living," *Time*, 97(May 3, 1971): 12-13.

6

THE RESERVES AND NATIONAL GUARD: THEIR CHANGING ROLE IN NATIONAL DEFENSE

John R. Probert

The military reserves of the United States, including the Army and Air National Guards, are comprised of personnel who are neither totally civilian nor totally military. For this reason our reserve forces potentially can perform unique roles in civil-military relations. By limiting the manpower and resources of the active forces, the reserves serve as a check on the size of the professional military establishment. They leaven military thought and action, by infusing civilian views and values into the overall military structure. These roles are emphasized in early constitutional doctrine and debate.

The reserves also link the professional military establishment to the civilian sector, communicating information and perspectives about military requirements to civilians and thereby making them more sensitive to military needs. In certain circumstances, they can function as quasi-military pressure groups outside the ordinary constraints of the military, acting upon Congress, the executive, and state and local organs as well. With their considerable independence of the regular military, the reserves can take issue with it; and the political ties and expertise acquired in civilian pursuits and over long periods of interest group activity can make them very successful in securing their aims.

The reserves often act as a vehicle for testing public opinion in a crisis, with possible effects both at home and abroad. The call-up of reserve forces affects the American public much more directly than the deployment of regular forces, and is a more dramatic, summary and visible policy move than increasing the draft call. Consequently, probable public acceptance or rejection of a particular policy initiative can be ascertained quickly by mobilizing all or significant portions of the reserves.

The Johnson administration's failure to call the reserves for service in Vietnam was a departure from precedent. The Nixon administration has returned to precedent, officially stating its intent to rely on the reserves as "the initial and primary source for augmentation of the active forces in any future emergency requiring a rapid and substantial expansion of the active forces." [1]

The recasting of the role of the reserves—beginning with the decision of the Johnson administration in July 1965, to rely on the draft rather than a reserve call-up to augment our forces in Vietnam—appears, over the long sweep of the history of the reserves, to be a temporary change, but one that had great significance for civil-military relations in the United States. The exact nature of this significance can best be determined by an examination of the historical precedent for the role of the reserves up to July 1965, together with the actual and potential effects of the abandonment of the traditional role of the reserves in the Vietnam War.

THE CITIZEN-SOLDIER: TRADITIONAL AND
IDEAL CIVIL-MILITARY RELATIONSHIP

The Historical Precedent

The minutemen of Lexington and Concord were not the
first citizen-soldiers of American history. In fact, the citizen-
soldier concept developed in England, where feudal relationships had early established the dual responsibility of the serf
to till the fields and stand ready to serve with his lord in the
defense of his lands. In early England "trained bands" were
established to quell civil disturbance or deal with invasion.
The concept and the arrangements, which were incorporated
into the common law, were the basis of the colonial militias,
some of which were precursors of today's Army National Guard
units.

After the Revolution, the United States provided by law
for the National Guard, placing the responsibility for command
and authority with the states. The national government re-
tained the right to set up uniform standards of training and
equipment, but rarely exercised this authority. Federal government financed support of the militias was also limited.

From its establishment by federal law in 1792, until the
War of 1812, the National Guard or militia played a central
role in national defense. Our regular forces were almost nonexistent. In fact, the state militias comprised the principal
defensive forces of the nation in the War of 1812. As the outcome of that war indicated, the militias were generally ineffective and by the time of the Mexican War the regular Army
had expanded, and state militias were used to a very limited
extent. This also was the case in the Civil War. It was only with
the coming of the first and second world wars, the Korean
conflict and the Berlin and Cuban crises that the National

Guard and the various reserve units of the armed forces again played substantial roles in our defense.[2]

But from their establishment in colonial days until the present, the basic purpose of the militia or National Guard, and later the various reserves, was to constitute "the initial and primary sources for augmentation of the active forces" in an emergency, to use the phrases of the Laird memorandum quoted earlier. While it is true that in the major wars in our history, especially where the reserve forces were insubstantial, there was a necessary and frequently concurrent resort to the draft, only in the case of Vietnam was there no reserve call-up of any substance. This exception is difficult to understand for several reasons: our reserves were substantial and, by any earlier standard, well trained; they also were comparatively well equipped; and the war in which we were involved was far away, slow developing, limited in scope and against a small and comparatively weak force.

The Reserves as Economical Military Forces

Major reliance on the citizen-soldier in our national defense posture was not, however, founded on precedent alone. As the foregoing account has indicated, the economics of the problem of defense down through the years has predisposed us to a principal role for the reserve. An underdeveloped society could ill afford the tremendous expense of large standing forces. Furthermore, the need for defense forces was not continuous, except in the early days of the frontier. Militias appeared best suited to repelling Indian attacks, quelling domestic disturbances, or dealing on a long-term basis with unpredictable threats. In fact, with great ocean barriers, a balance of power being maintained in Europe, and reasonably secure borders to the north and south, the United States spent little time worrying about external threats either immediate or in the distant future. Consequently the government appropriated little money for meeting them. Militias suffice in circumstances such as these, and militias, particularly neglected militias, are cheap.

To this day, economics would appear to work to favor reserve forces. To quote Secretary Laird: "In many instances the lower peacetime sustaining costs of reserve force units, compared to similar active units, can result in a larger total for a given budget or the same size force for a lesser budget. In addition, attention will be given to the fact that Guard and Reserve Forces can perform peacetime missions as a by-product or adjunct of training with significant manpower and monetary savings." [3]

Providing Military Assistance to Civil Authorities

The reserves, particularly the National Guard, are not only more economical, but possibly more versatile, than the active forces in providing military assistance to civil authorities. The reserves are available to cope with civil disturbances, natural disasters, and for civil defense in the event of hostile attack.

Of the various components of the reserves as we have defined them earlier, the National Guards, both Army and Air Force, are the most immediately available and probably the best suited to the demands for military assistance in civil disturbances, natural disasters and for civil defense. The Army and Air National Guards comprise the largest components of the Selected Reserve—that part of the total reserve forces most likely to be ready by virtue of training and equipment levels. The Army National Guard, which in recent years has never been far from its programmed strength of 400,000, includes many combat-type units; and the Air National Guard, with its programmed strength of 88,000, includes a large number of transport-type units. Units in these categories are most likely to be useful in civil disturbances and natural disasters, as well as for civil defense. While it is true that in the latter two instances of military support to civil authorities, engineer, medical, signal and other types of service personnel—as distinguished from combat arms—are most essential, military reserve personnel and units of these types are available in substantial numbers in the Army and Air Guards even though the Army, Navy and Air Force reserves are composed primarily of such service units.

The principal advantages of the Guard over the reserve forces lie in the ease of calling them to active duty and their geographical distribution. The Army and Air National Guard can be called by state governors as well as by the President; the Army, Navy, Air Force, Marine Corps and Coast Guard reserves by the President only, and then only if he declares a national emergency.[4] Army and Air National Guards are never on state and federal duty at the same time because the President's call supersedes that of a governor. Since 1945, the Army and Air National Guard units have been called to active duty in approximately 700 different instances to deal with a variety of civil disturbances and disasters. Numbers called have ranged from two to almost 17,000. In all but a few instances, the troops have been called initially by the state governor; in all but a few, they have served in a state status only, although in some of the major call-ups—particularly for civil disturbances—they have been federalized.[5]

Since every state has a militia unit of some kind, and since in most states the Army and Air National Guard units are, for a variety of reasons, dispersed, local units of the Guard are on hand and available to the governors for immediate use in most cases of military assistance to civil authorities.

Thus the composition and location of the Guard units, together with the fact that they can be called by the governors as well as the President into state or federal status, make this component of the reserve forces the workhorse in military assistance to civil authority. Recent training emphasis plus substantial infusions of equipment and supplies have substantially improved Guard and reserve ability to deal with civil disturbances.

Although military assistance in natural disasters and for civil defense is not provided by the same military channels as assistance in civil disturbances, the reserve forces components have similar functions, response capabilities and problems here. The Office of Emergency Preparedness (OEP) in the Executive Office of the President plays a leading role in planning for and meeting natural disasters, with the Army as executive agent for the military. The OEP and the Army are central agencies in civil defense planning also. Again it is the Guard which has greatest flexibility of command channels, variety of resources and advantage of location. State adjutants general are key officials in the organizational structure for dealing with natural disasters and in civil defense, and are also the immediate commanders of the state national guards.

The recent massive effort in training time and provision of equipment that has been made to upgrade the performance of the reserves in providing military assistance to civil authorities in domestic disturbances should need no documentation, for it has been reported widely in the communications media. The effectiveness of the effort is difficult to measure, although instances of the use of reserves in meeting civil disturbances since Kent State in 1970 would appear to indicate improvement.

That there have been substantial efforts to improve administration of military assistance to civil authority is attested to by the plethora of new directives and revisions of old ones at all levels from Washington down through the state capitals to the units in the reserve. Additionally, there have been, since Kent State (May 2-8, 1970), some 230 recorded instances of state and federal reaction to requests for military assistance throughout the United States and its possessions, and involving up to 4,000 troops in response to antiwar rallies, civil rights riots, hurricanes, floods, tornadoes and an almost infinite variety of other emergencies.[6] One would assume, therefore, that the organizational machinery has inevitably improved.

Regular military forces are available for military assistance to civil authorities as well, and their performance has been outstanding since the Little Rock crisis. Williams has written extensively in "The Army in Civil Disturbances: A Professional Dilemma?" on the subject.[7] Reserve forces appear to have numerous advantages, including location, knowledge of local conditions and less cost, but their principal advantages lay in specialization and preventing the professional military from becoming involved in domestic political situations. Weapons, training, tactics and certainly mental outlook differ between riot control and dealing with alien military forces, and as Williams points out, there is even a difference in approach between domestic and foreign riot control. The reserve forces can specialize in domestic military assistance to civil authorities without seriously affecting their capability to fight against enemy military forces. While some loss of proficiency in capacity to fight a strictly military action would appear inevitable, the reserves are second-line and therefore would have time to prepare themselves to meet changing demands.

Avoiding the Pitfalls of the "Garrison State"

The founding fathers, particularly George Washington, had reasons other than economics for favoring the reserves. While the framers of the Constitution were aware of the need to be prepared militarily if peace was to be maintained, they also knew the perils of the "garrison state." And they were aware that we had slim resources for defense. As early as 1783, General Washington maintained that "the only probable means of preventing hostility for any length of time and from being exempted from the consequent calamities of War, is to put the National Militia in such a condition that they may appear respectable in the Eyes of our Friends and formidable to those who would otherwise become our enemies." [8]

But Washington and the framers had other aspects of defense besides cost and continued readiness in mind. That they saw the threat of the military to our democratic institutions is evident from the phrases of the Constitution, *The Federalist* and other publications of the time. In *The Federalist*, Numbers 24 through 29, for example, Hamilton presents an extensive discussion of the dangers of a standing army and the advantages of a militia as an alternative.

Washington and the framers were preoccupied with the idea of a well-regulated militia, not only because the militia provided comparatively inexpensive security against invasion, domestic insurrection and Indians, but also because it appeared to insure the continuance of our democratic form of government against militarism. Down through the years reliance on the militia continued as a foundation of American national security until eventually, as Hamilton predicted in *The Federalist, Number 28*, we could afford and needed large standing forces. Even then, as Hamilton also advised in *The Federalist,* through the medium of the National Guard and reserves, the safeguard of citizen forces remained. And the reserves were available for initial augmentation of the armed forces in an emergency as well. As Hamilton put it in *The Federalist, Number 26,*

> It is not easy to conceive a possibility that dangers so formidable as a military takeover can assail the whole Union, as to demand a force considerable enough to place our liberties in the least jeopardy, especially if we take in our view the aid to be derived from the militia, *which ought always to be counted upon as a valuable and powerful auxiliary* [italics added].

Implicit in this point of view is the belief that from the citizen-soldier can and will come not only the effective deterrent to military domination, but also to military or politico-military adventurism. When we stopped counting upon the reserves as "a valuable and powerful auxiliary" for augmentation of the active forces in 1965, did we encourage our ill-fated overextension in Vietnam? Without the citizen-soldiers as part of our military forces in a time of large-scale military operations, are we missing a counterpoise, some pluralism at the level of military execution which a democracy ought always to possess? And will this be missing in an all-volunteer army unless we keep it small and continue to rely upon the reserves for initial and primary augmentation in emergencies?

The Reserves and Deterrence

Among other justifications for a major role of the reserves in our defense are the circumstances which a surging military technology has imposed upon our defense requirements. Closely related to the cost argument, George Washington would have found the essence of his pronouncement on the militia echoed in this rationale. The capacity of an industrialized nation with modern arms to strike devastating blows over long distances and in a variety of ways would appear to be increased with a highly trained reserve as a credible deterrent.

In 1961, the Kennedy administration undertook to develop a flexible military capacity to deal with threats to the national security. The idea of sole reliance on massive retaliation was discarded. Also announced was massive mobilization of the World War II type, which depended upon sufficient time to train forces prior to their deployment. A flexible response, requiring troops in a high state of readiness, made necessary a variety of military forces tailored to a diversity of possible defense situations.

"Graduated deterrence," as the strategy came to be called, put tremendous requirements on the military establishment in men, training and equipment. To implement this strategy through standing forces not only would have entailed exorbitant expenditure, but it would likely have been less credible as a deterrent. The Berlin crisis is a case in point. The substantial call-up (of 150,000 reservists) at the time of Khrushchev's threats to Berlin underscored, as no standing military could, the resolve and determination of the nation. This kind of capacity to call up well-trained reserves not only signifies the resolve of the leadership of a nation, but also the population's knowledge and general acceptance of the venture.

The Political Role of the Reserves

Though the Berlin call-up of 1961 had the desired effect upon Khrushchev, as George F. Eliot so clearly demonstrates in his book on the subject,[9] there were some outcries of complaint and even opposition from the reserves and civilians. The complaints concerned mainly administrative shortcomings and are probably inevitable in any call-up. The opposition to the strategy itself was minimal.

But what if, as in the *Pueblo* incident call-up of 1968, opposition to the basic strategy is involved in addition to complaints about inconveniences, interrupted career programs and education? As an examination of correspondence files in the Pentagon and the newspapers of the day will reveal, some re-servists and civilians objected to the limited 15,000-man mobi-lization on the grounds that our national security was not involved, that the Vietnam War was a civil war, and that if the reserves were committed there would be a loss of flexibility in meeting potential aggression from another quarter and no forces at home to deal with civil disturbances. Some reservists filed law suits to prohibit the call-up. Every level of officialdom was besieged with letters, telegrams and telephone calls as those involved, their relatives and friends, but also other reservists and their relatives, friends and sympathizers attempted to re-verse the decision or, at least, prevent any additional call-up.

Here we have a manifestation of the reserve's capacity for both good and evil. Reserve forces are made up of individuals established in the community. They are concerned, especially about foreign policy which is likely to affect them directly. The officers are organized, as are some of the enlisted personnel, especially the noncommissioned officers and specialist groups.[10] While it is true that reservists have used their political weight most frequently on those issues where they seek immediate ben-efits such as a larger reserve, retirement pay, hospitalization or PX privileges, they have entree to decision-making centers in their hometowns and in Washington where military policy can be affected. And they can use their political power for just such purposes.

Reservists, with roots in civilian communities across the land plus their continuing interest in foreign policy, can exert strong influence for preparedness, and indeed have exerted such influence, as a glance at any issue of the house organs of the Reserve Officers Association or the National Guard Association will show. Because of their predisposition to military discipline and stated policy, they might not be able to restrain possible military or politico-military adventurism or error, but they can and will voice opposition to the decisions of the regular forces. For example, in the 1968 call-ups of reserves, numerous object-ing reservists wrote to congressmen. Many of these letter-writers questioned the rationale of the call-ups and did not object simply on the grounds of injustice or inconvenience, as the files of the Office of the Deputy Assistant Secretary of Defense (Reserve Affairs) will show.

As part of a military organization which is basically authoritarian, the individual reservist may be more constrained to withhold critical views than is a civilian. But he is, after all, only a part-time soldier. Furthermore, the great variety of reserve units and the kinds of education, training and vocational pursuit represented in them, assure a broad spectrum of points of view. All levels of society economically and educationally, all geographic areas, all ages from 18 to 60, are to be found in our reserve structure, as can be proven by a look at any troop list or some of the studies of reserve personnel.[11] While the old "society troops" of the pre-World War II years are not quite as representative of the highly influential segments of society as they once were, there are still many business and professional men, from both officer and enlisted ranks, in the reserve. There are also many troops from less influential walks of life. And of particular significance, there are substantial percentages of federal, state and local government employees, both as officers and enlisted men. In our pluralistic society, a sizable reserve structure is likely to be both representative of that society and concerned and capable of making its views known and its desires felt.[12]

Yet the voice of the reserve is not likely to be overpowering. Though certain segments of the reserve, such as the civil affairs units in the Army Reserve and their association, the Civil Affairs Association, were vocal in support of a role in Vietnam, they were not called.[13] One would assume that a strongly hawkish sentiment would exist in the more influential levels of our reserve structure, and the Reserve Officers Association and the National Guard Association journals attest to this. Working closely with Armed Forces committees in House and Senate, the Reserve Officers Association and the National Guard Association have time and again been instrumental in maintaining a strong reserve.

In addition, as mentioned earlier, high percentages of reserve and Guard officers and enlisted men are government employees. They know how to get things done in government at all levels, where the pressure points are, and how to apply the leverage. That the Guard is active in politics is shown by the established practice in many states of patronage appointments to officer slots in the Guard. In some states, although this is difficult to document, there are close connections between the Guard and certain political factions.

Even with all this political support the reserve does not always achieve its full aims. The example of the position of the Civil Affairs Association concerning Vietnam policy was mentioned earlier. The case of the merger of the National Guard and the Army Reserve by McNamara is another case in point. Though the total merger was forestalled, a substantial portion of what Secretary of Defense McNamara sought to accomplish was achieved by abolishing hundreds of reserve units.[14]

Furthermore, the hawkish bias is countered in many influential and articulate reservists and guardsmen alike by a preference for reserve rather than active status. For most of those in the reserve structure, active duty, particularly for prolonged periods, is disadvantageous to career, family life, educational pursuits and more especially the pocketbook. Financial incentives are the most attractive single aspect of the reserve status for our reserves and guardsmen. Desire to serve the country is a close second, but one of the biggest single disadvantages is the chance of being called to active duty. Extended active duty would end the dual income status.

Reservists thus have reason to be critical of call-ups, and hence of adventurism overseas. The response of those in the reserve status to the call-ups in the *Pueblo* incident, referred to earlier, is germane here. And the reserve pressure groups have only after many years, with great difficulty and fortuitous developments in our foreign policy, succeeded in approaching the reserve force levels they have considered necessary.[15]

In sum, the reserve is uniquely constituted, situated and motivated to play a role in support of and in restraint upon national security policy that is most likely to redound to the advantage of the republic. It is possible that no other segment of our society is in a like situation. But unless the reserve is to be invariably "the initial and primary" augmentation for the active forces in a "rapid and substantial expansion" it probably will not be inspired to play its role fully. If it is liable to call, it will be more likely to react in a critical and evaluative way which should be salutary for our policy-making, either in support of or against the proposed policy. If in support, we should have a result similar to that in the Berlin crisis; if in opposition, the effects should be a cautioning, calling for secondary looks and reevaluation.

Flexibility and the Reserve

A series of DOD directives, refined over the years to incorporate lessons learned in previous emergencies and mobilizations, provides the administrative basis for a modern reserve system that is truly flexible and capable of being adapted to a wide range of situations.[16] The Selected Reserve Force category, developed several years ago for increasing the readiness of reserves with important roles in contingency plans by adding to the number of drill periods, is a good example of one way in which reserve proficiency can be raised. More recently, Secretary of Defense Laird, in his statement before the Senate Armed Services Committee on the 1972 defense budget, outlined marked progress in equipping the reserves and in advancing their state of readiness. By the end of fiscal year 1971, ten reserve brigades had full equipment allowances. Improved types of equipment and increased allowances markedly advanced the equipment status of reserve units. In addition, some reserve units now train with active duty units and others actually have been integrated with active duty units so that if contingency plans are put into effect, these reserve units will deploy immediately with the parent active units.[17] Currently, some reserve units have the same high priority in contingency plans as active units.

More recently, Secretary of Defense Laird, pointing out that 45 percent of the Army's total force will be reserve elements by fiscal 1974, reiterated that the Army alone had issued more than a billion dollars worth of combat-serviceable equipment to the Army Guard and reserve during fiscal years 1970 and 1971 and had programmed equipment issues in fiscal 1972 at a higher level than the $727 million of fiscal 1971. In fiscal year 1973 they were expected to exceed $1 billion. Assistant Secretary of the Army Hadlai A. Hull has pointed out that the equipment build-up and improvement in training exercises have enabled the reserves to achieve mobilization standards.[18]

Concurrently, Secretary of the Navy John H. Chafee, in announcing a policy of completely integrating the Naval Reserve into all future planning, was maintaining that the Naval Air Reserve presently has the highest peacetime combat readiness rating in its history and has "clearly demonstrated the capability for immediate deployment of fleet-sized air wings fully manned, equipped with combat capable aircraft, and operationally ready to perform all phases of carrier operations."[19] The Naval Reserve state of readiness and carrier operations in particular had earlier received a boost with Secretary Laird's suggestion that the Naval Reserve take over the operation of one or two aircraft carriers on a training basis.[20]

In spite of this evidence of increased readiness to accord with the enhanced role of the Guard and reserves—both as a larger part of the total defense force and primary source of augmentation in rapid military build-ups in future emergencies—there are threatening manpower shortages. Guard and reserve strength has fallen as the reduced imminence of the draft has shaved the number of volunteers for vacancies in Guard and reserve ranks. Late 1971 reports from DOD sources showed reserve strength down by 44,222 men.[21] Rapidly dwindling waiting lists characterized reserve units as well.

Though knowledgeable commentators venture dire predictions of manpower shortages in the Guard and reserves as we go to the all-volunteer armed force,[22] the services are moving on a broad front to prevent such predictions from coming to pass. The Chief, National Guard Bureau, Departments of the Army and Air Force, has called for a reenlistment bonus for the Army National Guard.[23] And the Army Reserve, with a peak demand this year of some 50,000 replacements for men whose terms of enlistment expire, has already gained approval for 65 new full-time technicians to serve on the staffs of major reserve commands as recruiters. Additionally, the Army Reserve has stepped up its advertising program for reservists, and the Active Army has expanded a highly successful in-service recruiting program which releases enlisted personnel up to 179 days early in exchange for accepting a unit assignment in the Army Reserve or National Guard. Economic incentives through increased pay, especially at lower enlisted and officer grades, have been provided, and an increased recruiting effort has been mounted for WACS, nurses, doctors and other specialists for the reserves. Also, proposals are currently being studied to extend Servicemen's Group Life Insurance to reservists at the same minimal cost as Active Army personnel, and expanded medical, dental, survivor, retirement and educational benefits for reservists are under consideration. Training for Guard and reserve forces is receiving major command attention in an attempt to make it more interesting and relevant, and to eliminate phases of it which detract from individual morale. Finally, substantial progress has been made in the improvement of reserve training facilities, with many new centers completed and a considerable number under construction or planned.[24]

Should all of the foregoing be to no avail, some individuals in the services, the Reserve and Guard Associations, and individual congressmen have advanced the possibility of a draft for the reserves and Guard. The idea has not gained widespread support, partially because the same groups and in some cases individuals support the continuance of the present draft. Should the new approaches being taken to establish an all-volunteer active armed forces succeed, and an all-volunteer approach to the reserves and Guard falter, a draft to support the latter would appear likely and feasible. The reserves and Guard in their new expanded role would have to be kept up to strength as their importance for immediate augmentation increases while the active forces dwindle. Quality would also be vital. In addition, reserve service would not be as demanding as active service in terms of time, dislocation, interruption of education, occupation or home life.

The evidence suggests that the reserves can be administered in a way that will develop the necessary readiness consistent with the resources available. Units and individual personnel whose capacities must be available on short notice can, it would appear, be brought to and maintained in a high state of readiness. Others, for whose services there is not the same urgent need, can be maintained on tap for long periods so that they can, with concentrated training, be brought to the necessary proficiency for active duty. The various combinations of drills, active duty, equipment levels and training in conjunction with the active forces where possible, make available means to ensure substantial flexibility in reserve response.

It would appear, then, that the reserve spectrum of readiness has been materially broadened and that we have not seen the limits of it to date. Though those involved in estimating the costs of various degrees of readiness by different types of reserve units maintain that the range extends all the way from 50 percent or less to 90 percent or 100 percent of active forces equivalents, depending upon weapons systems and degree of readiness required, it is apparent that the reserves are potentially remarkably versatile on the readiness score, while remaining basically reserves. The ultimate in maintaining reserve status without crossing the rather indistinct line to active status must be, one would suppose, some of the civilian technicians and aides who are simultaneously members of the Ready Reserve units for whom they work in a civilian capacity.

The Reserves as a Device for Maintaining the Availability of Required Skills and Expertise

There are certain types of skills and expertise required by the military on an occasional basis or in the event of emergency which are more likely to be maintained on tap through a reserve program. In spite of the fact that medical personnel are the only category currently in short supply in the Guard and reserves,[25] hundreds of doctors, dentists and other professional medical personnel find it possible to serve in reserve medical units on a voluntary basis. They would be lost to the immediate military requirements of the country if it were not for the nature of the reserves as a part-time affiliation. Other professional and skilled personnel of all kinds who find participation in the defense effort possible on a part-time basis would be unavailable if there were no option but an active status.

The advantage of the reserve, it seems likely, does not stop here. Doctors, engineers and technicians, but also certain other professions and less obvious technical specialties, such as public welfare and public education people, would find it difficult to remain abreast of developments in their areas of expertise as full-time military personnel. In a reserve status, in civil affairs and other types of units, they can practice their specialties as civilians and be available simultaneously for call to active duty by the military. Thus they bring into the active military the latest techniques and improvements and retain proficiency while doing it.

The Reserves as Counteractives of Antimilitarism and Isolationism

With one foot in the military camp, and the other in the civilian community, reservists can do much to counter those antimilitarist tendencies which are caused, to some extent, by the relative isolation of the active forces.

Reserve forces are increasingly active in their communities with projects of a public service nature of all kinds. A recent Pentagon news release of April 28, 1971, cited 30 units of the Guard and reserves for continuing efforts in support of community projects and domestic actions. These activities ranged from work in public health in areas of poverty and unemployment by an Army station hospital in Puerto Rico, to assistance to the mentally retarded by an Air National Guard unit in Steelton, Pennsylvania, and seminars on drug abuse to the youth of the Chicago area by the reservists at the Naval Air Station, Glenview, Illinois.[26]

The active forces of the United States have been characterized by high turnover rates, particularly in recent years, and most also have lived in civilian communities. They have, therefore, not been precluded from public service programs and such familiarity and contact with civilian society which might dispel antimilitarism and the adverse effects of such separatism as is inevitable. But the reservists all live in civilian communities, are basically civilians, and can do the job continuously without obtrusiveness, and hence with greater effectiveness.

Not all of these attributes of the reserves are relevant in each specific civil-military situation. But over time, and with changing circumstances, it is possible that all can serve to enhance the capacity of military forces to meet the needs of the nation.

VIETNAM AND EXTENSIVE RESERVE CALL-UP

A brief look at the possible results of reliance on the reserves in Vietnam provides a relevant case study here. Of course, some portion of the reserve call-up of January 1968, in connection with the *Pueblo* incident, was sent to Vietnam. But the total number involved was only about 15,000, and most of those reservists did not go to Vietnam. In May 1968, some additional units were mobilized to bring the total to some 37,000, not a very sizable portion of a Ready Reserve numbering about two million as of January 1968.[27] By contrast, we mobilized 26,000 National Guard and reserve personnel in the Post Office emergency of March 23, 1970.[28] And by further contrast, we mobilized over 630,000 of the Guard and reserves in the first year of the Korean conflict. By statute, the President may call to active duty for 24 months, one million of the Ready Reserves, simply upon declaration of a national emergency.[29]

Furthermore, the procedures for a reserve call-up had been tried and tested before. They had been reviewed in congressional hearings and revised on several occasions, actually after each preceding reserve call-up since World War II. While there would have been administrative errors committed in the process, some are inevitable and they would not have prevented the process from being executed effectively.

In 1965, when the Administration made the initial decision to expand the active forces via the draft rather than call the reserves, civil disturbances were at a minimum. If the Administration was trying to avoid overreacting, it could have called the reserves up in installments rather than wholesale. Or it could have called them wholesale for impact. Public opinion may not have been overwhelmingly in support of the move. But the Tonkin Gulf Resolution of some months earlier was backed overwhelmingly by Congress. Certainly the call-up of the reserves could have been accomplished more quickly, and probably more cheaply, than expansion of the active forces by means of the draft. While the Administration did not react to the Tonkin Gulf episode with large-scale military support for South Vietnam until six months later, the point is that the attitude of the country, cost, requisite flexibility, even readiness did not preclude use of a reserve call-up to enlarge U.S. forces in South Vietnam.

In fact, there are more inherent advantages which might have accrued through the use of the reserves in this situation. While the Ready Reserves were then and are now overwhelmingly comprised of young enlistees, 20 to 30 percent of them are career reservists, officers and men who are mostly long-time voluntary participants in the reserve program and veterans of previous wars. Presumably, as trained personnel, a significant portion of them, the leadership, older and wiser and more experienced and possessed of more varied and developed skills, could have gone to work immediately and with ingenuity and resourcefulness.

The Administration, of course, did not immediately move to large-scale expansion of our forces, as might have been expected by its reaction to Tonkin Gulf. Some ten months later, the build-up really began. By then, it may have wanted to avoid the appearance of all-out intentions concerning Vietnam which the necessary declaration of a national emergency by the President would imply. But if the declaration of a national emergency had come in the atmosphere of Tonkin Gulf, there probably would have been less fear of overreaction in Moscow and Peking. And then the President would have been free to call up the reserves rapidly or slowly as circumstances dictated.

Of course he did not have to make a basic decision on reserves versus draft in August 1964. The crunch did not come until July 1965, when the strategic reserve began to become thin and the uncertainty grew about the size of the commitment of forces we would have to make in Vietnam. But even then, calling the reserves with a played-down declaration of an emergency could have been effected. And it probably should have been, considering the precedent to the role of the reserves as an initial and primary source of augmentation in an expansion. Such a call might have provoked an outcry by reservists and civilians alike. Certainly there would have been more discussion of the whole involvement in Vietnam, especially in the now wider circles of those immediately effected.

And here is the point of this case study. No matter what ensued, in the face of such a hypothetical call-up, it appears in retrospect that it would have redounded to the advantage of the country.

If there was sufficient outcry by the public, an agonizing reappraisal by the Administration might have followed, with possible change of policy. Or the debate might have expanded support, gotten more consensus and resulted in more resolute and determined prosecution of the war.

If there had been an extensive call-up of the reserves, the progress of the war would have been watched more critically by the general public, with earlier disenchantment with its prosecution, or demands of changed strategy. It is likely that the reserves, if extensively involved in Vietnam, might have made their contribution to a change of strategy. Certainly they would have been more capable at and more strongly disposed to the nation-building facets of the job, and perhaps less inclined to observe clear-cut limits to the war.

At home the draft could have been utilized to reconstitute

the strategic reserves. At home, too, the dislocation of families, careers, and all the deprivations and sacrifices of a large-scale reserve call-up would have provoked discussion, critical reexamination and reevaluation and the invocation of all the salutary processes of a democracy at work.

It is unlikely that if we had used the reserves as we have traditionally, we would have as easily and even imperceptibly slid down the slippery slopes into the quagmire of Vietnam.

Vietnam was a politico-military misadventure, and this was one way it might possibly have been avoided. The reserves, and the families, friends and business associates of reservists, constitute another independent power center in our pluralistic society. Their interested, knowledgeable, influential and inevitably critical focus on Vietnam was not prompted as it should have been. If it had been, it is possible that the nation would have changed course earlier. The course of the Johnson administration might have been aborted. But more likely it would have been changed, if not overall, possibly insofar as military strategy in the field was concerned. It may have become more resolute if public opinion rallied and backed greater involvement. Sensing our demonstrated determination, who knows the Russian and Chinese reaction? But it is difficult to believe that the use of the reserve in its traditional capacity would have resulted in a more disastrous outcome in Vietnam than we have experienced.

In sum, reliance on the reserves, early in any emergency, would appear consistent with maintaining the health of our democratic state. Berlin is perhaps evidence of its effective deterrent capacity. The massive reliance of the Israelis on their reserves in their dire peril would appear the example *in extremis*. In our complex, pluralistic and diversified society, it would appear to be an institution and a precedent we should not lightly overlook or disregard.

Notes

1. Secretary of Defense Melvin R. Laird, in a memorandum of August 21, 1970, Subject: "Support for Guard and Reserve Forces," p. 2.

2. For a brief history of the reserve, see W. F. Levantrosser, *Management of the Reserve Forces* (Washington, D.C.: Industrial College of the Armed Forces, 1967), from which most of this resume comes. For a more extensive history of the National Guard, especially, see William H. Riker, *Soldiers of the States* (Washington, D.C.: Public Affairs Press, 1957).

3. Laird, "Support for Guard and Reserve Forces," p. 1.

4. U.S., United States Code, Title 10, Sects. 263, 331, 332, 333, 672, 673, 3500 and 8500.

5. Data supplied by Directorate of Military Support, Department of the Army.

6. Ibid.

7. In Robin Higham, *Bayonets in the Streets* (Lawrence, Kansas: The University Press of Kansas, 1969) Chap. 7.

8. From a paper by George Washington entitled *Sentiments on a Peace Establishment* written in 1783 and quoted in George F. Eliot, *Reserve Forces and the Kennedy Strategy* (Harrisburg, Pa.: Stackpole, 1962) p. 2.

9. Eliot, *Reserve Forces and the Kennedy Strategy.*

10. For example, the Reserve Officers Association, the National Guard Association, the Air Force Association, the Fleet Reserve and Naval Reserve Associations, and the Air Force Sergeants Association, to mention only a few.

11. One particularly, done by the Office of the Assistant Secretary of Defense (Manpower and Reserve Affairs) in the Pentagon in 1969, gives a good view of some significant characteristics of personnel in the Ready Reserve.

12. Prior to recent decisions by some of our prestigious institutions of higher education to discontinue ROTC, the regular military and the reserves could expect an input of officers from the upper-economic strata, the professions and the higher levels of intelligence. The certainty of this input is now reduced, although by no means precluded. To the extent that our reserve is composed entirely of the lower economic strata, the less influential vocations and the less intelligent members of our

society, it may be less of a restraining factor in national military policy formulation.

13. See issues of the Civil Affairs Association journal, until May-June 1971 entitled *Military Government Journal and Newsletter,* now called the *Civil Affairs Journal and Newsletter,* particularly the issue of June-July, 1970.

14. Levantrosser gives the complete account of the Reserve-National Guard merger struggle.

15. See Levantrosser and issues of *The Officer* (Reserve Officers Association journal) and *The National Guardsman* (National Guard Association journal) over the last five years.

16. See, for example, Numbers 1200.7 (July 2, 1970), 1205.1 (March 13, 1970), 1215.5 (August 25, 1969), 1215.6 (August 25, 1969), 1215.13 (January 9, 1969), 1225.6 (April 18, 1970), 1235.9 (September 13, 1967) and 1235.10 (October 27, 1970).

17. U.S. Department of Defense, Statement of Secretary of Defense Melvin R. Laird before the Senate Armed Services Committee, *Toward a National Security Strategy of Realistic Deterrence,* March 15, 1971, pp. 102-103.

18. Secretaries Laird and Hull before the October 1971 Annual Meeting of the Association of the U.S. Army in Washington, reported in *The Army Reserve Magazine* (November-December 1971), pp. 8-9.

19. *The Officer* (February 1972) p. 24.

20. *The Officer* (January 1972) p. 7.

21. *Commanders Digest* (December 2, 1971) p. 7.

22. See David E. Rosenbaum, "Draft: Its Days May Be Numbered," *New York Times,* February 6, 1972, p. E6.

23. *Commanders Digest* (December 2, 1971) p. 3.

24. *The Army Reserve Magazine,* (November-December 1971), pp. 4-5.

25. *Toward a National Security Strategy of Realistic Deterrence,* p. 135.

26. News Release, Office of the Assistant Secretary of Defense, (Washington, D.C.: Public Affairs, U.S. Department of Defense, April 28, 1971, No. 371-71).

27. *Annual Report of the Secretary of Defense on Reserve Forces, Fiscal Year 1969* (Washington, D.C.: U.S. Department of Defense, 1970) p. i, D-4.

28. *Annual Report of the Secretary of Defense on Reserve Forces, Fiscal Year 1970* (Washington, D.C.: U.S. Department of Defense, 1970) p. 5.

29. U.S., United States Code, Title 10, Sect. 673.

7

CIVILIAN-MILITARY RACISM IN THE SEVENTIES: THE CHALLENGE OF REDUCING CULTURAL DIFFERENCES THROUGH PLANNED CHANGE

Richard A. McGonigal

Peace Corps volunteers going overseas, policemen working outside their native precincts, suburban-raised teachers coming to the inner city, and military men trying to relate to host nationals overseas all experience the problem of learning to relate to a different culture, or a different subculture. Racism is an insidious form of the problem.[1] Its outward manifestations are based on stereotypical myths. Its inner motivations have to do with personal anxiety. Here we will focus upon racism as it is experienced within the military community and is nourished by the civilian community. Our intent is to predict trends and to indicate some sorely needed research and development during the 1970s.

    Consider one incident which took place in Koza, Okinawa. (It might just as easily happen tonight in Frankfurt, San Diego, or Cicero.) A white American soldier asked a black woman marine for a dance in a bar near "Four Corners." The woman marine's black soldier escort objected. Someone asked what a white soldier was doing in a "brothers'" bar, anyway. A fight began; knives appeared; and the white soldier ended up hospitalized. The black soldier was confined to the brig and assigned military legal counsel. The "blacks'" bar was placed off limits by the provost marshal, the Okinawan witnesses shook their heads and asked each other about American democracy.

Such incidents, while growing in number, do not immediately subvert our nation's military capabilities. These incidents do, however, embody four characteristics which together threaten to be major impediments to an all-volunteer military force in the 1970s.

The dating expectations, the necessity of providing legal counsel for the black soldier, and the fact that it is the blacks' bar which is placed off limits are evidences of *institutional racism.* Black soldiers hold different hierarchies of values from white soldiers. This *value dissonance* can be seen in their need for separate bars and in the white soldier's ignorance of the advisability of asking the black woman marine to dance.

Problems in communication are almost inevitable threads in this web as predominantly white authority figures move into a bar for blacks to see that "justice" is done. Lenses ground through years of bias cause distortion in the views of both sides.

Reduced numbers of personnel and reduced control of personnel are also automatic features of this incident. Two soldiers are temporarily unavailable for duty and neither has become more enthusiastic about reenlisting. When the other men get back to their barracks, the rumors will fly. Tomorrow night will require extra military police just to maintain tonight's poor level of control!

In a nutshell, this incident encapsulates the four trends we predict in civilian-military racism in the seventies: increased institutional racism; increased value dissonance; problems in communication; and reductions in the supply and control of personnel.

INSTITUTIONAL RACISM

Institutional racism in the military is a natural extension of racism in civilian institutions. Recruiting qualified blacks to become officers is difficult because of segregation and the allied inequities of our school systems.[2] Since tracking systems often favor white, middle-class-and-above students, recruiters looking for officer candidates among blacks are not likely to be successful. The institutional patterns which favor segregation of civilian housing areas increase the bitterness among black military personnel looking for off-base housing in the United States and abroad.[3] That northern urban schools and housing areas are becoming increasingly segregated portends ill-will toward recruiters armed with general aptitude tests normed on middle-class white populations.[4] The military's insistence upon college diplomas for its regular officer corps narrows the door even further.

The human relations teams which have been surveying racial unrest in each of the military services are less than alarmist when they say that unless the pious equality declarations of commanders are translated into effective action, "The next time there will be fire." [5] The spirit of Eldridge Cleaver seems to be finding new ears.

> The assassin's bullet not only killed Dr. King, it killed a period of history. It killed a hope and it killed a dream. That white America could produce the assassin of Dr. Martin Luther King is looked upon by black people—and not just those identified as black militants—as a final repudiation by white America of any hope of reconciliation, of any hope of change by peaceful and non-violent means.[6]

Students of history know that blessed few people ever surrender goods or power peaceably or nonviolently. We see the growing institutional racism of the seventies as a source of more violent conflict.

VALUE DISSONANCE

Apparently the 1970s are bringing a growing disparity between white and black value clusters. While reflected in music and verse, this is of a deeper significance than differences between "soul" and "country and western" music. Clusters of values become ideologies,[7] ideologies which can and do steer, direct and actually define needs. Recent studies by Commander Robert Bedingfield, CHC, USN, at three Marine Corps bases showed that the value clusters of black marines are centering more upon dignity, pride and the importance of individual liberty, while those of white marines are moving toward security, health and material wealth.[8] We ought not to be alarmed so much that these clusters are dissonant but that the value systems appear to be closing. The work of Robin Williams and Milton Rokeach focuses on the troublesomeness of closed value systems.[9] While not beyond modification, these clusters of values may be more difficult to sway in the seventies than they were in the sixties.

COMMUNICATION PROBLEMS

Since early 1970, there has been, by the miltary's own admission, an increase of misunderstanding among both whites and blacks about official policy.[10] Directives which seem patently clear and equitable to commanders are often seen as racist by blacks and as an extension of favoritism by whites.

Symbols such as the Confederate flag and the black clenched fist were well known in the sixties. Now there is a plethora of symbols of white and black separatism which seems to heighten anxieties when the intended meaning is unclear. Words such as "bad" (which means "pretty good"), "chuck" (a white), "off" (eliminate), "rip off" (steal) and "spade" (black) have ethnic meanings which seem especially irritating to one's counterparts.

Hair styles and off-duty clothing styles also seem to be focal points of misunderstanding. A man may wear a black arm band to mourn the death of a relative, but his associates may hurry to a calendar to see if he is protesting the death of Ché, Ho Chi Minh or George Rockwell. Sheer ignorance does little to help the situation. Consider, for example, the problems of the young, white lieutenant who thought that the Soledad Brothers were a kind of cough medicine and the captain who piped Stephen Foster medlies into the mess hall.

As we travel through military posts we get the feeling that each racial group is developing its own communication codes in order to preserve its group identity. If true, this would make considerable sense socio-emotionally. However, codes only heighten the anxiety of the uninformed. Thus, the overall effects of vague cues, combined with less interaction between races in off-duty hours, implies that interracial communication will become more and more difficult.

REDUCED SUPPLY AND CONTROL OF PERSONNEL

As the draft becomes less of a threat to young men, enlistment rates will probably drop off. Officer recruitment has been especially difficult in this decade and promises to be even more of a problem in the future. Army ROTC enrollments dropped from 165,000 in 1961 to 74,000 in 1971.[11] Retention rates from the three service academies have dropped seriously in the same time span. Re-enlistment of noncommissioned officers has fallen from 25 percent to 20 percent, and re-enlistment of draftees has dropped from 10 percent to less than 5 percent since 1961. The most severe falling off occurred in 1970 and 1971.[12]

Absences without leave (AWOL) and desertions have increased three- to fivefold in the first two years of the seventies. Drug abuse incidents have doubled. Larceny, often for financing drug habits, has also doubled. One of the most unsettling indicators of less control is known as "fragging," which occurs when disgruntled juniors roll grenades under the bunks of their seniors for allegedly harassing them unnecessarily. In 1969 there were 126 actual or possible fraggings reported. There were 271 in 1970. Some predicted that in 1971 there would be over 425 fraggings. The number of courts martial for insubordination also doubled from 1970-1971.[13] These figures seem to predict a smaller source of personnel and less control over those personnel who do enter the military in the seventies.

Traditionalists within the military often call for the old forms of control. Morris Janowitz observed that the turning point of military discipline actually came in 1905.[14] Janowitz feels that at that point authoritarian discipline gave way to discipline by persuasion, manipulation and group consensus.

Though this shift in discipline is true historically, it is equally evident that—as of late—discipline by persuasion, manipulation and group consensus has not been managed with sufficient acumen or sincerity. A key point is that for the last quarter century the trend of combat conditions has been away from large troop movements which called for tight supervision to small, platoon-sized, independent movements with scarcely any immediate supervision of officers above the rank of lieutenant. This calls for increased internal individual controls. Indeed, a failure to instill internalized discipline has resulted increasingly in acts of insubordination.

For the federal government to extend its will through its military forces in riot control at home or constabulary action overseas, it must be able to sustain its will *over* its military forces. This cannot be done without the internalization of critical norms by military personnel. Norms or policy commitments that are not sufficiently internalized will tend to be sacrificed during times of stress unless their relevance for immediate operational requirements is obvious to commanders. In the case of race relations policies, if they are viewed as important commitments to be implemented when operational conditions permit, rather than as internalized fixed commitments, there is a great temptation on the part of commanders to minimize the necessity for their implementation unless racial problems appear to have a direct bearing on operational effectiveness.

The rationale for action

Having predicted the problems which will be encountered in the seventies, we would do well to decide upon what grounds —if any—we should attempt remedial action. There are at least two glaring paradoxes facing anyone who would meddle with civilian-military racial interaction. There is the paradox of trying to increase egalitarianism within an autocratic organization whose governing sponsor often uses it for the perpetuation of inequalities. The second paradox is equally unsettling. Many regard intolerance as a form of group control based upon meaningless stereotypical criteria. The road to a group climate free of such controls may well require the imposition of more individual controls.

There can be no doubt that maintaining a military arm of our government can institutionalize and make permanent some inequalities. We may be fooling ourselves to think that anything else is possible. Two centuries ago Jean-Jacques Rousseau, a champion of human rights, pointed out that "from the moment one man needed the help of another . . . equality disappeared." [15]

For those who are willing to live with paradoxes, the supreme challenge is to achieve the maximum amount of equality within an institution destined to perpetuate some inequalities. By "equality" we are speaking of the basic right of people to be treated as equally important human beings. The key to living within the paradox may be in so manipulating those who manipulate that a reverse-identification is made from those most manipulated.

To put it another way, those who are sent to control revolutionaries can so identify with them that they, too, join the revolution. Likewise, those controlling the controllers can so identify with their charges that the equality revolution spreads even further. Pye has observed this in Burma. Humphries saw it in Korea. Hickey became part of it in South Vietnam. [16] People who were sent out to suppress revolutions joined them and only then began to find their direction.

There is a short leash on such phenomena. It would be fascinating to study at what critical point the establishment steps in to squelch such identification. Just such an event occurred with Carlson's Raiders during World War II. Carlson's men addressed each other by first names, voted on mission priorities and had one of the most valorous combat records of all time. But the unit was disbanded before the war was over; it was too strong a threat to more formally structured units.

Everett Rogers feels that the distinguishing feature of successful humanistic innovations lies in whether or not they can be presented to their sponsor as functional rather than structural changes, since functional changes are much less threatening to those in power.[17]

Within the paradox of seeking equality inside an institution which is being used to perpetuate inequalities is that second paradox: using more control to limit abusive control. Bruno Bettelheim pointed out that tolerance is itself a function of personal individual control. The greater the underlying anxieties of men, the more prejudiced they are, because these same anxieties weaken their personal controls.[18] Supported by racist institutions, weaker personalities often become more influenced by their social field and thus become more prejudiced. Tolerance may also be viewed as the conscious effort to assure that no arbitrary controls are imposed upon others simply because of such attributes as race or religion. Our manipulations, then, will try to promote egalitarianism within a racist institution and to increase personal controls within environments of undesirable group controls.

If we were to design a battle plan to combat the problems and paradoxes we have described, it might look like this:

PROBLEM	METHODOLOGY	GOALS
Institutional Racism	Circumvention and new legislation	New entries to authority and justice
Value Dissonance	Triggering dissonance toward modified behaviors	Greater value confidence among civilian and military minorities
Communication Difficulties	Simulations, empathy training	New methods of bargaining and reducing hostility
Reduction in Numbers and Control of Personnel	Strength bombardment, team building and goal setting	More highly motivated and self-controlled personnel

Institutional Racism

Institutional racism is not changed by good will alone. No group of people which has been oppressed over many years by a social system has ever escaped such oppression through a sudden change of heart of the power wielders. Most often, violently but sometimes nonviolently, the oppressed managed to find more direct lines of advancement. They find new safeguards to their legal rights.

In the last three years we have seen some minority leaders circumvent the traditional, closed, authority mechanisms. Special task forces, race relations councils and the Black Caucus of the House of Representatives have supplemented the traditional chain of command. Courts of inquiry have investigated why minorities have been denied equal representation on the senior rank levels. Other courts of inquiry have investigated why blacks seem to get more than their share of nonjudicial punishments and brig sentences.

Ways must be found to circumvent culturally biased criteria for officer corps selection. Legislation is needed to so revise the Uniform Code of Military Justice that institutional racism can be countered by proportionate representation on all courts martial.

It is an obscenity that today, as in our civilian prisons, military brigs and stockades have from 25 percent to 80 percent black populations when the parent command's larger population contains only 4.5 percent to 13 percent black servicemen.

Some commands have long used their sergeant major or chaplain as a kind of ombudsman to prevent such unfairness, but this is too passive an approach, since the sergeant major or chaplain is often co-opted by the establishment.

To solve problems of racism we need to impose new laws, regulations or new structures of control. Creating temporary investigation commissions at the service branch level will not by itself even begin to meet this need. Rather, new panels of representatives and permanently installed monitors are required to insure that blacks get more opportunities to enter positions of authority plus greater fairness in the judicial system.

As a matter of fact, some antagonism toward the military has already been mollified by the mere establishment of the Defense Department's Institute of Race Relations, investigative teams, etc.

A more long-term and more credible approach might include permanent minority group representation in the Defense Department at all levels of decision-making. There needs to be a synthesis and genuine enforcement of policy about off-base segregated housing and schools, discrimination in hiring for defense contracts, and selection procedures for entrance to military academies and ROTC programs. The Government Accounting Office has the ability to hurt contractors who blatantly steal from contract funds. We need an arm to prosecute those who would violate human rights.

Nothing will gain support faster than action motivated by genuine concern. Thus, credibility must be earned, not promised. Some recruiters have, for example, arranged to have black officers, in return for extra leave time, simply ride Chicago buses or New York subways in uniform to prove to black youth that there *are* black officers today who are alive and well.

Minority group representatives have already proven their ability to earn their own rewards. At the moment, we need to short-circuit the credibility gap and to accelerate minority promotions.

Value Dissonance

The race relations programs in the Navy and the Marine Corps are already capitalizing on the work of Festinger and others to channel value modification.[19] The first step is to point out the distance between our stated beliefs about equality and our actual behavior. When such dissonance is highlighted, we may expect men to shift either their beliefs or their behavior. The second step of the treatment is to provide rewards for shifting beliefs and behavior in the desired direction. Perhaps the most important reward is the perceived acceptance by one's peers for such a change.

It has been our experience that values have been modified when they were reinforced by group approval. The regard for the value of equality remained higher at one base in Virginia when "significant others" affirmed it as near the top of their list of values.

Communication

The military has depended upon communication specialists for its tactical needs. Public affairs officers are groomed to communicate with the public at large. Psychological operations technicians are schooled to employ propaganda with unfriendly populations. But, strangely enough, we assume that our leaders should know intuitively how to deal with the internal communication problems brought to the surface by powerful social change.

Take the business of bargaining or reducing hostility "within the family." Bargaining is almost a forgotten art within the military. Deutsch and Krauss defined bargaining as being genuine only when both parties benefit by an agreement, when both parties see the possibility of more than one possible agreement, and when both perceive each other as having opposed interests.[20] They go on to point out that verbal communication was of little effect in their study. Mere existence of communication channels was no guarantee that they would be used. Cooperative existence was more effective than competitive existence. Weapons detracted from bargaining. Reorientation was an essential phase for both parties.

Most military men know these things deep down inside. Without using the explosive label of "unionization" we need to ensure that genuine bargaining is to occur inside the present military establishment. "Working it out," a practice not unlike collective bargaining, is already in use in Vietnam to avert "fragging." [21]

Thibaut and Coules also found that communication alone

was not nearly as significant in reducing hostility as the initial set or orientation.[22]

We would do well to examine our ecology of space within the military environment with a sharp eye as to which spatial relationships promote cooperation and as to which promote conflict. Living space within barracks has often become segregated due to preferences for music or desires to "rap with brothers." Seating patterns in mess halls might well be studied with a mind toward which patterns promote cooperative rather than competitive settings. Robert Sommer's work in this area is an excellent pilot study.[23]

Providing more adequate discharge of tension is by itself not enough. As Bettelheim and Janowitz point out, we need to develop more integrated personalities,[24] and in line with such integration is the greatly overlooked area of humor. Humor in riot control is a promising area for social experimentation.[25]

It is the author's experience that racial unrest is often very high when troops are in "garrison," i.e., not in the field or in combat. Troops in Vietnam cooperated magnificiently under fire, only to fight viciously along racial lines when they returned to the rear. Roger Little confirmed this in his study in Korea. As risks declined, ritual activity increased, and with it came racial conflict.[26]

Along with bargaining, humor, release of hostility, modified spatial relationships, and new kinds of garrison life, we would do well to study the effects of time patterns and fatigue upon race relations. Alert educators have already spotted culturally specific time patterns which, when accommodated to, have relieved hostility. It is quite likely that many so-called absences without leave are also the result of the moral behavior of minority groups who must take care of their primary responsibilities. Often the white majority does not realize that it has structured work schedules to guarantee some men breaking one of two conflicting orders, e.g., the responsibility to remain free of debt and the responsibility to be aboard at a certain hour.

ENACTMENT OF EMPATHY TRAINING FROM THE TOP
DOWNWARD AND THE BOTTOM UP

The last decade has seen a myriad of "schools" develop in
the area of sensitivity training, cross-cultural communication
and human relations. This author believes that an eclectic
approach is needed to translate these civilian-oriented developments into viable military training. We have seen men of high
and low rank excited about participating in role-reversal problem-solving. We have used National Training Laboratories
leadership, gestalt techniques and even strength bombardment
exercises as developed by William Schutz. After six years of
meddling, frequent consultation with Peace Corps trainers and
employing outside expertise, we feel that the following learning
goals are central to our needs:
  1. Increased self-awareness and self-esteem
  2. Increased ability to reverse roles
  3. Increased tolerance for ambiguity or reduced dogmatism
  4. Increased communication skills (verbal and nonverbal)
  5. Acquisition of pertinent subcultural information
  6. Ideological motivation
  Experience with Navy and Marine Corps personnel has
shown that statistically significant improvement can be achieved
in all of these learning goals. However, we must establish ser-
vicewide bench marks for longitudinal studies and the evaluation
of particular training models. Unobtrusive behavioral measures
such as those designed by Webb, Campbell, Schwartz and
Sechrest are sorely needed tools for evaluating our training.[27]
  The task of incorporating this training into all levels of
rank is similar to the tedious task of preparing all ranks for any
new function. Unless senior officers are sensitized, the progress
among men of lower ranks is soon undone. The resocialization
of juniors with great empathy by seniors with little empathy is
almost as certain as the phenomenon of flood tide followed by
ebb tide.

What often becomes the key factor in whether such training is accepted is the "setting." If this training is presented as appropriate military activity, enhancing the legitimate functions of this arm of government, it tends to be assimilated more quickly. Terms such as "role playing" are better replaced by "simulation." "Sensitivity" is more wisely replaced by "effective communication." There are, in short, culturally specific factors within the military environment to which empathy training must be tailored if it is to gain creditability and acceptance.

We have tried to match our predictions about racism in the civilian-military milieu with appropriate actions needed to counter such threats. Increased institutional racism, more value dissonance between races, less accurate communication between races and reduced enlistment and control of minority groups are likely. Such problems may be reduced by creating new entries to authority for minority groups within the military, increasing trust levels toward the military in civilian minority groups, finding new methods of bargaining and hostility reduction, establishing empathy training at all levels of rank, and displacing dissonant values by new group goals.

These goals can be achieved. Building the bridge between the predictions and the goals and getting thousands of people across that bridge will depend upon the sincerity of commitment and the amount of resources our nation is willing to apply to the task.

NOTES

1. The technical term for the generic problem is "heterophily," pronounced "hetrafully." In contemporary usage, it denotes the "differentness" of a change agent (for example, a social worker, a Peace Corps volunteer) who tries to work in a culture or subculture different from his own. Early usage of the term by the Greeks described many degrees of differentness between people, including (in various derivatives of the term) differences of speech, mannerisms, and family custom. See Everett M. Rogers and Philip K. Bhomik, "Monophily–Heterophily: Rational Concepts for Communication Research," (Paper presented for the Association for Education in Journalism, Berkeley, California, August 1969).

2. See U.S. Commission on Civil Rights, *Racial Isolation in the Public Schools,* vol. 2, *Appendices* (Washington: U.S. Government Printing Office, 1967).

3. Note the recent problems of housing discrimination toward black American troops in West Germany in Thomas A. Johnson, "Army Judge Fighting Bias in Germany is Called Home for Talks at Pentagon," *New York Times,* March 14, 1971, Sect. 1, p. 3.

4. Fred M. Hechinger, "Some Old Friends are Dropping by the Wayside," *New York Times,* September 5, 1971, Sect. 4, p. 1.

5. Richard Halloran, "Armed Forces: There is Racism and It Is Ugly," *New York Times,* September 5, 1971, Sect. 4, p. 3.

6. Eldridge Cleaver, *Post Prison Writings and Speeches,* Robert Scheer ed. (New York: Random House, 1967) p. 74.

7. Robin Williams, "Individual and Group Values," *The Annals of the American Academy of Political and Social Science,* 1 (May 1967): 24.

8. From unpublished reports of the Human Relations Team, April 1971, at Quantico, Virginia, Camp Pendleton, California, and Camp LeJeune, North Carolina.

9. Williams, "Individual and Group Values," p. 29, and Milton Rokeach, *The Open and Closed Mind: Investigations into the Nature of Belief Systems* (New York: Basic Books, 1960).

10. See U.S. Marine Corps, "Directive for Marine Distribution (AOIK-bh-1)," (Washington, D.C.: Headquarters, U.S. Marine Corps, April 5, 1971).

11. *New York Times,* September 5, 1971, p. 36.

12. Ibid.

13. Ibid.

14. Morris Janowitz, *The Professional Soldier* (New York: Free Press, 1960) p. 38.

15. Jean-Jacques Rousseau, *The First and Second Discourses* ed. Roger D. Masters (New York: St. Martin's, 1964) p. 151.

16. R. A. McGonigal, "A Model for the Cross Cultural Interaction Training of Adults" (Ph.D. diss., Michigan State University, 1971) Chapter 2.

17. See Everett M. Rogers, *Modernization Among Peasants: The Impact of Communication* (New York: Holt, Rinehart and Winston, 1969).

18. Bruno Bettelheim and Morris Janowitz, *Social Change and Prejudice* (New York: Free Press, 1950) pp. 54, 275.

19. Leon Festinger, *A Theory of Cognitive Dissonance* (Stanford, Calif., Stanford University Press, 1957) pp. 75, 78.

20. Morton Deutsch and Robert M. Krauss, "Studies of Interpersonal

Bargaining," *Journal of Conflict Resolution,* 6 (March 1962) 1: 52-76.

21. *New York Times,* September 5, 1971, p. 36.

22. John W. Thibaut and John Coules, "The Role of Communication in the Reduction of Interpersonal Hostility," *Journal of Abnormal and Social Psychology,* 47 (October 1952): 770-777.

23. Robert Sommer, "Further Studies of Small Group Ecology" *Sociometry,* 28 (December 1965) 4: 337-348.

24. Bettelheim and Janowitz, *Social Change and Prejudice,* p. 286.

25. See Joseph F. Coates, "Wit and Humor: A Neglected Aid in Crowd and Mob Control" (Washington, D.C.: Institute for Defense Analyses Paper N-671 [R], June 1970).

26. Roger W. Little, "A Study of the Relationship Between Collective Solidarity and Combat Role Performance" (Ph.D. diss., Michigan State University, 1955).

27. Eugene J. Webb et al., *Unobtrusive Measures: Nonreactive Research in the Social Sciences* (Chicago: Rand McNally, 1966).

8

THE ROLE OF THE MILITARY IN AMERICAN SOCIETY VIS-A-VIS DRUG ABUSE: SCAPEGOAT, NATIONAL LABORATORY AND POTENTIAL CHANGE AGENT

M. Scott Peck

Military drug abuse has been a major topic in the headlines in recent years. Yet, despite its notoriety, drug abuse in the military cannot be said to be a new phenomenon. Addiction to morphine in troops at the end of the Civil War and in veterans during the following decade was sufficiently common to be referred to as "army disease." [1] Use of marijuana by American soldiers stationed in Panama during the 1920s was common, and the first American effort to study marijuana usage scientifically was performed by the military there, determining, incidentally, that the drug seemed relatively innocuous. [2] Although there is a dearth of literature about the abuse of drugs by

The opinions expressed herein are those of the author and do not necessarily reflect those of the Army Surgeon General's Office, the Department of Defense or any other government agency.

servicemen during World War II and the Korean War, we know that the problem was far from nonexistent.[3] Furthermore, to put things in perspective, it must be mentioned that alcohol is a drug which has been for centuries the soldier's friend and not infrequently his downfall, although there is no evidence to indicate that problem drinking and alcoholism are any more or any less common among servicemen than in the civilian community.

Drug abuse is not the same throughout the military. While the predominant problem in Vietnam in the early seventies was heroin, the predominant problem among servicemen in Europe at the same time has been hashish. Polydrug use is perhaps the major problem for young soldiers within the United States at this time, while in Korea the illegal drug of choice seems to be the barbiturates. Moreover, the prevalence of drug usage of whatever kind varies widely throughout the military community, depending at least upon the local availability of drugs, the nature of the surrounding civilian communities and the stress under which the soldiers are operating. The prevalence of illicit drug use in Vietnam has been considerably higher than in the United States or Europe, not only because of the unique availability of drugs at low cost in Vietnam but also because the twin stresses of boredom and danger have been greater there. Based on still tentative urinalysis figures, approximately three times as many recruits enter basic training with illicit drugs in their system at Fort Dix, New Jersey (which predominately receives recruits from the New York City and New England area) as do recruits who enter basic training at Fort Lewis, Washington (which predominately receives recruits from the Pacific Northwest). Also, the pattern of drug abuse within a military community, as in a civilian community, may shift with bewildering rapidity. Heroin use, almost nonexistent in Vietnam in 1969, became rampant in 1970, when the military was still focusing its law enforcement attentions upon marijuana. Judging from the medical complications observed, the major drug problem among American soldiers in Okinawa in 1967 was barbiturates; in 1968 it was the amphetamines; and in 1969 it was the hallucinogens.

Any attempt to ascertain the extent of a drug problem within a community, civilian or military, is fraught with difficulty. The fact that drug abuse is illegal makes questionable the results of any questionnaire, no matter how confidentially conducted, of self-admitted illicit drug use. Then, such surveys also vary in the type of drug abuse they measure, so that some have simply asked the respondent whether or not he has ever used illegal drugs (including marijuana) while others have focused more upon current use and yet still make inadequate distinction between heavy regular use and occasional light use. The same problems pertain to civilian as to military questionnaire surveys. When a headline proclaims that "Forty Percent of High School Students Use Drugs," we don't know whether that means that 40 percent once tried marijuana or 40 percent are currently and regularly using harder drugs. Similarly, we know that just as there are some drug users who will deny their use of drugs on these questionnaires, there is also an indeterminate number of students or young soldiers who will manufacture a nonexistent history of drug abuse for a variety of social or psychological reasons. One such reason may be an attempt to avoid the draft, which brings us to the question of how many servicemen import their drug problem into service from civilian life.

THE MILITARY AND DRUG ABUSE: SCOPE OF THE PROBLEM

If the military could show that almost all drug-abusing servicemen abused drugs prior to their entrance into service, it would be of practical significance, for it could then be argued that the services have relatively little obligation to provide expensive or extensive rehabilitative services. It would also be convenient for the parents of drug-abusing servicemen, for if the evidence clearly indicated that almost all their sons began abusing drugs after entrance into service, they might be relieved of the guilt and possibly the financial responsibility for their sons' behavior. Consequently, for the past several years, the issue of when and where soldiers begin to abuse drugs has been important. It is an issue which has generated more heat than light, for again there are no unambiguous statistics.

The military would like to be in a position where it did not have to induct any illicit drug users, but that is impossible for a variety of reasons. During the past three years, enough youths have attempted to avoid the draft by manufacturing or at least exaggerating a history of drug abuse that the Armed Forces Entrance Examining Stations (AFEES) have been forced to regard histories of drug abuse with considerable skepticism. If it is reasonably clear that an individual is physically or psychologically dependent upon drugs on the basis of evidence above and beyond his own testimony, then he is determined unfit for induction. If he appears to be a user of illicit drugs but not dependent upon them, then under present policy he is considered fit for induction. Consequently, many self-proclaimed drug abusers have been admitted into service.

With the end of the draft it might be possible to tighten the induction standards, but such a step cannot be taken easily. The use of illicit drugs by young people has become a sufficiently common experience that, at least in the case of marijuana, it can no longer be considered aberrant behavior, and exclusion from service on the basis of a past history of illicit drug use may simply not be practical in view of manpower requirements. Moreover, the number attempting to avoid the draft by manufacturing a history of drug abuse probably has been far exceeded by the number who do everything possible to hide their drug use in order that they might be enlisted. In a zero-draft environment there will be no reason to believe this will not remain a major problem. Statistics fail to indicate that drug abuse is any more common in draftees than enlistees, and physicians at the AFEES or reception centers occasionally see individuals severely addicted to heroin who have enlisted in the Army for the expressed purpose of receiving some kind of treatment or in the vague hope that somehow the service will help them to "get their head together." Such men, of course, are not enlisted, but most enlistees with a lesser involvement do get into service, for there is no good way to diagnose or detect the nonaddicted enlistee who wants to hide his drug abuse.

Once detected as a drug abuser, the soldier may be quite free in admitting his preservice drug use. But some are probably quite loathe to do so; because they want to blame the service for everything wrong with their lives or for the not-unrealistic reason that things may go better for them if it appears that their drug use is somehow "service connected." Finally, of course, the fact that someone does take drugs in the service and did not before does not necessarily mean that his drug use is "service connected" or "service aggravated" anymore than an eleventh grade teacher can be held responsible for the fact that a student who did not use drugs in the tenth grade begins using them in the eleventh.

The whole issue of where the responsibility lies is unclear (and perhaps even a moot issue) and the meaning of the statistics is equally ambiguous. As reliable and meaningful statistics as any are probably those of a Harris poll of 1965 Vietnam era veterans which showed that 17 percent of the sample at some time used illicit drugs (including marijuana) prior to service, 32 percent during service and 26 percent since leaving service.[4] Since surveys indicate a steady increase in illicit drug use over the past five years in both the civilian and military population, and since this survey tapped not-so-recent as well as recent Vietnam era veterans, it is probable that current prevalence figures are higher than those of the Harris poll, but the proportions indicated likely remain accurate.

The least ambiguous statistics should be those which come from the actual biochemical detection of the illicit drugs in the body fluids of soldiers; but here again a great deal of interpretation is necessary. First of all, there is no biochemical technology that can detect the presence of marijuana or hashish, LSD or the other hallucinogens or their byproducts in body fluids. Second, most of the drugs which can be detected in body fluids —such as morphine, opium, codeine, barbiturates and amphetamines—have their legitimate medical uses, and the simple presence of one of these drugs in a soldier's urine does not mean that he has taken the drug illicitly. Further clinical determination may be necessary and can, upon occasion, be difficult. Then, most technology has its limitations, and it appears that in somewhere between 1 and 2 percent of the cases where the presence of one of these drugs is indicated, the soldier has not actually taken the drug. In other words, the result is a "false positive," a phenomenon which can occur for a variety of complex reasons and which plagues physicians in areas other than drug abuse detection, such as the serological testing for syphilis. Finally, the use of this complicated technology on a mass scale requires a complex systems approach which simply has not yet been perfected anywhere except by the Army in Vietnam in the case of opiates. Truly accurate data on other drugs or opiate use in the military outside of Vietnam on the basis of biochemical testing are not yet available.

Bearing in mind the small incidence of false positives and a slightly larger incidence of false negative urines, what, then, are the statistics on opiate abuse as derived from the biochemical testing of Army soldiers' urine in Vietnam? (Statistics from Navy, Marine and Air Force personnel are not included because relatively few remain in Vietnam, because their available figures are markedly lower than the Army's, and because their testing and urine collection procedures differ very significantly from those of the Army.) Beginning in July 1971, when urine testing was begun on all servicemen leaving Vietnam at the end of their tour, approximately 5 percent of Army personnel showed opiates (usually heroin) in their urine collected at the debarkation center. Since that time this rate has gradually but steadily declined 50 percent, to mid-1972 where about 2.5 percent of the departing personnel have such opiate-positive urine. These figures do not indicate that all these soldiers were *addicted* to opiates, since the test will detect any significant amount of opiate taken within three or so days of the time of testing. On the other hand, since this urine test at the debarkation center is conducted at a very definite and well-known point in time in the soldier's tour, the soldier can predict when he is to be tested. Clinical observation of the individuals detected through this urine screen (facetiously referred to by the troops as "Operation Golden Flow") reveals the vast majority of them are either sufficiently "hooked" that they are unable to stop their use or sufficiently impulsive, for whatever reason, that they are unable or unwilling to plan their heroin intake around this testing event. A positive urine is known to result in a certain amount of "hassle" and a delay of up to a week or so in their departure from Vietnam. Those individuals who are detected through this urine screen are generally in need of at least some rehabilitation and are currently being offered some such services.

Large numbers of soldiers have been discharged upon their return from Vietnam, with virtually no reliable estimates as to their ability to function well in civilian life. We have not known whether they will renew their pattern of opiate abuse on "the street" in America, where heroin is at least ten times as expensive as in Vietnam or whether, as almost all of them claim, their use of heroin in Vietnam is a "sometime thing" caused by the stresses and strains of surviving in a disenchanting war in a foreign land where pure heroin is virtually ubiquitous. In any case it seems clear that occasional users of heroin who can plan ahead and even regular users who are able to withdraw in sufficient time before the test, are able to "beat" the urine screen at the time of their Vietnam departure and go undetected. While we may be detecting most of the heroin-dependent soldiers at the time of their departure, and most of those in need of rehabilitation, the departure statistics certainly do not reflect the total prevalence of heroin use in Vietnam.

Since mid-autumn 1971 the Army has been conducting unannounced urine tests of whole company size units on a random basis in mid-tour in Vietnam. The average unit tested has approximately 5 percent of its men found to be opiate positive, and this prevalence rate has remained relatively stable to date. A striking feature has been the variability of units in this regard, with some units having only 1 percent of their men and other units up to 20 percent of their men opiate positive. There are many factors which could account for this variability, including the mission of the unit, its location and the local availability of heroin, its morale and the possibility that some units either had advance warning of the test or that the urine collection procedures may have been faulty for a particular unit.

Consequently, this 5 percent figure, which is the best we have for prevalence rate of opiate abuse in Vietnam based upon physiological testing, is also subject to interpretation, and it is probable that the actual prevalence rate is somewhat higher.[5]

FROM SCAPEGOAT TO NATIONAL LABORATORY

Having elaborated upon some of the great difficulties in trying to assess precisely the scope of drug problems in either a civilian or a military community, let me examine some of the relationships between the military and the civilian communities vis-à-vis drug abuse: specifically, the role that the military performs for the larger community. In the past role, now essentially completed, the military has played the scapegoat. From roughly the beginning of 1970 until the middle of June 1971, it was the primary scapegoat for the national drug abuse problem.

Let me review the dynamics of scapegoating. The usual initial response of a group to a significant internal problem is denial or minimization. The problem, or its significance, is simply not recognized. Efforts on the part of individual members to ignore or avoid the problem go unchallenged by other members. Throughout 1968 and 1969 neither the nation nor the DOD fully perceived the extent of the growing drug problem. Until the beginning of 1970 the nation was not terribly interested in recognizing its drug abuse problem, even in the armed forces.

When a problem increases in intensity to a point where it can no longer be denied, the group's next response is to ascribe the problem to one of its members as a means of continuing to avoid recognizing it as a problem of the group as a whole. So it was that in the spring of 1970 drug abuse became news. The problem was out in the open, only it was primarily identified as a military problem. Everyone knew about drug abuse. But while all thoughtful students recognized drug abuse as a national problem, with its roots diffuse and pervasive, America in

1970 felt secure with the idea that it was largely and primarily a military problem. Military ineffectiveness in controlling drug traffic in Southeast Asia was charged. Punitive, nontherapeutic and unconstructive military techniques of treating and disposing with the drug abuser in uniform were decried. Mothers across the land cried out: "You took my boy away from me and turned him into an addict." America saw herself as contaminated by a military which by some kind of hideous mismanagement took wholesome American youth and cranked them out two years later as confirmed degenerates.

But this was scapegoating. No matter how poorly the military may have managed the drug abuse problem, the rest of the nation was managing it just as poorly. While decrying the way in which the military was fumbling with its numbers, the rest of the nation was hardly even trying to keep statistics. Although chastising the military for its simplistic and inhumane "lock 'em up or kick 'em out" approach, civilian communities were doing just the same to their own citizens on a vaster scale. While they believed themselves contaminated by GIs returning from the Orient with heroin in their duffle bags, they said relatively little about the continued overproduction of uppers and downers by the "legitimate" drug firms and media advertising of "better living through chemistry." This is not to say that the military has been victimized, or that, as some military men have liked to believe, the services have been polluted by the products of a permissive society rather than *vice versa*. What I do mean to say is that no one part of our society has polluted any other part. Drug abuse is a phenomenon of the entire society; when you take an extremely large number of American adolescents in 1970 and crowd them together in rather austere circumstances, as the military does, drug problems are inevitable. One hardly has to put on a uniform to be exposed to the drug scene, as almost any high school teacher knows. Yet if one analyzes the drug abuse headlines during 1970 and the first half of 1971, I believe he would find approximately half pertaining to the 1 percent of the population in uniform. At one point during the spring of 1971 three congressional subcommittees were simultaneously investigating drug abuse in the armed services, yet none were then examining the same phenomenon in the rest of the nation.

Why did the nation choose the military as its scapegoat? There are two reasons: deviance and vulnerability.

All things being equal, a group will choose to scapegoat its most deviant or unpopular member. Traditionally the military has hardly been regarded as a deviant segment of American society. Moreover, as long as it is draft based and with a civilian leadership nominated by an elected President and confirmed by an elected Senate it is a particularly difficult institution to envision as deviant. Yet the extreme unpopularity of the Vietnam War, coupled with a growing tendency of many elements of society (which actually predated the war) toward pacifism and internationalism, has overcome this traditional view of the military. Generals—depicted as bumbling, mad with power or totally infantile—have replaced the psychiatrist as the favorite caricature of cartoons. Brave and noble warrior in World War II, the American soldier is seen as a villain after Vietnam.

Yet not all who are deviant or unpopular end up being scapegoated. It is possible (and not infrequent) that the leader of a group is both deviant and unpopular. For instance, the wealthy class is commonly deviant from and highly unpopular with the masses, and while revolutions may happen, often they do not. Instead, one picks on the weak and vulnerable. Even though one does not tend to think of the military as weak and vulnerable, for the purposes of Congress in 1970 in regard to drug abuse, it was at least relatively so. Drug abuse is a touchy topic which may involve corruption, selective law enforcement, inadequate health care, governmental ineffectiveness and public apathy. The military was the one broad segment of American society in which drug abuse could be most easily investigated. I do not mean to imply that any congressman would deliberately scapegoat the military for America's drug problem. On the contrary, Senator Harold Hughes, the undisputed leader of the battle against this problem, opened or closed most of his various hearings into drug abuse in the military with some acknowledgment that the military was responding to the problem as effectively, if not more so, than the civilian sector. But whatever their intentions, the effect of Congress's investigations into drug abuse in the military was to identify the problem, at least initially, as a military one more than a national one. Drug abuse was brought into public awareness on the back of the military.

The process of scapegoating is a vicious cycle. Once the label "deviant" has been attached to a group, it becomes tempting the next time problems arise to attribute them to the "deviant" group. However, the cycle of scapegoating can be broken. Reliance on scapegoating may grow to the point that members of the society find allegations absurd that previously seemed plausible. Or, the scapegoated group itself may alter its behavior in ways that enable it to lose the deviant label. Both of these tendencies currently are underway in societal and military response to the drug problem, and the scapegoating of the military, at least in this problem area, has come to an end.

In June 1971, the President created a special agency to combat the drug abuse problem: the Special Action Office for Drug Abuse Prevention (SAODAP). As director of this agency he picked Dr. Jerome Jaffe. The choice was an important one, for Dr. Jaffe is both a medical man and an expert with great experience in the drug field. The choice of a medical man settled, for the moment at least, the chronic disagreement within the departments of Justice and Health, Education and Welfare about whether the primary direction of the nation's efforts should be toward law enforcement or education and treatment. The choice of an expert signalled, for the moment at least, an end to scapegoating. Dr. Jaffe has a broad and sophisticated understanding of the drug abuse problem which leaves little room for scapegoating. SAODAP is constructed as a national agency to meet the needs of the nation as a whole. Some, still laboring under the myth that the military is the Typhoid Mary of the drug abuse scene, have urged that SAODAP be given direct control over the drug programs of the DOD. Dr. Jaffe has pointedly denied the need for such extraordinary authority. He may have many motives for doing

so, but there really is no more need—indeed even less need—
for him to have direct control over military programs than for
him to have direct control over 50 different state programs.

Although SAODAP has eschewed direct control over the
DOD drug programs and is clearly national in scope, this does
not mean that its interest in the military is slight. On the contrary, its interest is proportionately greater than the size of the
military. At least four SAODAP executives are currently de-
voting their full attention to the service programs. The reason
for this intense concern is that SAODAP is using the military
as a laboratory for the development of drug abuse programs for
the nation. Almost overnight the military has switched from
the role of scapegoat to the role of laboratory and testing
ground for the society as a whole.

In May 1971, a bold but predictable decision was made to
test the urine of servicemen for the presence of illegal drugs.
This decision may well prove in the light of history to be one
of the most dramatic of the decade. For several years a number
of civilian treatment programs, including Dr. Jaffe's own programs in Illinois, had been testing the urine of their patients as
a way of monitoring their treatment, and while not inexpensive
the procedure had proven both feasible and clinically useful.
For over a year a variety of organizations had been rather sur-
reptitiously testing the urine of prospective employees for drugs
as part of their routine physical examination. For over a year
considerable pressure had been exerted both by Congress and by
military leaders themselves upon the Army Surgeon General's
Office to test the urine of potential inductees at the Armed Forces
Entrance Examining Stations. In early 1971, after consulting with
members of the White House staff, the DOD conducted a study
for drugs in the urine of a large sample of servicemen who were
being outprocessed into civilian life at the separation centers
upon completion of their tour in Vietnam. We all knew that
there were an increasingly large number of such soldiers returning to civilian life with significant heroin habits, and the
military was being criticized increasingly for contributing to
crime in the streets. The pressure was on and the technology was
available. These facts, coupled with an American tendency to

use technology whenever it becomes available, made the decision to begin testing servicemen, at least those returning from heroin-endemic Vietnam, almost inevitable.

However, despite all that I have said, in some respects this decision was unprecedented. Both civilian and military populations have been mandatorily subjected to various types of medical analyses and treatments, from skin tests and x-rays for tuberculosis to innoculations and malaria prophylaxis, in the interests of public health. Yet these conditions are all considered by a unanimity of public and medical opinion to be diseases for which the victim bore no responsibility, diseases which are legal and indeed even entitle the victim to certain rights and privileges ranging from free medical care to pensions. At one time, soldiers had been subjected to certain penalties for being discovered to be infected with venereal disease, but 20 years ago such practices were discarded as being destructive and unethical. Breath analysis and blood alcohol determinations have always been matters of heated medicolegal controversy, and even then are concerned not so much with the drug, which is legal, as with illegal forms of behavior which may or may not be drug related.

The decision to mandatorily test the urine of soldiers for heroin and other drugs as a kind of public health measure comes at a time when neither the public nor the medical profession have any consensus that drug taking is a disease. On the contrary, the presence of such illicit drugs in the urine, while not in itself a crime, is *prima facie* evidence that the individual has committed a crime, perhaps a major crime as defined in many jurisdictions. Many legal and medical authorities have cogent reasons to consider mandatory urine testing for the presence of illicit drugs, insofar as such testing would result in treating an individual as a criminal, as a clear violation of the Fifth Amendment to the Constitution.

The enormity of the decision to institute mandatory urine testing for the presence of drugs in servicemen may begin now to be appreciated. Some feel it is a grand experiment to see if, by using the armed forces and their authority over the very bodies of their members, the nation could get away with violating the Constitution on a mass scale in its war against drug abuse. Actually, the experiment is far more broad, exciting and visionary. For there are ways to mandatorily test the urine of a population for illegal drugs without violating the Constitution. One was to do nothing with the results of such tests other than to compile nameless incidence statistics. Such statistics, no matter how useful in defining the problem, do nothing to attack it, however, and America in June of 1971 was not in the mood for a go-slow, do-nothing approach toward the military and the nation's drug problem. Another alternative was to use scrupulously the urine results only for some purpose other than legal prosecution, namely treatment. That is the real nature of the experiment presently being conducted with the military.

It is a terribly bold experiment for three reasons. One is that to scrupulously avoid using the test results for prosecution tends to decriminalize drug abuse. To avoid using urine test results for prosecution means foregoing not only the immediate prosecution but also the initiation on the basis of the test of any kind of surveillance which might lead to prosecution. Furthermore, it means, by a reasonable construction of the Fifth Amendment, the foregoing of any adverse quasi-legal administrative action on the basis of test results. It is for this reason that the DOD has declared, in the summer of 1971, that no one can be separated administratively from the service under less than honorable conditions for drug abuse alone, thereby reversing a long-standing policy that addicts be discharged punitively. It is in part for this reason that at least one commanding general has recently decreed that the fact of known drug abuse will not in itself be prejudicial to promotion in his command, and it is in part for this reason that no one can now be separated administratively from the Army for drug abuse unless adequate rehabilitative efforts have been made and demonstrated to fail. While the military services are still undergoing a period of transition in this regard, and are moving at different rates, it is clear that the direction is toward a society in which the "crime" of personal drug use (as distinct from the pushing of drugs which will remain criminal behavior) will be weighed carefully against the perhaps greater evil of permitting undetected drug use.

This is not to say that drug use will become acceptable behavior since the drug user will be expected to receive treatment, to undergo rehabilitative therapy. Yet this too is a grand experiment. For the truth of the matter is that the military is embarking upon a vast program of treatment at a time when an effective model of treatment is not known. Indeed, it is becoming a mission of the military not simply to treat drug abusers, but to develop a successful and model treatment program on behalf of the nation. Difficult though this may seem, the military, by virtue of its high degree of social control, is in a better position to develop such a model than any other segment of our society. For as we look at the problem with our current state of expertise, the key seems to be not so much any specific treatment modality—such as antabuse of AA, methadone or cyclazocine, confrontation therapy or behavioral therapy, etc.— as the way in which we deliver these health care services. In other words, the problem is not the treatment per se but how to get the patient into treatment, how to choose the specific form of treatment for him as an individual, how to maintain and retain him in the treatment process and how to provide adequate follow-up care—in short, how to develop an ideal system of care delivery. Such a system can be developed only if the total community is involved in the task. For the present such total community involvement can probably be obtained only in an authoritarian, mission-oriented society—namely the military—where community resources can be directed to the task by order, by compulsory education, by centralized planning and by other pressures not generally available to civilian communities.

One aspect of this health care delivery system needs special mention because of itself it is particularly experimental. Having identified a man through urine testing or other means as having a significant drug dependency problem and having given up the option of ostracizing him or putting him in jail, society is demanding of the military that he be treated for his problem. Yet most of our models of health care are based on the principle of voluntarism. Health care professionals are used to having their patients come to them voluntarily seeking treatment for a condition they themselves define as a problem, and the patient's gratitude when relieved of the problem is indeed part of the physician's payment. Moreover, it is a well-established, unwritten principle, almost a sacred cow of psychiatry, that only deeply motivated persons can respond to psychotherapy, that one can change only if he wants to change. But the average drug-dependent individual is not overtly anxious to change. Usually he does not see himself as having a problem. Rather, one of the characteristics of the drug-dependent individual is his capacity to deny his problem and to avoid meaningful involvement with people and programs who would seek to take from him that which he does not want to give up. Almost all civilian drug treatment programs are voluntary ones and for that reason affect only a minority of the population which presumably needs their services. The military, however, is now involved in an experiment of involuntary treatment or, as I would rather look at it, an experiment to develop a unique system of care delivery so constructed that it not only provides care but motivates the target population for that care.

To date, the majority of personnel found to be abusing drugs by the compulsory urine screening program have not been motivated to accept rehabilitative services. Generally, they do not see themselves as having any significant problem or else they think that their problem can be relieved only by their rapid early discharge from active duty. With judicious management and exposure to rehabilitation services, some shortly do recognize their need for help, and the number of such men can probably be increased as the rehabilitation services improve. Surprisingly, hardly any individuals have objected to the compulsory urine testing or viewed it as an unnecessary infringement of their civil liberties. Almost all who are detected by the program, despite their general denial of the need for rehabilitative services, see the urine testing as an appropriate and constructive measure. They frequently voice such thoughts as, "Finally the military is doing something realistic about drug abuse" and, "While I don't really have a problem, I was glad to have the chance to get off the stuff." Similarly, to date, objection to the urine testing program from other sources such as parents, professional societies or Congress has been slight.

In summary, the military is no longer the scapegoat for the nation's drug problem. Instead it has become its hope, an enormous laboratory with the mission of developing a model program for the country. Currently, four vast and interrelated social experiments are being conducted simultaneously in this laboratory: the use of biochemical technology for case finding through compulsory screening; the partial decriminalization of personal drug use; the institution of a health care delivery system involving not simply medical professionals and paraprofessionals but the entire community; and the development of techniques and systems to motivate the unmotivated. If these experiments prove successful they more than likely will be extended in part at least into the civilian community. Dr. Jaffe himself supported this analysis of the current role of the military in the drug abuse scene in a speech to the Army World Wide Drug Abuse and Alcoholism Conference in September 1971:

> The relationship between the Special Action Office for Drug Abuse Prevention and the military services is an integral factor in the success of our endeavor. As the President recognizes, the drug problem in the military is a reflection of the drug problem in our society as a whole. As such, its seriousness cannot be denied. However, those critics who isolate and overemphasize this issue are looking for an excuse to malign the military and are ignoring the real problem. The President has observed that many times the military has been able to find solutions for unique medical problems and to benefit society by channeling this knowledge to civilian medicine. We hope to be able to use the unique potential of the military to find better ways to deal with drug abuse, in civilian society as well as in the services. Methods of treatment can be controlled and studied much more closely for drug dependent servicemen than for civilians under treatment, so that the most effective modalities may ultimately be discovered. Therefore, a close and cooperative working relationship between the military services and the Special Action Office is of utmost importance.[6]

To change and be changed

The business of working with drug users—and it is becoming a business—changes people. When you attempt to relate genuinely to young people (as you must if you are going to be successful) you soon find yourself questioning the sanctity of your own maturity and traditional ideals. When you work with the poor and the ghetto black you begin to wonder about the price you have paid to be successful and white. When you genuinely try to cure the criminal you begin to doubt your own supposed honesty. As a matter of fact, in their use of drugs the youth of America have unconsciously chosen a brilliant tool to revolutionize our society. They are saying "If you want to cure me of my ecstatic hedonism, which seems so upsetting to you, then you must show me something more sweet and more meaningful than you have managed to show me until now in your lives." So in trying to cure the revolutionaries we ourselves are being revolutionized. It is not just we as individuals who are changed but also our institutions. We find that these street children whom we magnanimously desire to help do not want our sterile hospital corridors, our elaborate record keeping and bureaucratic filing systems, or our bills and insurance forms. So we have had to establish the free clinics, and in so doing the very practice of medicine is being revolutionized.

Colonel Tom Harris, chaplain to the Army Surgeon General's Office, put it well when he said to an audience of high-ranking officers, "The struggle to reclaim or rehabilitate one whose life and whose patterns of thought have been built around drug usage is the struggle to rehabilitate you and me." [7] If the military succeeds in its task of rehabilitating drug users it will never again be the same. Its practices of personnel management will never be the same. The whole ethos of the military will be changed.

The resistance which many career military personnel display to the vast expenditure of money, time and talent necessary to effectively combat drug abuse is based on the rationale that rehabilitation is not a proper mission of the armed forces. The historical fact of the Civilian Conservation Corps (CCC), the somewhat tentative efforts of Project 100,000 and the more successful efforts of Project Transition suggest that this reasoning may be based more upon stereotypical images of drug abusers than a clear analysis of the situation. Nevertheless, there is a real question about the priority of human resources development tasks when compared with what is still regarded as the primary mission of the military: defense of the nation by arms. Yet not since the CCC, and perhaps not ever, has a human development mission for the military been afforded such priority by the President as drug abuse prevention and rehabilitation. Moreover, in order to succeed in this mission, some are beginning to suggest that it will be necessary to increase further the military's role in domestic civic action programs so as to provide the youthful drug user with some organizational purposes "more sweet and meaningful" than the traditional garrison exercises and maneuvers. Should the military succeed with its drug abuse mission, it is not unlikely that it will be assigned other missions of human resources development and domestic civic action. If this all comes to pass then there will have occurred not only a vast change within the military but also in the relationship between the military and society and within the society as a whole.

At this point, career military personnel are resentful or at least ambivalent about this strange additional new mission which has been imposed upon them. But it is possible that they will come to embrace it with enthusiasm, finding in this mission a new meaning in their careers and their organization. In the final speech of the Army World Wide Drug Abuse and Alcoholism Conference in September 1971, General William Westmoreland, the Army Chief of Staff, concluded by saying:

> I may be overly optimistic, but I see President Nixon's drug abuse program as a possible rallying point for the people of our country to confront the root problems of our society—and to rectify them. I see this program serving as a catalyst—an opportunity for our nation to correct

some of the ills of our society, and to restore the moral standards which made our country great. A concerned effort by the people of our country could create a moral Renaissance in which an ethical regeneration of our society takes place. I know not what will eventually come from these efforts. But I do know that the Army will be in the vanguard of our country's efforts to correct this national problem of alcoholism and drug abuse. Just as the Army led the nation in a massive effort in social welfare during the great Depression with the Civilian Conservation Corps —just as the Army has led this nation in its efforts to achieve a truly integrated society in which any man can advance in accordance with his demonstrated abilities— the Army fully intends to lead the way in meeting the national challenge of alcoholism and drug abuse.[8]

It is possible to interpret such remarks as politically inspired and empty rhetoric. But although it may be that the Chief of Staff was "overly optimistic," his speech also indicates that intuitively the military leadership, at least in part, seems to sense the dramatic changes in their not-too-distant future.

NOTES

1. Charles E. Terry, M.D., and Mildred Pellens, *The Opium Problem* (New York: Committee on Drug Addictions in collaboration with The Bureau of Social Hygiene, Inc., 1928) p. 69.

2. Report of the Panama Canal Zone Governor's Committee, "Marijuana Smoking in Panama," *The Military Surgeon* 72 (1933): 159-169.

3. Colonel Albert J. Glass, M.D., "Drug Addiction and Alcoholism— Psychiatric Considerations" (Symposium on Recent Advances in Medicine and Surgery, Walter Reed Army Medical Center, Washington, D.C. April 27, 1954), pp. 159-169.

4. Louis Harris Poll, reported in *The Washington Post*, February 21, 1972, p. E-5.

5. U.S. Congress, Senate, Subcommittee of the Committee on Armed Services, *Hearings, Drug Abuse in the Military*, 92nd Cong., 2d Sess., 1972.

6. Jerome H. Jaffe, M.D., "The National Drug Abuse Control Program" (Address delivered at the Army World Wide Drug Abuse Conference, National War College, Fort McNair, Washington, D.C., September 27, 1971).

7. Chaplain Thomas A. Harris, "A Chaplain Looks at Drug Abuse," Army Conference. (Address delivered at the Army World Wide Drug Abuse Conference, Washington, D.C., September 27, 1971).

8. General William C. Westmoreland, "Closing Remarks," (Address delivered at the Army World Wide Drug Abuse Conference, Washington, D.C., September 29, 1971).

NATIONAL SECURITY POLITICS AT TOP POLICY LEVELS

9

NATO NUCLEAR POLICY-MAKING

Robert M. Krone

NUCLEAR WEAPONS FOR WHAT?

How to think about nuclear weapons—and, indeed, whether to think about nuclear weapons—have been constant questions since Hiroshima. The controversy over these subjects reached a peak after the 1960 publication of Herman Kahn's *On Thermonuclear War* which "attempted to direct attention to the possibility of a thermonuclear war, to ways of reducing the likelihood of such a war, and to methods for coping with the consequences should war occur despite our efforts to avoid it." [1] Kahn's following book, *Thinking About the Unthinkable,* was an analytical response to the emotional reaction of many of his

The opinions expressed in this chapter are those of the author and do not necessarily reflect the official positions of the United States Air Force, DOD, SHAPE or NATO. The comments of Lawrence S. Finkelstein, Harvard University Center for International Affairs, on an earlier draft are gratefully acknowledged.

critics that it was immoral to write about such things and, in fact, might make thermonuclear war more possible or acceptable by doing so.[2] Now that the controversy has largely passed from the scene, the ten additional years that nuclear weapons have been in existence have brought a slowly evolving realization that such weapons may help to prevent war. The terrible consequences of nuclear war make the search for peaceful alternatives absolutely essential.

Kahn, Brodie and others also explored some new ideas— that the use of nuclear weapons in warfare would not necessarily result in escalation to a nuclear Armageddon and that peacetime preparations could well be decisive in the survival of large portions of a population or of a nation itself.[3] These lessons are a part of the tacit knowledge of NATO nuclear policymakers. Thus, nuclear weapons affect all NATO military operations, plans, tactics and strategy; it is impossible to isolate alliance military strategy from national and international politics (see Exhibit 1).

However, differing views regarding the fundamental purpose of a NATO nuclear arsenal (defense? deterrence? bargaining power? prestige?) have led to differing approaches to related policy issues. The contrasting orientations of military officials on the one hand, and of political officials on the other, illustrate the point at hand. Military authorities have the responsibility for maintaining the military effectiveness of NATO's forces, while the political authorities, in conjunction with the heads of state of nuclear powers, have responsibility for the decision to use nuclear weapons in defense of NATO. Because political authorities tend to value influence and prestige more than deterrence or defense, and deterrence more than the defense, there can never be complete agreement between political and military officials on approaches to nuclear policy. The military authorities will always be concerned that military flexibility and effectiveness will suffer through the natural inclination of political authorities to increase measures for control over military nuclear procedures, plans and exercises.

As in any pluralistic democratic polity, the values and tacit theories of political and military authorities, combined with their jurisdictional responsibilities, produce competition for control and allocation of scarce resources. The military approach to planning must be conservative, consider the worst case possible, and be based primarily on enemy capabilities. Military requirements are never completely met. The political approach will usually be less conservative, include more of a proclivity for bargaining, and include explicit or implicit estimates of risk and enemy intentions which then guide decisions on establishing priorities for allocating resources. For political authorities, resources for this allocation are never adequate.

Another aspect of the dilemma about the purpose of nuclear weapons is the disparity between the two basic functions of nuclear weapons—deterrence and use—and the strategic and tactical connotations of each of these functions. Most theorists agree that mutual and stable deterrence on the strategic nuclear level has been achieved between the United States and the Soviet Union, since neither has an assured first-strike capability that would deny the other a capability to respond effectively. As the United States possesses a high percentage of NATO weapons and the Soviet Union all of the Warsaw Pact weapons, and since a strategic exchange would destroy both countries, it is "unthinkable" that such an exchange would occur. Furthermore, deterrence (including strategic and tactical components) has worked in the past, is working now, and shows good indications of continuing to work in the future.[4]

Deterrence, however, is based to a considerable extent on subjective and extra-rational factors such as threats, uncertainties, estimates of intentions, strategy and doctrine.[5] All of these factors are nonquantifiable, noncomparable and very difficult to analyze; they can hardly be the basis for explicit policy. Defense factors present a completely different picture, however. The use of nuclear weapons for defense can be analyzed because it is possible to think about objective, quantifiable and comparable factors such as warheads, delivery systems, numbers of weapons, yields and weapons' effects. Furthermore the technology is predictable to a certain degree. These tangible components which can be precisely compared ("their capability" vs. "ours") make thinking about nuclear weapons easier.

The irony is that the employment analysis may be much less relevant than the deterrence analysis because the employment analysis is almost entirely theoretical, what Secretary McNamara called "a vast unknown." There are, fortunately, no nuclear wars from which to extract experience and data.

Most strategic studies and war games concentrate on hypothesizing scenarios for the employment of nuclear weapons because such data can be fed into computers and compared. Since deterrence aspects are subjective and nonquantifiable they tend to get less attention despite their greater relevance. Furthermore, the deterrence aspects and employment aspects of nuclear weapons cannot be separated without violating the reality of any hypothesized scenario except a full-scale strategic exchange in which deterrence factors have all failed to prevent or limit war.

The programs of the NATO Nuclear Planning Group (NPG) suffer from this concentration on employment to the neglect of deterrence. One reason for this is that since the military physically possesses the weapons and has the organized staff to do research it seems natural for political authorities to ask them to engage in studies. The military is best equipped to analyze the employment aspects through strategic-type studies. Analysis of the use of deterrence for war prevention or war termination involves investigating many variables for which the political authorities are primarily responsible. There appears to be no final solution to this dilemma, which is a product of the nuclear age and the relatively short period of time that international political-military nuclear concepts have been under development and experimentation.

The evolution of purpose within the Alliance itself complicates matters even further. Tacit theories which give a participant an answer to the question, NATO for what? also influence that participant's view of the role of nuclear weapons in NATO.[6] There seem to be five fundamental purposes of the Atlantic Alliance which have evolved over the years of NATO's existence: collective security for the military defense of Western Europe and the containment of communist expansion; political cooperation and solidarity of the 15 nations of the Alliance; scientific, technical, economic and cultural cooperation; detente between East and West Europe; and the search for solutions to societal and environmental problems.

As would be expected, there is a spectrum of viewpoints on the relative priorities of these purposes. Coincident with that spectrum of viewpoints is the range of viewpoints toward the question, Nuclear weapons for what? Although this is a very important problem in NATO nuclear planning, its significance should not be overemphasized. Despite it the NPG political-military consultations process reaches consensus on difficult and sensitive matters of nuclear policy.

What types of nuclear weapons?

Related to the question, Nuclear weapons for what? is the question, What types of nuclear weapons should be developed and deployed? The issue is one with numerous dimensions, ranging from technology to strategy and tactics, politics and morality.

According to one way of thinking, the bigger and dirtier the weapons the more apt they are to deter enemy aggression. To another, large-yield dirty weapons would provide no alternatives to general nuclear war and conventional defeat or even preemptive surrender.

To one way of thinking small, clean and accurately delivered tactical nuclear weapons are the essential link between conventional weapons and strategic nuclear weapons. Moreover the problems of civilian casualties and unwanted collateral damage would be minimized. To another way of thinking small clean weapons would dangerously lower the nuclear threshold by eliminating the distinction between nuclear and conventional armaments, making nuclear weapons more "acceptable," and opening the door to an early use of nuclear weapons in a conflict with rapid and uncontrolled escalation.

To some the stockpiling of small clean weapons would insure the credibility of the deterrent. To others such a development would be an unjustifiable expenditure of funds and scientific expertise and merely mean another round in the nuclear arms race. This dilemma, like the others, will not be resolved easily—if at all. How a participant would wish to resolve this dilemma strongly colors his judgments on what the alternatives for the NATO nuclear planning system should be.

THE NUCLEAR THRESHOLD

Another omnipresent issue concerns just where and when nuclear weapons might be used should the necessity arrive: the nuclear threshold issue. Under the massive retaliation strategy of the 1950s there was no ambiguity on this point. Any enemy aggression would, presumably, act as a tripwire and be met by nuclear response—a response which the Soviet Union was not then capable of countering.

With the change to the strategy of flexible response in the 1960s (formally in 1967) immediate nuclear response by NATO is not assumed, although immediate military response to stop the aggression is assumed. Just what this strategy might, would or should mean in terms of graduated response, a raised nuclear threshold and the number of conventional forces needed, became the subject of a controversy on both sides of the Atlantic in the 1960s referred to as "The Great Debate." [7] That debate will not be resurrected here. It is enough to say that the various perspectives on the problem and how it should be resolved keep the nuclear threshold issue alive. The first variable influencing national views on the nuclear threshold is proximity to the threat—the nations having common borders with Warsaw Pact countries tend to favor policy positions which assure a lower threshold (earlier use) than the Nordic or North American countries.[8] The United States is in a unique position on this issue since escalation to a strategic exchange would have a major impact on American cities and populations. The Germans, on the other hand, do not like the idea that the necessary force to stop a Central European Warsaw Pact aggression might be withheld until German territory was overrun, thus presenting two unpalatable options, using a large number of nuclear weapons on their own soil or conceding defeat.[9] The second variable is the nation's position on conventional forces—if the position is that nuclear weapons are a replacement for conventional forces then the acceptable nuclear threshold will be lower than if conventional forces are considered essential. This position is complicated by the inevitable accompanying domestic national political orientation which includes economic, social and moral pressures resulting in a configuration of national priorities which will dictate a peacetime strategy toward conventional forces versus nuclear power. The third variable is national parochialism (the French model) versus internationalism (the Atlantic Alliance model with U.S. nuclear protection); this variable gets to the heart of Alliance rationale. To the extent that Alliance solidarity and successful consultation to maintain solidarity are shared goals, ambiguity over a precise definition of the nuclear threshold will be accepted. The French did not have such a goal, and so used the nuclear threshold issue as one rationale for opting out of the NATO military structure in 1966. Since then there has been tacit consensus that the nuclear threshold should not be precisely defined for two good reasons: the first is that Alliance solidarity might suffer, and second is that the Warsaw Pact's uncertainty with regard to NATO's exact nuclear threshold is an important part of deterrence.

CONTROL OF NUCLEAR WEAPONS

Related to each of the issues thus far identified is the fundamental one of the control by member nations of nuclear weapons (with control translating into prestige and ability to mold policy). Because the NPG is the institutional manifestation of a long and continuing debate over control of nuclear

Exhibit 1: ISSUE INTERRELATIONSHIPS IN NATO*

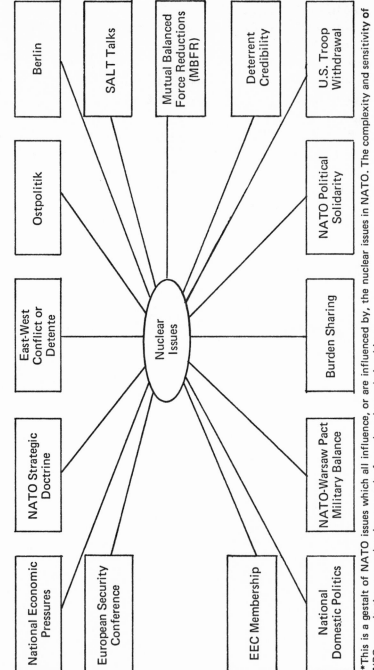

*This is a gestalt of NATO issues which all influence, or are influenced by, the nuclear issues in NATO. The complexity and sensitivity of NPG consultation on nuclear issues results from these interrelationships.

weapons, some discussion of the evolution of the debate, and of the structure and processes that characterize the NPG, is necessary to clarify the current status of the issue.[10]

The interest of European Alliance nations (including the United Kingdom) in active participation in nuclear planning has steadily increased over the past two decades due to a number of post-World War II international trends. In NATO's first decade, the 1950s, American supremacy over the Soviet Union in strategic nuclear weapons, the Eisenhower administration's emphasis on massive nuclear response in the event of Warsaw Pact aggression,[11] the Cold War, and Western Europe's preoccupation with its postwar economic and political reconstruction left American leadership unchallenged in nuclear planning for the Alliance. The U.S. strategic nuclear umbrella was universally accepted in the Alliance as providing the security within which Western European economic and political recovery could progress without expensive nuclear research and development programs. With almost exclusive ownership of NATO's nuclear weapons, delivery systems and knowledge, the American government forged NATO's nuclear strategy single-handedly.[12]

A combination of events beginning in the late 1950s and extending through the 1960s changed this situation. In October 1957, the Soviet Union orbited Sputnik I and thereby demonstrated that it was only a matter of time until the U.S. homeland would be vulnerable to strategic attack.

The following December, at the North Atlantic Council meeting attended by heads of government, President Eisenhower made a formal proposal to NATO for the introduction of nuclear weaponry into Europe for non-United States European forces. These weapons were to be distinct from and in addition to the U.S. strategic weapons.[13]

NATO accepted this proposal, which led to bilateral stockpile arrangements, providing nuclear systems to Europe and training European personnel in the use of nuclear delivery systems. This was the beginning of the nuclear capability for Allied Command Europe (ACE) which was to grow to 7,000 warheads over the following ten years.[14] The Soviet ICBM capability increased throughout the decade to the point where the "missile gap" became a major issue in the presidential elections of 1960.[15] The new Kennedy administration, and particularly Secretary of Defense Robert S. McNamara, became convinced that massive retaliation was an unrealistic strategy which left the United States and the Alliance no options between all-out nuclear war and surrender in the face of any Warsaw Pact aggression.[16] In spite of the fact that neither the oversimplified term "missile gap" or "massive retaliation" was an accurate reflection of reality, a new strategy of "flexible response" was devised to provide defense alternatives from conventional warfare to strategic nuclear exchange. Considerable political pressure was applied to the Alliance by the United States to have European members increase their conventional forces committed to the defense of NATO to the point where defense against an "all out Soviet attack could be accomplished by NATO without resort to tactical nuclear weapons. . . ." [17]

The combination of increasing Soviet strategic nuclear weapons capabilities and the new U.S. emphasis on conventional forces created doubts in Europe concerning American willingness to risk the sacrifice of its own cities and populations to save Europe.[18] Except for the German forces build-up and successive qualitative improvements in weapons systems the Alliance largely resisted U.S. pressures for conventional forces increases.[19] U.S. reluctance to share nuclear information, planning or control served to increase European suspicions. France was the leader of the opposition to the American nuclear monopoly, and it was primarily over the nuclear strategy and planning issue that France later withdrew from the military side of NATO.[20]

Still other factors in the 1960s which influenced attitudes toward nuclear negotiations were the continual efforts by some nuclear powers to achieve international agreements concerning disarmament, nuclear tests and nuclear proliferation. The Treaty Banning Nuclear Weapons Tests in the Atmosphere, in Outer Space and Under Water was signed on August 5, 1963. Nonproliferation treaty negotiations took place throughout the 1960s,[21] and in 1967 negotiations began toward a treaty to keep the seabed free of nuclear weapons.[22] These various pressures and trends motivated the United States to search for ways to provide its NATO allies a role in nuclear matters without actually turning over control of the weapons or encouraging them to develop national nuclear capabilities.

From 1960 to 1965 a series of American nuclear hardware sharing solutions were proposed to the Alliance. These included offering the strike capability of Polaris submarines under the control of NATO;[23] an interallied nuclear force to include United Kingdom Vulcan bombers, Polaris submarines and other nuclear elements; a railroad car or truck-drawn trailer-mounted mobile medium-range ballistic missile force;[24] and finally President Kennedy's Multi-Lateral Force (MLF) proposal whereby a fleet of multinationally manned nuclear-capable surface ships would cruise in NATO waters.[25] Although some of these proposals were highly developed and actively championed by the United States—particularly the MLF—none of them satisfied growing European interests in the fundamental problem of control and policy formulation. American pressures to have them accepted in the Alliance often caused divisiveness and internal political problems for national governments. President Johnson, in 1964, became sensitive to these problems and allowed the MLF idea to begin a process of natural death by removing U.S. pressure on the European allies. European support also dissolved and by 1966 the MLF, the last weapons system sharing proposal, was no longer an active issue.

Well before the MLF had been completely phased out of NATO deliberations, in December 1966, the staff of the office of U.S. Secretary of Defense McNamara was looking for alternatives. In early 1965 McNamara himself reached the decision that something new must be added to America's European nuclear policy.[26] He presented his new nuclear sharing solution to the NATO Defense Ministers meeting in Paris on May 31, 1965, by recommending that a "Special Committee of Defense Ministers" be established and composed of four or five member nations to investigate ways in which the allies could expand their participation in nuclear planning. The official communique of the meeting stated:

The Ministers . . . agreed that further consideration should
be given to a proposal for ways in which consultation
might be improved and participation by interested allied
countries extended in the planning of nuclear forces, including strategic forces.[27]

The special committee was established, and during the late
summer and fall of 1965 divided into three working groups
(for communications, data exchange and intelligence, and nuclear planning). The working groups formulated plans for a
new structure in NATO during 1966, which was a chaotic and
dynamic year for NATO, with the French announcement that
ties with the NATO integrated military system would be sev-
ered in 1967 [28]; with United States and Soviet increased interest in a nonproliferation treaty; and with the MLF idea rapidly
losing what remaining support it had.

In this political environment, and with French opposition
toward joint nuclear planning removed, the Defense Planning
Committee (DPC), meeting in ministerial session on December 14, 1966 in Paris, approved the special committee's proposal
and established the Nuclear Defense Affairs Committee
(NDAC) and its subordinate action body, the Nuclear Planning
Group (NPG), as the permanent NATO structure to replace
the temporary special committee.

Since its establishment and first meeting in April 1967, the
NPG has met in ministerial session 11 times (see Exhibit 2).
The ministerial meetings are held twice a year, in the spring
and fall.[29]

NPG STRUCTURE

The current NATO policy-making system and the relationship of nuclear policy-making within that system is shown in
Exhibit 3. The Exhibit shows the structure of the NATO
policy-making system divided by the vertical dotted line in the
center of the page into the political structure (on the left) and
the military structure (on the right). This, of course, represents

only the formal structure. The arrows marked "civil-military cooperation" are representative of a very complicated inter-action of political and military roles and functions at all levels of NATO.

The NDAC can be seen on the left as one of 16 functional committees of NATO which carry on their business and report to either the DPC, the North Atlantic Council (NAC) or both. The DPC considers defense matters and does not include France, while the NAC is composed of all 15 member nations and is the highest authority in NATO. Only NAC and DPC were provided for by the North Atlantic Treaty (Article 9) signed in Washington on April 4, 1949. The remainder of the NATO structure was designed or evolved through subsequent agreements and protocols or decisions of the NAC/DPC. These latter two groups are the policy-making bodies of NATO, while the functional committees (as well as the NATO Military Agencies shown on the right of the chart) have no decision-making authority. The NDAC and the NPG recommend policy while the NAC/DPC decides policy.

Exhibit 2. NUCLEAR PLANNING GROUP MEMBERSHIP HISTORY*

NPG Countries	1967		1968		1969		1970		1971		1972
	1	2	3	4	5	6	7	8	9	10	11
Permanent											
Germany	⊕	⊕	⊕	⊕	⊕	⊕	⊕	⊕	⊕	⊕	⊕
Italy	⊕	⊕	⊕	⊕	⊕	⊕	⊕	⊕	⊕	⊕	⊕
United Kingdom	⊕	⊕	⊕	⊕	⊕	⊕	⊕	⊕	⊕	⊕	⊕
United States	⊕	⊕	⊕	⊕	⊕	⊕	⊕	⊕	⊕	⊕	⊕
Rotating											
Belgium					⊕	⊕	⊕			⊕	⊕
Canada	⊕	⊕	⊕				⊕	⊕	⊕		
Denmark					⊕	⊕	⊕			⊕	⊕
Greece			⊕	⊕			⊕	⊕	⊕		
Netherlands	⊕	⊕	⊕				⊕	⊕	⊕		
Norway							⊕	⊕	⊕		
Turkey	⊕	⊕			⊕	⊕	⊕				⊕

*Numbers 1 through 11 indicate the meeting number and an ⊕ indicates attendance at the NPG ministerial meeting.

Exhibit 3: NATO POLICY-MAKING STRUCTURE

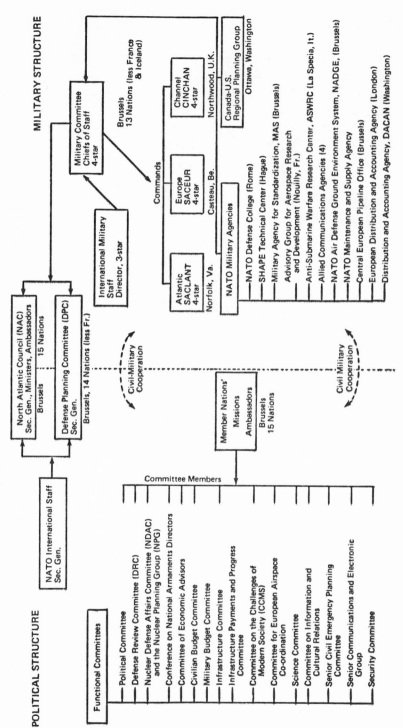

POLITICAL STRUCTURE

MILITARY STRUCTURE

NATO International Staff
Sec. Gen.

North Atlantic Council (NAC)
Sec. Gen., Ministers, Ambassadors
Brussels   15 Nations

Defense Planning Committee (DPC)
Sec. Gen.
Brussels, 14 Nations (less Fr.)

Military Committee
Chiefs of Staff
4-star
Brussels
13 Nations (less France & Iceland)

International Military
Staff
Director, 3-star

Commands

Atlantic
SACLANT
4-star
Norfolk, Va.

Europe
SACEUR
4-star
Casteau, Be.

Channel
CINCHAN
4-star
Northwood, U.K.

Canada-U.S.
Regional Planning Group
Ottawa, Washington

NATO Military Agencies

NATO Defense College (Rome)

SHAPE Technical Center (Hague)

Military Agency for Standardization, MAS (Brussels)

Advisory Group for Aerospace Research and Development (Neuilly, Fr.)

Anti-Submarine Warfare Research Center, ASWRC (La Specia, It.)

Allied Communications Agencies (4)

NATO Air Defense Ground Environment System, NADGE, (Brussels)

NATO Maintenance and Supply Agency

Central European Pipeline Office (Brussels)

European Distribution and Accounting Agency (London)

Distribution and Accounting Agency, DACAN (Washington)

Civil-Military Cooperation

Civil Military Cooperation

Member Nations'
Missions
Ambassadors
Brussels
15 Nations

Committee Members

Functional Committees

Political Committee

Defense Review Committee (DRC)

Nuclear Defense Affairs Committee (NDAC) and the Nuclear Planning Group (NPG)

Conference on National Armaments Directors

Committee of Economic Advisors

Civilian Budget Committee

Military Budget Committee

Infrastructure Committee

Infrastructure Payments and Progress Committee

Committee on the Challenges of Modern Society (CCMS)

Committee for European Airspace Co-ordination

Science Committee

Committee on Information and Cultural Relations

Senior Civil Emergency Planning Committee

Senior Communications and Electronic Group

Security Committee

Exhibit 4 concentrates exclusively on the structure of the NATO nuclear planning system. The political structure includes the NDAC and the NPG—in its three levels of operation —shown on the left of the chart. The military structure, with lines showing military representation to the three NPG levels, is portrayed on the right side of the chart.

To date the major formal role of the NDAC has been to allow NATO's nuclear planning to comply with the fundamental NATO operating philosophy of equality. All nations of the Alliance have the right to participate in any consultations. The NDAC provides this opportunity for the 12 nations which have elected to participate in nuclear planning. In practice it has been the exception for a substantive issue to be raised during an NDAC meeting.

As the ministers representing nations are the same for the NDAC or the DPC the few meetings of the NDAC to date have been scheduled sometime during one of the two-day NAC/DPC meetings which occur twice a year. In theory any member nation of the NDAC not a current member of the NPG ministerial level meetings could place a reservation on a proposal as it was passed from NPG through the NDAC to the DPC for approval.

Such a reservation has not occurred so far in the short history of the NDAC because ample opportunity exists for airing national views in the three levels of the NPG mechanism (i.e., the ministerial, the permanent representatives and the staff group) where a minister of defense, an ambassador to NATO or a representative from the national delegation at NATO headquarters in Brussels presents his capital's position in the consultation process. In this manner the issues are debated and resolved prior to their reaching the NDAC level on their way to the DPC for final approval. All NDAC member nations with the exception of Portugal participate at the two lower levels of the NPG, and if the Portuguese government felt the need of a greater voice in NATO's nuclear planning it could request active participation within the NPG. In addition to the principle of equality another fundamental NATO operating principle is unanimity. All participating nations must agree before

Exhibit 4: THE NATO NUCLEAR PLANNING GROUP

POLITICAL STRUCTURE

MILITARY STRUCTURE

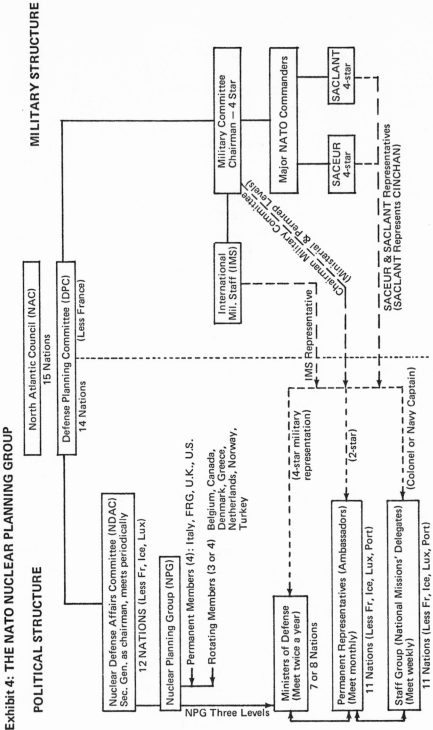

a policy can be approved by the DPC or the NAC. Agreement does not have to be overt. Silence, or the absence of an objection, is adequate to maintain the unanimity principle. Both the NDAC and NPG consultation processes conform to these two principles.

The highest level of effective nuclear planning consultation in NATO is the ministerial level of the NPG, which is chaired by the Secretary General. Twice a year ministers of defense from seven or eight NPG nations meet, usually in a national capital, to discuss nuclear planning and policy issues, to approve the work accomplished by the two lower levels and national capitals over the preceding six months, and to give direction for the future work program of the NPG.

The permanent representatives (or Permreps) are the national ambassadors to NATO and meet on the average of once a month with more frequent meetings as the time for the ministerial meeting approaches. These meetings are also chaired by the Secretary General. The Permreps may discuss any study, report or recommendation which will be on the agenda for ministers.

The NPG staff group, composed of delegates from the member nations' missions to NATO, meets weekly throughout the year and accomplishes the bulk of document formulation and administration for the NPG. The chairman of the staff group is an international staff officer who is also the director of nuclear planning (see Exhibit 5). The staff group was not explicitly provided for in the December 1966 decision to establish the NPG but has developed as a necessary initial consultative body to draft NPG documents and begin the difficult process of obtaining the political and military consensus of 11 sovereign nations on matters of nuclear planning and policy.

The military side of NATO is represented at all levels of NPG meetings by either the chairman of the Military Committee, at ministerial or Permrep level, or by a representative of the International Military Staff at staff group level (see the right hand side of Exhibit 4). The chairman of the Military Committee presides over the highest military authority in NATO (the Military Committee). He is usually a four-star gen-

Exhibit 5: NATO INTERNATIONAL STAFF

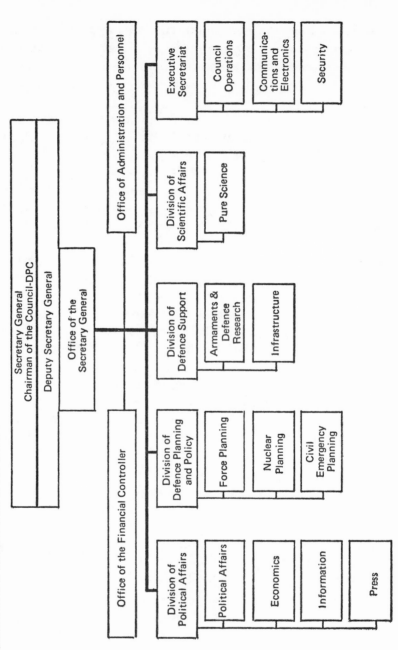

eral or flag officer, and the position rotates among the nations. To date officers from the Netherlands, Germany, Belgium and the United Kingdom have held the position.

SHAPE and the Headquarters of the Allied Command Atlantic (ACLANT) are also represented at NPG meetings through observers. At ministerial level meetings SACEUR (Supreme Allied Commander Europe) and SACLANT (Supreme Allied Commander Atlantic) are traditionally invited. At Permrep level these commanders are normally represented by two-star officers and at staff group level by officers of colonel or naval captain rank. The chairman of the Military Committee or International Military Staff representatives provide the senior military voice at NPG meetings, but in practice the SHAPE and ACLANT representatives participate, as well as the Supreme Commanders themselves, SACEUR and SACLANT, at ministerial meetings.[30]

PROCESS [31]

There are no rules for the introduction of subjects into the NPG for discussion, although most agenda items stem from long-range work programs. Any member nation or combination of nations can introduce a subject through its representatives at any level of NPG consultations. The military side of NATO can also make proposals or state positions through its representatives. In addition, the Secretary General, through the prestige of his office, can offer a subject of his own for NPG consideration. Once a subject has been agreed upon as appropriate, however, there is an accepted procedure for processing it through the consultation machinery to the final decision authority which is the Council/DPC.[32]

The first step occurs in the staff group, where preliminary discussion on the subject takes place. This is normally exploratory and without guidance from national capitals. The advantage of this sort of consultation is that views can be expressed as "trial balloons" so that other staff group representatives' reactions can be observed and the problem can be clarified on a working level.

Next the International Staff Office of the NPG staff group, under the direction of the chairman of the staff group, prepares a first draft document which attempts to reflect any discussions to date. This is a critical point for the future of the subject, as this first paper can set a direction influential to the procedural and the substantive aspects of the problem under discussion. The chairman makes every effort to avoid presenting the subject in a manner which will be obviously unacceptable to any of the national or international authorities of the Alliance. This in itself requires considerable finesse as any issue worthy of discussion by the NPG will have impact on national capitals as well as on the civil and military sides of NATO. Once this document is drafted it is scheduled as an agenda item for discussion at a weekly meeting of the staff group.[33] In most cases the first time a subject is addressed the paper will be a proposal to the Permreps or ministers for the procedural handling of the subject rather than for the substance of the issues involved. Even this is not a simple task, as in most cases the definition of a problem and the identification of a method to approach it has significant influence over the outcome of ministerial discussion.

The wording of the draft paper will be revised during the staff group meeting with additions, deletions or changes subject to the principle of unanimity. Any wording which is unacceptable to a representative of a member nation will be revised to his satisfaction unless the revision is unacceptable to another national representative. The absence of an expressed opposition is considered as "silent consensus." Military representatives' recommended changes are considered by the staff group, but the military observer status places them outside the unanimity principle. In other words, if a military recommendation is not accepted by a consensus of the staff group the military representative does not have the prerogative to place a reservation on the paper with regard to his objection. National representatives have this prerogative.[34]

If the consultative bargaining within the staff group does

not produce a consensus the chairman has two alternatives. He can recommend that discussion end on that paper to allow him to produce a revised draft paper which will, hopefully, be an acceptable compromise; or he can recommend that the paper be distributed to national capitals with the contested points indicated by alternative wording to represent the views expressed within the staff group.

He will choose the first alternative as long as there is the possibility that a compromise can be reached. That determination is primarily one of judgment depending upon a number of factors: how much previous debate there has been on the subject; whether or not a staff group representative's position might be susceptible to alteration through more dialogue within his national delegation or between his delegation and its capital; whether or not informal consultation between a small number of national representatives holds promise of breaking the deadlock; and timing considerations of the NPG work program.

As soon as consensus is reached, the draft paper is distributed to national capitals for official comment. If consensus continues after this step the paper is submitted to the Permreps, who normally approve it for inclusion on the next ministerial meeting agenda, or merely note it if ministerial discussion is not considered necessary.

If, after national capital review, there are still divergences of views the problem will be turned over to the Permreps to be debated at the higher consultative level. At this level a process of consultation and debate similar to that within the staff group occurs. Positions may be softened or hardened depending upon the political bargaining possibilities of the situation, the personalities and influence of the ambassadors, and the guidance received from national capitals—where the issue is being reviewed by correspondingly higher levels of authority in the respective ministries of defense and foreign affairs.

If Permreps cannot produce consensus, the issue will be turned over to ministers for resolution, be returned to the staff group for more clarification of the issues or shelved. If it is a report, study or other document which has been specifically requested by the ministers (which is often the case) a report must go forward which either complies with the request, provides a progress report, explains why the request cannot be fulfilled or presents divergent views for ministerial discussion and resolution.

The intensity of Permrep and staff group consultations and preparations increases as the spring or fall ministerial meetings approach and as the agenda for the next meeting receives final approval in capitals. This approval also may require a lengthy process of consultation as national capitals invariably pursue or avoid political, military or economic motivations which are related to issues inherent in the agenda items.

At the ministerial meeting the ministers will be asked to note the agenda items which are informational in nature (e.g., the briefing of a study, a work program status report or an informational presentation) and approve for submission to the DPC through the NDAC those agenda items which call for policy decisions which will affect the nuclear planning, military forces or political consultative process of NATO.

If ministers cannot reach consensus in their discussions for a decision, the agenda item is not accepted and must be reworked at the lower levels of NPG consultation for resubmission at a future ministerial meeting. If ministers cannot agree on guidance to give Permreps for further action the subject cannot be pursued. Thus, the unanimity principle, in its strict application, is observed only at the ministerial level of the NPG. If NPG ministers cannot agree, nothing will go forward to the NDAC and DPC for final NATO approval.

The equality principle is also evident in the NPG process. All NPG nations have an equal opportunity to influence the eventual policy resulting from consultation at the three levels of the NPG structure, and although everyone involved is very much aware of the special position of the United States in providing the overwhelming majority of the nuclear delivery systems available to NATO—the use of which must be approved by the President of the United States [35]—and of the U.S. laws which restrict the type and amount of information which can be released on nuclear weapons technology, these facts do not inhibit other NPG nations from expressing their positions forecfully and effectively within the NPG forum.

A final important distinction between the NPG process and other NATO bodies is that the NPG has no specific responsibilities or military tasks which become repetitive and routine—such as reviewing annual force proposals or infrastructure programs. The NPG is free to range as far across the nuclear planning, policy and strategy area as imagination, emerging problems and political feasibility dictate. A major objective of the staff group and Permrep consultation process is to insure that trivial items are not included on the ministerial agenda for the ministers' scarce time must be reserved for the important role of nuclear policy advisory body to the DPC. It is only through the personal involvement of ministers in frank, uninhibited and unrecorded discussion on issues whose final resolution has not been predetermined that the NPG remains a viable and dynamic part of NATO.[36] As the former U.S. ambassador to NATO, Harlan Cleveland, noted, "Instead of mixmanning the hardware, NPG mix-mans the policy." [37]

Assessment of the NPG

Views of the usefulness of the NPG fill a spectrum between the two extremes of: "the NPG is an indispensable part of NATO" and the NPG is "useless, if not detrimental." Just where in that spectrum a participant's views fall depends upon where he is located in the NATO nuclear policy-making system and the particular set of values he might bring to nuclear questions. The current structure and process of the NPG is a result of a long and difficult international political-military bargaining process within the Alliance.

NATO's principles of unanimity and equality in consultatation, combined with the fact that political consultation takes place at Brussels sequentially and in an environment of continual communication and feedback to national capitals for advice and policy positions, results in NPG's characteristically

slow and incremental progress toward consensus on issues.[38]
(I am describing here the normal nuclear policy-making process.
Crisis decision-making procedures also exist in NATO, but the
NPG, as an integral body, would not be involved.)

Political feasibility is the major operational criterion of the
NPG, and the current NPG structure has proved to be politically feasible. Discontinuing nuclear planning in NATO would
not be politically feasible because of the importance which
allied nations place on nuclear matters. Changing the current
structure and process which accomplishes nuclear planning
might be feasible, but the changes themselves would have to
be consistent with the "incrementalist" approach to policy-
making in NATO. Attempts to do otherwise would produce
divisions within the Alliance which the NATO structure itself
would have difficulty handling.

The present structure and process of the NPG have a number of limitations, but before agreement on structural changes
could be reached, agreement also would have to be reached
on the goals of the NPG. Five explicit and implicit goals of the
NPG are: to raise the level of knowledge in the Alliance on
nuclear weapons matters; to formulate policy guidelines; to
act as a pressure relief valve [39]; to provide an alternative to
nuclear weapons proliferation as a solution to the nuclear
sharing dilemma; and to provide an informal privileged forum
for high-level political-military consultation.

The NPG, as can be noted from these goals, is only partially a policy-making group. Its functions of education, international pressure relief, discouragement of nuclear weapons
proliferation and provision of a top-level political-military
forum accomplish other goals which must be considered and
evaluated when alternatives are contemplated. The United
States has maintained from the beginning that the highly classi-
fied and sensitive issues of nuclear planning should be addressed
in a small informal forum of ministers who are presented problems, not solutions, by their national and international staffs.
The U.S. position has been that enlarging the permanent membership would hinder the policy-making process and that, in
effect, all NPG member nations have a voice in all issues

through the ambassadorial and staff group levels. An additional U.S. motivation is that exerting influence in a smaller group is less difficult. This position has relaxed somewhat over the last five years.

The opposing position, espoused by the nonnuclear, smaller and rotating members, is that the NATO principle of equality should be applied and that all 11 NPG nations have a legitimate interest and right to participate at ministerial level. As previously noted this issue has more to do with national prestige and influence than with the quality of nuclear policy-making.

Structural alternatives range from elimination of the NPG from the NATO structure to the full participation of all ministers at every meeting. It is quite clear that the trend of increasing interest in nuclear-related matters precludes removing nuclear consultation from the Alliance. Without the NPG some other part of the structure would have to accomplish the nuclear planning function. That could be the NDAC, the DPC or some other working group reporting to the DPC. Without an agreed alternative to the NPG, however, any attempt to remove it from the structure would be a highly divisive issue.

The alternative of enlarging the structure to include all 11 NPG nations at ministerial meetings is not currently politically feasible, although political feasibility in international political-military affairs is ephemeral and usually unpredictable. Europe today provides the dynamism that can alter political feasibility overnight. Increased pressures for NPG expansion could well be counterproductive from the standpoint of effective nuclear policy-making and Alliance solidarity if the United States considered that the intimate nature of the NPG had been eroded through such an expansion. Needless to say, if the major nuclear power in NATO concluded that the NPG was no longer a viable or useful forum and withdrew active support, the NPG role would wither. This would not be in the interest of any individual nation or of the Alliance as a whole.

If consultation, in itself, is considered the major benefit resulting from the existence of a permanent forum for international political-military dialogue on nuclear matters, then the efficiency or output of the process is largely irrelevant and the slow incrementalist approach to business can be considered a virtue. In other words, when the means are the major benefit, attempts to produce efficiency toward achieving ends can be dysfunctional to the system. However, the viability of the NPG does depend on some perceptible movement toward achieving the programmatic ends established. The overt milestones of progress tend to be the completion of program phases leading toward political guidelines rather than the intangibles of the implicit goals.

CONCLUSIONS

The discrete issues addressed by the NPG in its 11 ministerial meetings to date are provided in the appendix which follows. Fundamental problems such as the nuclear threshold and NPG membership issues are undercurrents for the entire nuclear consultation process. Others continue as unresolvable dilemmas such as the answer to the question, Nuclear weapons for what?; the conflict of national interests with Alliance interests; the problem of specificity or ambiguity with regard to nuclear matters; and the questions of deterrence. The overall nuclear problem of the Alliance—the nuclear sharing dilemma —is the reason for the existence of the NPG.

The NPG, in its short life-span, has met the test of satisfying the demands of the varying political and military interest groups of the Alliance by careful selection of its objectives and through slow and incremental progress to achieve consensus. It has a planning and policy function only, so does not get involved in crisis management, nor would it function should NATO be faced with the decision to use nuclear weapons in defense. This latter decision would be the responsibility of the nuclear powers in coordination with the NAC and DPC.

The functions the NPG now performs will persist as long as nuclear weapons exist and NATO strategy and defense rely on their existence and potential use. Survival of the NPG it-

self is considered to be in the interests of individual NATO
nations and the Alliance collectively. The very existence of the
NPG is a factor in deterrence.[40]

NOTES

1. Herman Kahn, *On Thermonuclear War* (Princeton, N.J.: Prince-
ton University Press, 1960). The quote is from Chapter 1, "In Defense of
Thinking," from *Thinking About the Unthinkable* (New York: Avon
Books, 1962) p. 20.

2. Kahn, *Thinking About the Unthinkable.*

3. In addition to Kahn's works previously noted, his *On Escalation*
(New York: Praeger, 1965), is pertinent to the point made here. Bernard
Brodie has detailed this view in the preface to the paperback edition
of *Strategy in the Missile Age* (Princeton, N.J.: Princeton University
Press, 1965) p. vii and his *Escalation and the Nuclear Option* (Prince-
ton, N.J.: Princeton University Press, 1966).

4. There is ample evidence that nuclear weapons have been a major
reason for the evolution of communist doctrine from the idea of inevitable conflict to peaceful co-existence. Obviously, peace in Europe has
been due not only to the deterrent qualities of nuclear weapons; rather,
complex factors have been responsible. However, the significance placed
by leaders on both sides of the Iron Curtain on the nuclear balance
supports the utility of deterrence.

5. Effective deterrence also requires a credible military capability as
a foundation from which these subjective elements can operate, but the
discussion here concerns the conceptual distinction made between that
capability as a deterrent and that same capability actually being used in
nuclear warfare.

6. The form of the question is a reference to Robert S. Lynd's classic
investigation into the rationale for social sciences, *Knowledge for What?:
The Place of Social Science in American Culture* (Princeton, N.J.: Princeton University Press, 1939).

7. This reference came from the title of an influential book by the
French sociologist and political scientist Raymond Aron: *The Great
Debate: Theories of Nuclear Strategy* (New York: Doubleday, 1965),
first published in French in 1963 by Calmann-Levy.

8. Quite obviously, no national capital, or, for that matter, the Alliance itself, will precisely define its position on the nuclear threshold. To
do so would forfeit political and military flexibility for both internal and

external actions. Furthermore, no government could predict with any certainty what course of action it might take as the enemy could select any one of an infinite number of military options. The question of What is the nuclear threshold? is one of those nuclear unanswerables which should remain unanswered. Even when one hypothetical scenario is chosen for study, agreement on when, where and how many nuclear weapons should be used is rare, and such consensus is meaningless since it can only apply to that one isolated scenario.

9. This view can be found in the sources cited in footnote 12 (e.g., Kissinger, *The Troubled Partnership*, Chapter 14, as well as in various German writings). See, for example, Franz Josef Strauss, *Challenge and Response: A Program for Europe* (New York: Atheneum, 1970) Chapter 3.

10. The events leading up to the establishment of the NPG are provided in more detail in Robert M. Krone, "NATO Nuclear Policymaking" (Ph.D. diss., University of California, Los Angeles, 1972), Chapter 2.

11. The word "emphasis" was carefully chosen here because there has been an ambiguous relationship between strategy and forces over the past 20 years. Although the Eisenhower-Dulles administration is identified with the massive retaliation strategy and did stress nuclear capability and response in its policy toward the Warsaw Pact, there were actually more troops and fewer nuclear weapons committed to NATO during the 1950s than in the 1960s, when the Kennedy administration ushered in the "flexible response" strategy. President Kennedy and Secretary of Defense McNamara put a high explicit priority on conventional forces, but actually reduced U.S. conventional forces in the 1960s, while increasing the number of nuclear weapons in NATO Europe by 100 percent. For a description of this nuclear weapons increase see Robert S. McNamara, *The Essence of Security* (New York: Harper and Row, 1968) p. 86.

12. The American foreign policy approach to Europe in the post-World War II period and the strategic environment existing at the time are not reviewed in detail in this study. For an insight into these areas and for analyses which describe the relationship of nuclear weapons to NATO strategy see: Henry A. Kissinger, *Nuclear Weapons and Foreign Policy* (New York: Harper, 1957); Kissinger, *The Troubled Partnership: A Re-Appraisal of the Atlantic Alliance* (New York: Doubleday Anchor Books, 1966); Walter F. Hahn and John C. Neff, eds., *American Strategy for the Nuclear Age* (New York: Doubleday Anchor Books, 1960); Stanley Hoffmann, *Gulliver's Troubles, or the Setting of American Foreign Policy* (New York: McGraw-Hill, 1968), particularly Chapters 5 and 11; Harold van B. Cleveland, *The Atlantic Idea and Its European Rivals* (New York: McGraw-Hill, 1966); Brodie, *Escalation and the Nuclear Option;* Karl H. Cerney and Henry W. Briefs, eds., *NATO in Quest of Cohesion* (New York: Praeger, 1965). An exhaustive survey of Atlantic area sources to 1967 can be found in Michael Boury, "A Guide

to Atlantic Studies," mimeographed (Los Angeles, Cal., Dept. of Political Science, UCLA, October, 1967).

13. NATO, *NATO Final Communiques, 1949-1970* (Brussels: NATO Information Service, 1971) p. 105.

14. For a discussion of the nature of these 7,000 warheads see *The Military Balance, 1971-1972* (London: Institute for Strategic Studies, 1972) p. 79.

15. John F. Kennedy claimed that the United States fell far behind the Soviet Union in number of missiles (the so-called "missile gap"), but it was actually another ten years before the Soviet Union came close to a situation of strategic nuclear parity and not until the 1970s that the Soviet Union passed the United States in numbers of land based ICBMs. See *The Military Balance, 1970-1971*, which credits the Soviet Union with 1,510 ICBMs to the United States' 1,054.

16. See McNamara, *The Essence of Security*, pp. 68-86. The term "massive retaliation" was more a reflection of the will to use nuclear weapons in defense of NATO during the Cold War period of the 1950s than of the Alliance's incapability to combat aggression. After World War II demobilization (1946) the United States still had 391,000 men in Europe under arms, and the United Kingdom 488,000 men. See NATO, *NATO Facts and Figures* (Brussels: NATO Information Service, 1969), p. 14. The U.S. number remained around 400,000 until the second half of the 1960s, when the number dropped slowly to the present 310,000. After West German entry to NATO in 1955 the West German armed forces rapidly built up to a strength of half a million men. Although the Soviet Union and Warsaw Pact have always had larger numbers of conventional forces than NATO, the Alliance has never been in the position of being unable to respond to aggression with anything but massive retaliation of nuclear weapons. For a view of the McNamara efforts to have the flexible response strategy implemented in NATO, see Henry L. Trewhitt, *McNamara: His Ordeal in the Pentagon* (New York: Harper & Row, 1971) pp. 188-192.

17. Statement of Secretary of Defense Robert S. McNamara before the House Armed Services Committee, January 30, 1963. Trewhitt describes this U.S. pressure on the Allies in *McNamara: His Ordeal*, Chapters 5 and 7.

18. See the works cited in Note 12 for the evolution of these doubts.

19. Bernard Brodie wrote a much-quoted critique of the new U.S. conventional force oriented strategy entitled, "What Price Conventional Capabilities in Europe?" *The Reporter* (May 23, 1963) pp. 25-33. In it he accurately predicted that Europeans would not make large conventional force increases and stated: "Thus, appeals to our NATO allies

to increase their military effort must be based on something more objective than the fact that we have shifted to a new strategic philosophy,
especially one that must appear to them to cost more and at the same
time diminish deterrence." There was, of course, a German forces
buildup.

20. It could be said that the primary reason was French opposition
to acknowledging U.S. leadership in any area influencing French pride,
prestige and nationalism under de Gaulle, and that the nuclear issue
was the major overt one with regard to French withdrawal from the
military side of NATO. For the French position on nuclear weapons see
Ciro Zoppo, "France as a Nuclear Power," in *The Dispersion of Nuclear
Weapons: Strategy and Politics* ed. R. M. Rosecrance, (New York: Columbia University Press, 1964) pp. 113-156.

21. The nonproliferation treaty went into force on March 5, 1970,
when the United States and the Soviet Union deposited their instruments
of ratification. The United Kingdom had ratified earlier.

22. On October 7, 1969, the United States and the Soviet Union presented a joint draft treaty under which the parties would undertake "not
to emplant or emplace on the sea-bed and the ocean floor . . . any objects
with nuclear weapons or any other types of weapons of mass destruction. . . ." Disarmament Conference document. CCD/269.

23. Text of communique, *Department of State Bulletin*, 44 (January
9, 1961): 40. Also John F. Kennedy, "The Common Aims of Canada and
the United States," *Department of State Bulletin*, 44 (June 5, 1961): 841.
This offer was not to physically turn over the Polaris submarines to the
Alliance but to have their strike capability under control of NATO. The
United States would retain full control of its warheads. For a well-
documented review of U.S. offers at this time see Zoppo, "France as a
Nuclear Power," p. 144. The offer was eventually implemented. Robert
S. McNamara reviewed these various offers in a news conference of
April 3, 1967, in Washington prior to the first meeting of the NPG
(April 6-7). *Department of State Bulletin*, 55 (May 1, 1967): 686.

24. Ibid.

25. Kissinger, *The Troubled Partnership*, pp. 130 and 142. For a good
analysis of the MLF issue from the German point of view, see John N.
Zedler, "The Multilateral Force: A Misreading of German Aspirations,"
Security Studies Paper No. 14 (Los Angeles, Calif.: UCLA, 1968).

26. For a description of McNamara's shift from the MLF to the
nuclear Special Committee concept see Trewhitt, *McNamara: His Ordeal*,
pp. 79-85.

27. *NATO Final Communiques*, p. 157.

28. *New York Times*, February 22, 1966. The text of the aide memoire
to the allies can be found in "U.S. Ready to Consult with France and

NATO on French Demands," *Department of State Bulletin*, 54 (May 2, 1966): 702-703. Fourteen NATO members responded formally on March 18th stating their support for the North Atlantic Treaty and the principle of military integration. See "Fourteen NATO Nations Declare Alliance Essential to Common Security," *Department of State Bulletin*, 54 (April 4, 1966): 536.

29. The Appendix to this chapter summarizes these 11 meetings.

30. In time of war SACEUR, SACLANT, and CINCHAN (Commander in Chief Channel) would command all NATO military forces through a hierarchy of subordinate commanders. In peacetime they are responsible for NATO military planning, training and exercises. There is a fourth military body, the Canada-U.S. Regional Planning Group, which is sometimes shown on organization charts as being of equal status with the major commands, but which actually has a far less significant role to play in the military structure (see Exhibit 3).

31. It should be noted here that the focus of the study on the international NPG consultative process means that the considerable amount of direct involvement of national capitals, and particularly staffs in ministries of defense, is not covered.

32. The source for the majority of the following discussion on process is the author's personal participation as the SHAPE representative to the NPG staff group during the period June 1971 to December 1972.

33. The staff group evolved from the necessity for preparations to be made prior to Permrep and ministerial meetings. The nuclear planning staff of NATO performed this function even before the first NPG Meeting in April 1967, but on an informal basis. The position of chairman, NPG staff group, was established in the summer of 1967, and the position was filled the following fall. The title "staff group" emerged in early 1968, and the participation of all NPG nations occurred even before the Hague formula was approved in April 1968. The staff group is now listed in the NATO pamphlet, "Conference Service: List of NATO Committees and Working Groups" (Brussels: North Atlantic Council, A3-D(72)1/1, January 1972), p. 6, but still has no officially published charter. Source: discussion with Mr. Harvey Seim, chairman, NPG staff group, February 17, 1972.

34. The word "veto" is not used in NATO consultation, and no voting takes place. A reservation by a nation accomplishes the same function as a veto, since a reservation indicates a lack of consensus. The consensus principle applies only to positive actions. For negative actions one nation's disapproval is all that is required.

35. The same restrictions apply to the weapons of the United Kingdom, the use of which must always be approved by the Prime Minister.

36. There are no formal verbatim minutes taken of NPG meetings

and no distribution of results of the meetings other than an Agreed Minute which summarizes decisions reached and agenda items noted.

37. Cleveland, *NATO: The Transatlantic Bargain*, p. 53.

38. On incrementalism see Charles E. Lindblom, "The Science of 'Muddling Through,'" *Public Administration Review*, 19 (1959): 79-88; David Braybrooke and Charles E. Lindblom, *The Intelligence of Democracy: Decision Making Through Mutual Adjustment* (New York: Free Press, 1965). For a critical analysis of this method of policy-making and its applicability to modern world problems see Yehezkel Dror, "Muddling Through—Science or Inertia?" *Public Administration Review*, 24 (September 1964): 154. Dror has developed the critique further in his various policy sciences works and particularly in *Public Policymaking Reexamined* (San Francisco: Chandler, 1968). For an analysis of the NPG using a typology of existing policy-making models in the literature of political science, the social sciences and policy sciences as well as a more complete discussion of alternatives see my dissertation, "NATO Nuclear Policymaking," Chapter 5.

39. This goal (or function) embraces a large number of pressures by nonnuclear nations and NPG rotating member nations for more participation in nuclear planning.

40. This assertion is supported by Timothy W. Stanley, "The Military Balance," in *U.S. Troops in Europe: Issues, Costs and Choices,* ed. John Newhouse, et al. (Washington, D.C.: Brookings, 1971), Chapter 3, p. 45.

APPENDIX
SUMMARY OF NPG MEETINGS*

Meeting	Date	Place	Discussion Items/Agreements
1.	April 6-7, 1967	Washington, D.C., U.S.A.	Strategic nuclear forces of the Alliance and of the threat (concluded that the size of existing strategic nuclear forces and the plans for employing them are adequate to the need); antiballistic missiles (ABMs); arms control efforts; tactical nuclear forces (agreed that number of tactical nuclear weapons available is adequate but distribution should be kept under review); initiated studies related to use of tactical nuclear weapons; atomic demolition munitions (ADMs); the role of host countries; future work program.
2.	Sept. 28-29, 1967	Ankara, Turkey	ADMs; possible tactical use of nuclear weapons; ABMs; arms limitation efforts; national participation in military nuclear planning; the role of the NATO Military Committee; future work program.
3.	April 18-19, 1968	The Hague, Netherlands	ABMs (agreed that circumstances did not justify deployment of an ABM system in Europe); arms limitations efforts; studies of use of various types of nuclear weapons; gave directions for elaboration of further guidelines for the NATO Military Authorities with regard to the tactical use of nuclear weapons; national participation in military nuclear planning.
4.	Oct. 10-11, 1968	Bonn, Germany	Studies commissioned at Hague meeting (April 1968) with regard to the tactical use of nuclear weapons in defense of North Atlantic Treaty area as a part of the NATO strategy of a flexible and balanced conventional and nuclear response to aggression.

5.	May 29-30, 1969	London, England	Further guidelines for the NATO Military Authorities with respect to the tactical use of nuclear weapons in defense of the North Atlantic Treaty area; strategic aspects of NATO's nuclear defense; further arrangements for consultation within the Alliance on the possible use of nuclear weapons.
6.	Nov. 11-12, 1969	Arlington, Virginia, U.S.A.	Approved political guidelines for the possible tactical use of nuclear weapons in defense of the Treaty area as a basis for future military planning; initiated a further program of studies; completed a review of the Alliance's procedures for consultation on the possible use of nuclear weapons in defense of NATO; discussed strategic aspects of NATO's nuclear defense.
7.	June 8-9, 1970	Venice, Italy	Policy issues pertaining to the possible defensive employment of nuclear weapons; review of studies and reports; future work program designed toward formulation of policy proposals to be considered by NDAC and DPC.
8.	Oct. 29-30, 1970	Ottawa, Canada	Balance of strategic forces; reviewed military planning; refined political guidelines for the initial defensive tactical use of nuclear weapons which had been adopted a year ago (meeting no. 6 above); agreed on political guidelines covering the possible use of ADMs; reaffirmed the importance of the NPG; noted progress on ongoing studies.
9.	May 25-26, 1971	Mittenwald, Germany	Balance of strategic nuclear forces; confirmed that NATO military plans were in conformity with the policy guidance which the DPC had approved in December 1970 (see meeting no. 8 above); ongoing studies for further policy recommendations.

Meeting	Date	Place	Discussion Items/Agreements
10.	Oct. 26-27, 1971	Brussels, Belgium	Balance of strategic nuclear forces; reviewed the military procedures developed in conformity with the political guidelines for the initial defensive tactical use of nuclear weapons which were approved in 1969; discussed requirements essential to effective Alliance consultation and decision-making; examined studies designed to explore in greater depth the possible tactical use of nuclear weapons in defense of NATO; and the further work program.
11.	May 18-19, 1971	Copenhagen, Denmark	Balance of strategic nuclear forces with emphasis on the buildup of Soviet capabilities; reviewed the arrangements for facilitating effective consultation in circumstances where NATO might be faced with the necessity for considering the defensive use of nuclear weapons; discussed studies, which were part of a comprehensive work program, that might provide a basis for further refinement and elaboration of political guidelines.

*Sources: NATO Final Communiques, 1949-1970, (Brussels: NATO Information Service, 1971). These official sources have been augmented by articles in The New York Times, The International Herald Tribune, the NATO Letter (published monthly by NATO Information Service); Harlan Cleveland, NATO, The Transatlantic Bargain, (New York: Harper and Row, 1970), and Harry George Harris, "The Special Committee of NATO Defense Ministers," (Ph.D. diss., Harvard University, 1970).

10

THE OFFICE OF THE SECRETARY OF DEFENSE: THE LAIRD AND MCNAMARA STYLES

James M. Roherty

Towards the end of Robert S. McNamara's term as Secretary of Defense a prominent political scientist wrote that

> the Pentagon has been led by genius or near genius; the cost accounting methods that have been established within it and the assertion of civilian supremacy over the military that have been established by the new team will go down in history among the great and lasting reforms within the American government.[1]

This rather hyperbolic assessment is typical of reactions to the McNamara performance at the end of the sixties. By and large social scientists have tended to suspend their critical faculties in evaluating the McNamara term. This chapter is not intended to redress the balance, but to compare the McNamara stewardship of the Pentagon with that of his Republican successor, Melvin R. Laird, who was Secretary of Defense during the first term of the Nixon Administration.

Laird was a member of Congress during McNamara's term and served as a searching yet responsible critic of his predecessor. Laird was thus prepared to be a different kind of Secretary of Defense. Not only did he have a different view of politics from McNamara, he also had a different style of administration. The concept of varying types of administrative style led to the assumption that the personality of the Secretary of Defense makes a real difference, since significant changes in organizational performance stem from variations in style at the top.

In our analysis of secretarial style as a factor explaining change in the Pentagon we shall compare McNamara's and Laird's performance at two levels: how each understood or attempted to cope with the system as a whole, and how each in turn performed as director of that system. That is to say, how each man performs in relation to the external world (as institutional representative) will not only bear on, but in large measure explain how each performs in relation to the internal world (as institutional director).[2] We can postulate that the environment consists of uncertainty factors which are not susceptible to the same degree of control as internal system components. For the Secretary of Defense the environment is made up of two major sectors, each with its own unique uncertainty factors: the international sector presents both "threats" (potential enemies) and "add-on resources" (potential allies); while the domestic sector consists of the major elements in the domestic political process, namely, the presidency, the Congress and the public. Both sectors of the environment deeply affect the bureaucratic system over which the Secretary presides. While the Secretary of Defense presumably faces the internal world of the Pentagon with more confidence than he does the external world, the defense establishment presents unparalleled challenges for him as system director.

The management of the defense bureaucracy is the management of the largest single allocation of resources in the world; it is the management of a complex of professions both civilian and military; it is a commitment to maintain the supremacy of civilian rule over the critical function of the controlled application of force. The roles of institutional representative and system director, while conceptually distinguishable, become inextricable in practice.

Since our purpose is to show a relationship between changes in organizational performance and changes in secretarial style, we will focus on a key area in which the two men, both in their roles of institutional representative (coping with the environment) and institutional director (managing the bureaucracy), have differed significantly. In their assessment of the Soviet threat, their understanding of the strategic balance, on the one hand, and their approach to managing the research and development-weapons acquisition process, on the other, McNamara and Laird best point up this relationship.

COPING WITH THE ENVIRONMENT

The problem of coping with the environment has been for both Secretary McNamara and Secretary Laird, first and foremost, the problem of understanding the Soviet threat. The two Secretaries have differed in important ways in their assessment and response to this threat. Some of the differences, no doubt, stem simply from the passage of time (the seventies present a different environment from the sixties), but for the most part they appear to result from differing intellectual convictions. Secretary McNamara committed himself to a concept of stable deterrence as a means of bringing the enormity of the nuclear confrontation between the Soviet Union and the United States within the bounds of rationality. The effort was in many respects an academic exercise in which a tightly drawn model resting on rather explicit assumptions was constructed. While it may be said that the objective was to deter the Soviet Union from employing its strategic nuclear weapons against the United States, in a more fundamental sense the objective was to impose a degree of order on a chaotic and frightening scene. In short, McNamara, who sought to remove uncertainties from whatever corner, undertook to render the external realm—as well as the internal world of the Pentagon—more manageable.

The assumptions which McNamara had to make about the real world in order to construct his stable deterrence model were, of course, critical. In a model that made stability its objective, the fundamental assumption was stability. McNamara found stability had many aspects. The problem, to begin with, was in its essence bilateral and uncomplicated by numerous players. The Soviet Union and the United States as the two superpowers in the world had an important commonality of interests and could be expected to behave rationally insofar as those common interests were concerned. Inasmuch as the most dreaded possibility in the real world was the resort to nuclear weapons (especially in a strategic bilateral exchange), the most fundamental objective was to avoid the use of nuclear weapons.[3] What followed during the term of Secretary McNamara has been described by Bernard Brodie as both "noteworthy" and "remarkable":

> An especially noteworthy characteristic of our national military policy since the advent of the Kennedy Administration in 1961 has been the attempt to reject, or at least seal off, nuclear weapons as the basic element in our military power—a move which contrasted markedly with that adopted under President Eisenhower and then known as the "new look," sometimes identified with the phrase "massive retaliation." It is remarkable that the nation which led the world in nuclear power should also have led the attempt to dispense with the use of that power, seeking even to reduce its significance as a latent threat. Much of this movement can be identified with the leadership of specific persons, especially President John F. Kennedy and Secretary of Defense Robert S. McNamara. . . .[4]

David Halberstam, who may be counted among the disaffected devotees of McNamara, makes this point even more bluntly:

> We had sold the idea of nuclear retaliation to the Europeans, our whole budget was based on it, and yet here was the Secretary of Defense (McNamara) who did not believe in it. If the word got out of his doubts, it would mean in

effect that the U.S. was virtually disarmed, and he would not be able to stay in office.[5]

Halberstam and others have gone on to note the ironic connection between Mr. McNamara's view on nuclear weapons and his advocacy of large-scale conventional forces:

it is one of the smaller ironies of his years as Secretary of Defense that in making his relentless arguments against nuclear weapons, he had to make counter arguments *for* conventional forces. If the Joint Chiefs wanted to send American combat troops to Viet Nam without nuclear weapons, he had to go along, since he had developed the mystique of what conventional weapons could do with the new mobility.[6]

Brodie, finding it difficult today to recall the mood of the early sixties, refers to the "lightheartedness" that underlay the notion of "putting out brushfires" with a minimum application of conventional force. He underscores a lesson which was not lost on Secretary of Defense Laird:

Among the things we have learned is that restraint in the application of force—in order to keep that application compatible with its purpose—may make the force applied ineffective for its purpose. Thus to grant sanctuary and to withhold tactical nuclear weapons may be correct policy, but such restraints have to be recognized as being costly, possibly very costly, in military effectiveness. For the future, this is bound to mean not fewer limitations upon the use of force, but rather fewer occasions for applying force under circumstances requiring restraint.[7]

It is impossible at this juncture to summarize McNamara's role in the conduct of the Vietnam conflict. Although Vietnam was a crucial aspect of the McNamara story, more importantly for the matter at hand it offers a striking point of contrast with Laird's conduct of the war. One is tempted to say that Vietnam was an anvil on which McNamara broke more than one of his lances. This was a testing ground not so much for his cherished schemes (electronic barriers and the like) as it was for his most fundamental tenets. McNamara undertook to exercise authority, direction and control over the military establishment under conditions of peace. Vietnam tested his authority, direction and control under conditions of war, conditions he could exert little or no control over. There is little dispute that Vietnam was a steadily expanding source of confusion and frustration for McNamara. The root of his frustration was the gap between the premises of peace management (with which he felt comfortable) and the premises of war management (for which he was not only unprepared but which he disdained). This dichotomy might be put another way, this time with the emphasis on political rather than administrative factors: Vietnam mixed political and military considerations as perhaps no other incident in our history; the most sophisticated practitioners of politics, war and diplomacy were all sorely tried; McNamara, who had no background in such matters and no taste for them, was the most sorely tried of all.[8]

No doubt the most painful problem was Secretary McNamara's relationship with Congress. David Halberstam has observed that "McNamara had no following on the Hill." [9] This somewhat understates the matter: there was a notable lack of mutual understanding and communication. McNamara's tendency to enter a situation with "homework done," "decisions made" and "a fixed position" had led him to gather similar men around himself inside the Pentagon. However, these characteristics also led to his running warfare with Congress. McNamara's passionate loyalty to the presidency has been described as one of the results of this unhappy state of affairs. Secretary McNamara functioned effectively first with President Kennedy and then, for a period, with President Johnson. In the former case there was an element of personal attachment to the Kennedy clan (where the contrast of personality was little less than startling). With President Johnson it was a matter of a top deputy skillfully providing "analyses" of complex problems; there was no personal bond. In the course of time Vietnam came between the two men. Secretary Laird has stated that "Mr. McNamara served too long"—a mistake he intends not to make.[10] Whether or not there is a Vietnam, a Secretary of Defense stands exposed to too many perils, in Laird's view, to venture beyond four years in office. This is the perspective of a long-time member of Congress who, whatever his administrative abilities might be, has some appreciation of what both the environment and the system hold for a Secretary of Defense. McNamara, on the contrary, seemed persistently unaware of possible pitfalls.

Secretary Laird has been ahead of the President in his efforts to extricate American forces from Vietnam. His reasons are the quintessence of practicality, suggesting a marginal utility approach all the more remarkable when seen against McNamara's failure to apply such an approach in this instance. Whether one considers dollar costs, manpower utilization, domestic priorities or a shifting international scene, Laird felt that the costs of maintaining a large-scale American presence in Vietnam exceeded the gains, probably while McNamara was still in office, but certainly by 1968-1969. Hanoi's capability to overrun the South by dint of force had been essentially destroyed. However, withdrawal of American forces must be accompanied by a more intensive effort to strengthen the military forces of Saigon than had been the case under the previous administration. Withdrawal must not in any way lead to a "last battle" military victory for Hanoi. Withdrawal and Vietnamization would go hand in hand, but both would proceed forthwith. Secretary Laird, more attuned to domestic political currents than to international politics, from the beginning had seen major gains for the Nixon administration in such a twofold policy. On the international level Laird's earnestness in disengaging from Vietnam comes back once more to the Soviet Union. More of the defense dollar (more, indeed, than "the Vietnam dividend") must be allocated to the strategic sector in response to Soviet activity.

Washington does not see the Soviet threat in the early seventies in the same way that it did in the early sixties. This is due largely to actions taken by the Soviet Union in recent years, but the changed perception of the threat is due also to the fact that there is a new President and a new Secretary of Defense. From the outset Laird has made the changing strategic equation—the fundamental strategic relationship between the

United States and the Soviet Union—as his primary concern. Intensive effort has been devoted to a detailed assessment of Soviet "warmaking capabilities." Two major factors explain this approach: an enhanced intelligence data-gathering capability; and, more important, a decision to subject the root premises of deterrence to critical reappraisal. Laird has not sought to postulate a model wherein the variables of the United States-Soviet Union confrontation would be contained and interrelated. Rather, he appears to feel that this most serious of all strategic relationships is not grist for game theory or action-reaction analysis, but must be looked at as a unique case. The Soviet Union, in his view, is committed to a significantly more aggressive foreign policy than in the aftermath years of Cuba. One could date this new development from the 1968 Czech invasion or the establishment of a major presence in Egypt following the 1967 fiasco. But it is the backdrop of expanding strategic capability against which Soviet moves are staged that is his major concern.

Laird sees the Soviets simultaneously proceeding to discuss strategic ams limitation (SALT) and deploying strategic offensive forces, not on a principle of sufficiency or parity (which would be playing the game) but on the traditional principle of superiority. In other words, there is strong evidence that the Soviet Union is driven by its own imperatives and does not wish "to play our games." At the same time, Secretary Laird is in the forefront of those who recognize certain imperatives at work in the United States if not in the West as a whole. Powerful constraints on military budgets are operating; pressure to reduce military manpower levels make McNamara's conventional-force concepts impossible, whatever view one has of their merits. If Scylla is a new Soviet aggressiveness, backed by a thrust for strategic weapons superiority, and Charybdis is a downswing, particularly in U.S. conventional force levels, then the course set in the McNamara years must be changed. Precisely because it must limit further those occasions in which the restrained use of conventional forces is called for, the United States must have strategic superiority. The concept of sufficiency is part of the baggage of deterrence and assured destruction; it is not particularly relevant in the present context.

The superiority that Laird has supported—and in today's defense lexicon a less contentious word, no doubt, would be preferable—is a strategic capability that would make it impossible for the United States to be effectively disarmed. The possibility that the United States might be put in a position where it could be disarmed, or even be vulnerable to the threat of a disarming strike by the Soviet Union, continues to constitute the gravest of all threats to world stability.[11] Unlike his predecessor, Secretary Laird sees weapons technology as a highly dynamic if not volatile factor in the strategic equation, and unlike McNamara he finds no economic advantages in reliance on "state of the art" technology at the expense of diversification and investment in research. On the contrary, the United States can expect to assert a kind of supremacy through a strategy of technology exploitation perhaps better than in any other quarter. New initiatives in weapons technology has been a hallmark of the Laird administration; it does not necessarily imply major deployments of new systems, but it is a quest for superiority in research and development. It is in this light that we look particularly at research and development administration as we turn to Laird's efforts to cope with the defense bureaucracy.

MANAGING THE PENTAGON

Robert S. McNamara strove with determination if not success for one-man rule of the Pentagon. He believed with an intensity unmatched in other Secretaries that this was both possible and desirable. In contrast the most significant, certainly the most obvious, management development under Secretary of Defense Melvin R. Laird was the establishment at the top of the Pentagon of a triad: Laird-Packard-Foster. Laird, of course, has all the authority, direction and control vested in him that McNamara had. But the former congressman from Wisconsin, astute as a politician, experienced in the machinations of the military establishment (from his vantage point on

the House Appropriations Committee), and recognizing that
he was not a bureaucrat, made a predictable decision when he
went "across the river": he would manage the Pentagon through
key associates whose experience he valued and in such a way as
would permit him, as Secretary of Defense, to concentrate on
major policy questions. This was his own bent to begin with; it
represented the advice of close congressional associates experienced in defense matters and such "former defense persons"
from the Eisenhower years as Tom Gates and Wilfred J. McNeil;
but it was made possible in the final analysis by the discovery
of David Packard and by the impressive performance of an in-
cumbent, John S. Foster, Jr.

While he was Deputy Secretary of Defense, David Packard
told the House Defense Appropriations Subcommittee of the
thinking that underlay the Laird-Packard-Foster triad: "I think
it is important to realize that management has been moving in
the direction of having a chief executive who is not just a single
executive, but sometimes several people . . . recognizing that
if you have capable people in top offices, they can and will work
together. . . ." [12]

Secretary Laird refers to this as "participatory management," and while he sees the concept extending down into the
system, it is most striking in the relationships among the triad
at the top. Laird and Packard, particularly, developed what
probably has been the most effective working relationship between Secretary and Deputy Secretary since the establishment
of the department in 1947. The Secretary of Defense did not
find Packard's top-level management experience with a major
defense contractor a liability; on the contrary he sought to
capitalize on it to the maximum. Packard had direct responsibilities for implementing "participatory management" in the
Pentagon, with special attention directed to logistics systems
policies, and above all to the renovation of research and development and weapons acquisition policies.

Both men rejected the recommendation of the Blue Ribbon Defense Panel (BRDP) that three deputy secretaries be
created with responsibilities divided along functional lines.[13]
Laird has been explicit in his views on the matter:

We feel that such a compartmentalization of functions at the deputy secretarial level would inevitably lead to greater centralization of authority and decisionmaking. This would run counter to our proposals to decentralize decisionmaking to the lowest practical level, and to restore appropriate authority to the military departments. We do not feel that the principles of participatory management would be enhanced by a further division of functions at another, and higher, level within the Office of the Secretary of Defense. We want to improve the access which the military Secretaries and JCS have for personal contact with the Secretary in order that they may personally present their views and recommendations to him. Placing deputies in functional positions would tend to inhibit that access.[14]

However, Laird found a need for a second deputy secretary. In the words of one top defense official, "If you have a David Packard working on the West Coast you need another one on the East Coast."[15] The Secretary of Defense, himself, has been somewhat more specific:

I feel that I spend far too little time conferring with the Secretaries of the military departments and the JCS. I simply am limited by the time I can afford to take from the multitude of problems and issues that require my and the Deputy Secretary's attention. An additional deputy would relieve me of a great deal of this workload and actually improve the access to me that the military Secretaries and JCS need.[16]

Laird's retention of John S. Foster, Jr., as director of Defense Research and Engineering was a strong indicator of how he would undertake to manage the Pentagon and of the view he would take about the strategic weapons balance with the Soviet Union. Foster had held the position of director since October 1965, when he was appointed by McNamara to succeed Harold Brown. The Office of Director, Defense Research and Engineering, had been established in the 1958 amendments to the National Security Act so that the Office of the Secretary of Defense (OSD) might have a "direct" responsibility for weapons development and acquisition. It gave promise in the final years of the Eisenhower administration of becoming a dominant element in OSD. However, in the McNamara term, the Office of Defense Research and Engineering lost momentum and soon was clearly in the eclipse of the Office of Systems Analysis (formerly the Office of the Comptroller). McNamara had made Charles Hitch and his deputy, Alain Enthoven, his major management aides to preside over the implementation of a new "Planning-Programming-Budgeting System." But the decline of Defense Research and Engineering was due only in part to shifting emphases in organization and management. These simply reflected a more profound shift in policy as McNamara succeeded Secretary of Defense Thomas S. Gates. McNamara, as we have pointed out, did not wish to undertake a policy or strategy of technology exploitation. He saw more than a sufficient number of weapons options within the state of the art, that is, already developed and awaiting utilization. Technology at the outset of the sixties appeared stable to him rather than "dynamic," and in any case it was important to take steps to level off the arms race. An important element in a policy of minimizing risk would be a cautious approach to research and development. This kind of thinking provided the foundations for the analyses that would issue from the Hitch and Enthoven offices, where "technological proliferation" and "scarcity of resources" were the bywords. The emphases in ODDR&E were of a different order. This was the habitat of the engineer with an orientation to hardware application and, to a somewhat lesser degree, the physical scientist whose basic research had application rather than knowledge per se as its end point. In either case it was a far remove from the world of economic analysis with its emphasis on mere units of force. Here capabilities, quality and performance were critical considerations. Foster, more than his two predecessors from Livermore (Herbert York and Harold Brown), embodied this outlook, and at the close of the McNamara term was better able to give expression to it. He had, moreover, the unqualified support of Edward Teller, and was very much to the liking of David Packard. Foster more than anyone else combined a scientific background and knowledge of Soviet developments in his support of new technological initiatives.[17]

Secretary Laird's attempt to give more attention to the major issues is well illustrated in his management approach to research and development. John Foster has described it as follows:

> It seems to me that the most important thing that Secretary Laird and Secretary Packard have done since coming into office, at least as regards research and development, was to clarify the roles and missions of the Office of the Secretary of Defense and the roles of the services. In particular they have indicated that, when it comes to implementing a program, that is the responsibility of the services, and that function should be delegated to the services.
>
> We [ODDR&E] have gotten out of the business of detailed management of individual programs, even the larger ones, and into the business of looking at the broader aspects of research and development for the Department of Defense . . . one of the results of that work [is] . . . the technical assessment of the Soviet Union's effort versus that of the United States. What ODDR&E undertakes to do today is map out and organize "large areas of research." [18]

Policy questions ("the broader aspects of R&D") are examined through two series of technical papers: technology coordinating papers, which look to the long-range advancement of the technology base, e.g., propulsion systems, materials, etc.; and area coordinating papers, which concentrate on particular warfare areas and put forward optimal development plans in each area. This is the net technical assessment function which the BRDP suggested should lie directly with the Secretary of Defense. Instead it lies with Foster and with his deputy for Research and Advanced Technology.

If further evidence is needed that Foster is very much part of a management triad running the Pentagon today, one need only look at the BRDP's recommendation for an independent Defense Test Agency. Indeed, it was around this proposal and the proposal for three functionally distinct deputy secretaries of defense that the Blue Ribbon Defense Panel would have wholly

dismantled the Directorate of Defense Research and Engineering
—a statutory part of DOD. Not only was ODDR&E not dismantled, it is far stronger today than at any point in its history,
with its "total supervisory role" over all research and development. In June 1971, Foster was given a new deputy director
for Test and Evaluation, but in responding to the point raised
by the BRDP Foster points out that those who test are not those
who finally judge. Weapons selection is the prerogative of the
Secretary of Defense. The procedures by which ODDR&E super-
vises research and development are illustrative of the Laird
management. The total acquisition process from earliest concept definition to ultimate deployment is keyed to such devices
as the development concept paper (DCP), management reviews, especially through the Defense Systems Acquisition Review Council, milestone contracting, and "prototyping." The
development concept paper was initiated in Foster's office at
the end of the McNamara term to cover new weapons projects
at a time when draft presidential memoranda (DPM) originat-
ing in the Office of Systems Analysis were the basic planning
documents for the Secretary of Defense. Weapons projects were,
to put the matter bluntly, culled out of the jurisdiction of Systems Analysis. Today the DPMs are gone but the DCPs are
flourishing, and in character with the new regime DCPs origi-
nate with the interested service rather than with ODDR&E.
Each service has the responsibility for initiating concept definition of new weapons. But it must also write a DCP to highlight
key milestones or thresholds in the total development process
for management review purposes. Very quickly after coming
into office Deputy Secretary Packard saw the necessity for an
improved mechanism for major systems and established the
Defense Systems Acquisition Review Council (DSARC).
DSARC advises the Secretary of Defense at each critical milestone on the question of proceeding to the next phase. In the
event of a failure to reach a given threshold the DSARC rec-
ommends that the Secretary of Defense make any necessary decisions.[19] The council is a device which coordinates technology
initiatives with the broader imperatives of national security. It
departs most radically from devices of the McNamara period in

the degree to which it encourages the professionalism of the services.

The most notable of the new procedures is in the contracting area and appears to signal a return to old-fashioned, pre-McNamara methods. The term the Nixon administration uses to sum up its approach to contracting for weapons is "prototyping." All three members of the management triad are staunch advocates of an approach that was traditional in the services until the decade of the sixties. The hallmark of weapons contracting under McNamara was "total package procurement." In a "single buy" one secured not only the end-item piece of hardware but, beginning with the very "concept definition," all the "RDT&E" (research, development, testing and evaluation) as well. Buying a lot of paper as well as the hardware itself, meant that cost measurement became almost impossible. Moreover, competition among contractors on the basis of finished products was ruled out when the product was essentially a concept. Even at the very end of the Johnson administration, after some painful lessons with total package procurement, the Defense Department negotiated with Grumman Aerospace Corporation for the F-14 Navy fighter when the engine scheduled for most of the units was still "in development." Deputy Secretary Packard made no effort to disguise his displeasure with having to live with that contract.

The new contracting procedure which Packard assumed a personal responsibility for has most often been referred to as "fly-before-you-buy." The concept of prototyping means that competing contractors produce a limited number of finished end-items for demonstration-testing, with the production contract going to the winner. Laird realized that it is not feasible to adhere to this concept exclusively. For example, it is not plausible to take this approach in ship procurement. In high-cost aircraft programs such as the B-1 a modified version of prototyping is followed. A single contractor is called upon to produce prototypes; the production contract depends upon a DOD decision which follows successful completion of tests. Even then, a production contract, which is best understood as a decision to deploy the aircraft, may be rejected. Genuine prototyping is followed in the case of the new (AX) tactical fighter and many smaller systems. One aspect of this not-so-new departure in contracting that should be underscored is a DOD effort to encourage the establishment of more or less permanent weapons design teams with major contractors to enhance competitive prototyping. Packard, in particular, feels that this is the prime avenue for securing the best weapons system. Within DOD new emphasis has been put on two personnel areas where major improvements in the weapons acquisition process are expected, namely, project managers and procurement contract officers.

The significance of style

We have paid more attention to Secretary Laird than to Secretary McNamara in the two preceding sections. However, even this limited analysis should be sufficient to permit us to conclude with some suggestions about style at the apex of the Pentagon. The Secretary of Defense is the principal role player in a complex organizational setting. Studies focused on the Secretary should aid in our understanding of the total national security policy process in addition to providing greater depth to the theoretical enterprise of modeling organizations, particularly in the public sector. Of course, excess proliferation of models is dysfunctional. Rather, students of bureaucracy should test those existing paradigms that appear to be useful rather than attempt to spawn new ones. Existing models, no doubt, will be found inadequate in some ways. The most useful models will be those refinements which emerge from this testing process.

A few years ago I attempted to clarify the role(s) of the Secretary of Defense based on the testimony and conclusions of the secretaries who had preceded McNamara. My purpose was: to establish a point of departure for an analysis of McNamara's unprecedented tenure; and to confirm or modify Huntington's conclusion in 1957 that "no one role for the Secretary and no one pattern of civil-military relations has yet emerged as dominant." Two role formulations emerge from a study of accumulated practice through 1960: "generalist" and "functionalist." The generalist conceptualization

> arises inductively from experience for the most part; it is notably bare of preconceptions and illusion. It is reserved and taciturn about men and human judgment; at the same time it provides a certain witness to the variety of human accomplishment. The objective factors which impinge most sharply on this conceptualization of the Secretary's role are policy, professionalism, and responsibility.[20]

The "generalist" Secretary was placed solidly in a framework of bureaucratic politics, but his place was at the apex. He must assure the primacy of policy through the establishment of effective policy processes: "Not only must policy rest on an objective assessment of the present day world, it must also be made operative through processes which have proved practicable in the experience of men who have been associated with and responsible for policy."[21]

The proposition concerning policy anticipates the role of the professional and the generalist Secretary's response to it. He will not portray or represent any one of a wide array of professions in the national security policy process, "but will take account of and rely on all," recognizing in particular the unique province of the military and the problems which it presents. Finally this Secretary is most concerned with his responsibility for the coordination and integration of judgments from various levels and professions within the organization. What is required is ample authority and "an inner conviction about men." The generalists par excellence were Forrestal, Lovett and Gates.

The functionalist Secretary is primarily concerned with the consolidation of managerial control at the top. In this role formulation

> the elaboration of the authority of the Secretary is equated with the clustering of functions in the office of the secretary and his direct participation in them. Under the rubric of management, he becomes primus inter pares in each

functional-professional group which subjects its judgments
to his own as a prior step to coordination and integration.[22]
Management aims to produce effective national security measures guided by policy set outside the management apparatus.
There is, to be sure, "an inner conviction about men" that
marks the functionalist Secretary, but his ethos is markedly different from that of the generalist. It is derived essentially from
American industry and has had striking embodiment in Charles
Wilson and Neil McElroy, but more importantly in the history
of the Department of Defense in Dwight D. Eisenhower and
Nelson A. Rockefeller.

The generalist/functionalist formulation of secretarial roles
is intended to be dichotomous and point up significant differences. Notwithstanding this, however, both secretarial roles are
played out in a pluralistic, transactional world. If nothing else,
a study of McNamara's term makes this clear. My basic conclusion about the 1961-1968 period turned on the supreme effort
by McNamara's group to displace the political/bargaining processes of their predecessors and "bring the policy, strategy, resources, and operations continuum within the terms of an a
priori system." [23]

The antiseptic character of the rational policy model is
well recognized. For what may be obvious reasons it is, nonetheless, tempting to employ it where McNamara is concerned,
for the Secretary made a massive effort to establish a system
approximating the rational policy model. Indeed, McNamara's
major decisions were made in terms of that model. To put the
rational policy model in terms most congenial to the McNamara
management system one would contend that there was value-
maximizing behavior by a unitary actor who chose among alternatives on the basis of cost/benefit ratios. McNamara and
his remarkably like-minded colleagues tried to establish "scientific due process" or unitary, as opposed to pluralistic, administrative processes. There was an intensive effort to establish
internal consistency, to set the very terms of discourse by which
the management of defense would proceed. Hammond, Kaplan and others have written of the "success" of this undertaking.
Yet the vital connection that one must find between model and

decision to establish the utility of the former is not to be found: the major end-decisions of Secretary McNamara were so adulterated as to be unrecognizable as system-outputs.

In a detailed study of the McNamara decision process Major Richard G. Head, USAF, found that in "Decision-Making on the A-7 Aircraft Program" [24] the Office of Systems Analysis "seemed to repeatedly use a variation of the Rational Policy Model" but that this did not extend to other parts of the Pentagon. Head found that a rational policy model is not adequate to explain the McNamara system or McNamara himself. In an excellent example of model refinement through testing he concludes that an adaptation of a bureaucratic politics model (his own adaptation growing out of the A-7 study) fits reasonably well. Head adjusted the conventional bureaucratic politics model somewhat. On the basis of his investigations he contends that within the broader context of pluralist bargaining, emphasis should be placed on individuals in the process. Analysis should be directed to the players, their positions and their personalities. Head reformulates the bureaucratic politics model as an individual influence model, not to detract from it but simply to put stress on the person. Thus McNamara is cast as a role player subject to the vicissitudes of the military establishment, the Congress, the President and not least of all his own unique personality.

The premise of this chapter, that "It makes a difference *who* the Secretary of Defense is" requires that we concentrate on the actor as an element in the model. I have already referred to Major Head's study in this connection. In his essays on *Alliance Politics* [25] Richard Neustadt refers to work in the Kennedy Institute of Politics at Harvard aimed at the "clarification of conceptual models." In particular he notes the development of a so-called Model IV which "focuses attention on the fixed ideas men carry in their heads and use to screen out information." [26] James D. Thompson has given considerable attention to the exercise of discretion by human actors within organizational frameworks.[27] What we wish to take note of at this point are the aspirations, standards, beliefs and, not least of all, knowledge that the individual brings to the organization—and how these are affected in turn by the organization. One difficulty in studying top managers from this point of view, and particularly Secretaries of Defense, is that they invariably spend a short period in the top management role (McNamara, perhaps, the sole exception). At any event, it is probably more profitable to focus on the intellectual baggage which a Secretary brings to the Pentagon more than on how these ideas are transmuted in the encounter with the system.

The Halberstam account of McNamara "the man" has some exultant paragraphs about McNamara the statistician, McNamara the financial manager, whose forte was "a mathematical kind of sanity." Not only did McNamara believe in rationality, affirms Halberstam, "he loved it." Yet this picture portrays a man of small proportions: "when the mathematical version of sanity did not work out, when it turned out that the computer had not fed back the right answers and had underestimated those funny little far off men in their raggedy pajamas, he would be stricken with the profound sense of failure." And finally on style:

> something in his overall style, perhaps the very thing that made him so effective, bothered many of his colleagues. This was a relentlessness, a total belief in what he was doing, a willingness to knock down anything which stood in his way. So that other men, who were sometimes wiser, given to greater doubt, would be pushed aside.[28]

McNamara was not at ease with uncertainty; he sought constantly to translate it into manageable terms; this is to say that he had great difficulty with the environment in which he sought to make "his system" function. McNamara, in a word, was not a political man.

After Laird had been in office two years, William Beecher of the *New York Times* contended, perhaps somewhat extravagantly, that "The Pentagon of Secretary Melvin R. Laird is *vastly different* [emphasis added], in style and substance, from the establishment molded over a seven year period by Mr. McNamara." Beecher noted particularly the relationships which obtained between the Secretary of Defense and the Joint Chiefs of Staff, which he attributed to "the mutual respect and warmth

. . . that obviously was lacking on both sides during the Mc-Namara era." [29] Perhaps of equal importance in this regard is the fact that Laird has provided early fiscal guidance to the Chiefs so that they know "the ballpark figures" within which to make decisions. Since 1969 the budget process has not been "an exercise" for the Chiefs, but one in which they have been real players. This has imposed responsibilities on the Chiefs which Laird feels are rightly theirs, with the result that, today, much of the time spent on budgetary matters has to do with the refinement of cost estimates and not with soul-jarring struggles between civilian and military "shops" over major systems. On the Hill there is a harmony between the Secretary and "the committees" that has not been evident since Tom Gates. Whether Democrat or Republican, the moguls of the defense committees "like Mel Laird." As George Mahon puts it "you cannot have a violent disagreement with Mr. Laird. He does not behave that way." [30] The part of the environment represented by Congress is one which Laird can negotiate with easily; no thought is wasted on attempting to control it. The presidency, the elaborate National Security Council structure in particular, is a different matter.

Laird's own views on the Soviet threat, Vietnamization and withdrawal, the NATO structure and how these issues impinge on the national military establishment in some respects, of course, diverge from those of the White House. The major foreign policy statements of the President represent in broad outline the thinking of the Secretary of Defense. But there are important differences of emphasis and nuance which come to the fore in that complex of working groups which today is the National Security Council. Here Laird must deal not only with Henry Kissinger and his staff but with, most notably, State and Treasury. A senior civilian at the Pentagon has indicated that the DOD practice of sending experts to NSC Working Group meetings only to be confronted with a good deal of rank has not been altogether useful.[31] As a result, Laird has occasionally had to deal directly and frankly with the President. Still unresolved at the highest level are major issues relating to the makeup of the strategic forces in the seventies and eighties, new fleet construction and military manpower, especially concerning the Army, to mention only three areas.

What Thompson calls the natural system model may be the most useful paradigm in a study of the Secretary of Defense. "Approached as a natural system the complex organization is a set of interdependent parts which together make up a whole because each contribute something from the whole, which in turn is interdependent with some larger environment." [32] Here the emphasis is on the organization reacting and adapting to its environment with a view to its continuing existence. This, taken with the emphasis on the internal interdependence of parts, strongly suggests Laird's attitudes and approach. At the same time, Thompson, recognizing the dilemma of having to choose between one or the other of the two conventional models, notes the work of Simon, March and Cyert, which attempts to draw upon both. Here the organization is seen as a problem-facing and problem-solving entity. "The focus is on organizational processes related to choices of courses of action in an environment which does not fully disclose the alternatives available or the consequences of those alternatives." Thus, to deal with highly complex situations organizations must develop processes "for searching and learning as well as for deciding." [33] Yet any organization must set limits here; that is, set limits on the effort of defining situations, recognizing that it must make decisions "in bounded rationality."

The criterion of "satisfactory accomplishment" must take the place of "maximum efficiency." Thus, if we "conceive of complex organizations as open systems, hence indeterminate and faced with uncertainty, but at the same time as subject to criteria of rationality and hence needing determinateness and certainty," [34] we have a basis for distinguishing the performance of McNamara and Laird in terms satisfactory for theory.

The central problem of complex organizations is coping with uncertainty; that is, the unique role of the top manager is one of adapting the organization to the environment. It is as institutional representative that we see the Secretary performing this function most explicitly. As institutional director the Secretary undertakes to establish predictability and control within the system more than outside of it. He must, of course, encompass both of these roles as Secretary of Defense, but we underscore here the primacy of the former, i.e., the institutional representative. We have seen that McNamara gave himself assiduously to the effort of establishing predictability and control within the system; that he had explicit notions of how the system should be directed and structured; that he sought to surround himself with men similarly directed. McNamara's role as institutional representative was subordinated to and inspired by his role of institutional director. On the other hand, we have found Laird highly attuned to the environment, coping with it as a kind of bargaining agent. Because of his clear preference for the role of representative, he has dealt with the internal world of the Pentagon primarily through key associates. He sees the task of directing the bureaucracy as one of mediating between system and environment by those who have some understanding of each; it is not an effort to prescribe rationality. It is in such terms that we would distinguish the style of Secretary McNamara from that of Secretary Laird. If it is the style of Secretary Laird that accords more with a natural system model, it is also the case that in the final analysis we must examine the results of the two terms over a longer time period before definitive judgments can be rendered.

NOTES

1. Morton A. Kaplan, review of C. W. Borklund, *Men of the Pentagon: From Forrestal to McNamara* (New York: Praeger, 1966) in *Bulletin of the Atomic Scientists* (December 1967) pp. 32-33. William W. Kaufmann, *The McNamara Strategy* (New York: Harper and Row, 1964) is another early and, perhaps, premature appraisal; and Henry L. Trewhitt, *McNamara: His Ordeal in the Pentagon* (New York: Harper and Row, 1971) suggests tthat the euphoria of a decade ago lingers on in some quarters.

2. As will be evident throughout this essay I am indebted to James D. Thompson's lucid analysis of the problems of "modelling" organizations. See particularly, *Organizations in Action* (New York: McGraw-Hill, 1967). Also of particular value in the preparation of this paper were

the following: Herbert Simon, *Administrative Behavior*, 2nd ed. (New York: Free Press, 1957); Sir Geoffrey Vickers, *The Art of Judgment: A Study of Policy Making* (New York: Basic Books, 1965); and Frederick C. Mosher, *Democracy and the Public Service* (New York: Oxford University Press, 1968).

3. There is a considerable literature on strategic doctrine in the sixties, especially where McNamara is concerned. I have summarized much of it in *Decisions of Robert S. McNamara, A Study of the Role of the Secretary of Defense* (Coral Gables: University of Miami Press, 1970), esp. Chapter III. Three recent short studies having an important revisionist tone are: Johan Jorgen Holst, *Comparative U.S. and Soviet Deployments, Doctrines, and Arms Limitation*, an occasional paper (Chicago: University of Chicago Center for Policy Study, 1971); Bernard Brodie, *Strategy and National Interests* (New York: National Strategy Information Center, 1971); and William R. Kintner and Robert L. Pfaltzgraff, Jr., *Soviet Military Trends: Implications for U.S. Security* (Washington: American Enterprise Institute for Public Policy Research, 1971). Probably the most valuable new study is Fred Charles Ikle, *Every War Must End* (New York: Columbia University Press, 1971).

4. Brodie, *Strategy and National Interests*, p. 7.

5. David Halberstam, "The Programming of Robert McNamara," *Harper's Magazine* (February 1971), p. 53.

6. Ibid., p. 52.

7. Brodie, p. 18.

8. It is not necessary to cite the so-called "Pentagon Papers." An "inside account" with less notoriety is Townsend Hoopes, *The Limits of Intervention* (New York: McKay, 1969). The latter, it must be noted, is strikingly free of documentation.

9. Halberstam, p. 53.

10. At this writing Laird had not made his future plans clear except to limit himself to four years at the Pentagon.

11. For Laird's views the 1971 "Posture Statement" is a good summation: Statement of Secretary of Defense Melvin R. Laird on the *Fiscal Year 1972-76 Defense Program and the 1972 Defense Budget*, before the House Armed Services Committee, March 9, 1971 (Washington, D.C.: G.P.O., 1971). However, it must be noted that what I have chosen to call the revisionist literature is something of an intellectual base for much of Laird's thought on strategic matters. Among the scores of interviews which he has given to the press over the last three years the following are useful: The *Washington Post*, May 9, 1969 (George C. Wilson); *Newsweek*, December 14, 1970 (Lloyd Norman); the *New York Times*, January 21, 1971 (William Beecher); *Army*, February 1971 (Lloyd Norman); *U.S. News & World Report*, May 17, 1971 (Editorial Staff); and the

New York Times Magazine, June 13, 1971 (Julius Duscha). One might also consult Melvin R. Laird, *A House Divided* (Chicago: Regnery, 1962) and a study commissioned by Laird when he was with the House Republican Policy Committee: U.S., House of Representatives, Republican Policy Committee, *American Strategy and Strength* (Washington, D.C.: Government Printing Office, 1964). The writer was principal author of the latter.

12. U.S., Congress, House, Committee on Appropriations, Subcommittee on Department of Defense, *Hearings on Department of Defense Appropriations for 1972,* 92nd Congress, 1st Sess., 1971, Part II, p. 127.

13. *Report to the President and the Secretary of Defense on the Department of Defense by the Blue Ribbon Defense Panel* (Washington, D.C.: Government Printing Office, 1970). This author was a member of the research staff of the panel and most often found himself in agreement with the dissenting members of the panel. The staff director, J. Fred Buzhardt, has since become General Counsel of the DOD although not with an assignment to implement the recommendations of the panel. The panel report proved too rigid, even doctrinaire for Laird. Wilfred J. McNeil's dissenting views were more attuned to his own thinking.

14. *Hearings,* Subcommittee on DOD, 1971, Part I, p. 368.

15. Interviews were conducted with "senior" civilian officials in the Office of the Secretary of Defense on March 18, April 8 and July 23, 1971.

16. *Hearings,* Subcommittee on DOD, 1971, Part I, pp. 368-369.

17. See Roherty, *Decisions of Robert S. McNamara,* especially Chapters II-III. Foster's advocacy of the Safeguard ABM deployment is a major case in point. See, for example, his address before the Aviation/Space Writers' Association meeting, Dayton, Ohio, May 12, 1969 (Washington, D.C.: Office ASD/Public Affairs, May 12, 1969). The SALT "bargaining position" which allows for a deployment of 300 ABMs can be credited in part to the "management triad" at DOD which includes Foster. See the *New York Times,* July 23, 1971, p. 1.

18. *Hearings,* Subcommittee on DOD, 1971, Part VI, pp. 93, 100, 94.

19. Ibid., Parts I, II and IV for detailed discussion of these procedures. The BRDP gave considerable attention to procurement and contracting procedures although Secretary Laird had instituted major changes prior to the issuing of the panel report. For example, the DSARC was established May 30, 1969, more than a year before the panel reported. The *Defense Acquisition Study* of the National Security Industrial Association (Washington, D.C.) was issued in the same month as the BRDP report (July 1970) and on the acquisition process, itself is perhaps more pertinent.

20. Roherty, *Decisions of Robert S. McNamara,* pp. 61-62.

21. Ibid., p. 62.

22. Ibid, p. 64.

23. Ibid., p. 101.

24. Doctoral dissertation, Syracuse University, 1970.

25. Richard Neustadt, *Alliance Politics* (New York: Columbia University Press, 1970). For an aspect of this work see Graham T. Allison, "Conceptual Models and the Cuban Missile Crisis," *American Political Science Review,* 63 (September 1969): 689-718; also the full-length study, *Essence of Decision* (Boston: Little, Brown, 1971).

26. Neustadt, *Alliance Politics,* p. 140.

27. *Organizations in Action,* pp. 101-102. Paul Hammond has noted the difficulties in the application of models to the bureaucratic process in the Pentagon and undertaken his own "functional analysis." See "A Functional Analysis of Defense Department Decision-Making in the McNamara Administration," *American Political Science Review,* 62 (March 1968): 57-69. I am indebted to Professor Hammond for his comments on this essay.

28. Halberstam, "Programming of McNamara," p. 38.

29. The *New York Times,* January 21, 1971, pp. 1 and 12.

30. *Newsweek,* December 14, 1970, p. 34.

31. Interviews (see Note 15).

32. Thompson, *Organizations in Action,* p. 6.

33. *Ibid.,* pp. 6-7; also Hammond, "A Functional Analysis."

34. Thompson, *Organizations in Action,* pp. 10 and 13.

11

THE SECRETARY OF DEFENSE AND THE JOINT CHIEFS OF STAFF IN THE NIXON ADMINISTRATION: THE METHOD AND THE MEN

Lawrence J. Korb

Civilian and military leaders interact at many levels of the policy-making process in the American political system. Nowhere is this interaction or relationship more critical than at the Secretary of Defense–Joint Chiefs of Staff (JCS) level. For the Secretary of Defense is entrusted with the prime responsibility for defense policy-making and for exercising civilian control over the military establishment, while the JCS, who are his principal military advisers, are the highest-ranking uniformed military officials in the nation and the military chiefs of their individual services.

The Secretary of Defense–JCS relationship began in 1947, when the National Security Act brought the Departments of War and Navy together into a single Department of Defense.

Throughout the two decades from the creation of the Department of Defense (DOD) until the Vietnam War, the relationship has been highly unsatisfactory in several respects. President Truman and his Secretaries of Defense so politicized their chiefs, i.e., turned them into advocates for their own policy preferences, that Eisenhower fired them en masse when he took office. President Eisenhower himself accused his own appointees to the JCS of "legalized insubordination" [1] because of their attitude toward his Secretaries and himself. The majority of congressmen who served on the military subcommittees during the 1960s denounced Secretary Robert McNamara for concentrating too much power in his own office and ignoring his military advisers. [2] McNamara was so dissatisfied with some of his chiefs that he fired two of them and kicked a third upstairs. [3]

If DOD is to adapt successfully to the harsh post-Vietnam realities, it would seem that changes in the Secretary of Defense– JCS relationship are necessary. Two of the most obvious ways change could be effected are by modifying the way in which defense policy is made and by selecting different types of men for the JCS. [4] The purpose of this chapter is to analyze the extent to which the Nixon administration, faced with the task of adapting to post-Vietnam realities, has altered the policy-making and the selection processes, and thus the Secretary–JCS relationship.

Examination of the Secretary–JCS relationship across the entire spectrum of the defense policy-making process would be too vast an undertaking, so this study will examine the relationship only as it has existed within the budgetary process. The choice of this phase of military policy-making was dictated by four considerations. First, budgeting is the only constantly occurring activity of DOD and thus is the most comparable. Some administrations have been involved in wartime situations. Others were in office during crisis periods. But all had to produce a budget annually. Second, soldiers, scholars and statesmen have been unanimous in pointing out the overriding importance of the budgetary phase. There is little disagreement over the fact that, in defense, "dollars are policy." [5] Third, data on the Secretary–JCS relationship during the budgetary phase is more readily available than information on other phases of defense activity.[6] Fourth, the unsatisfactory elements of the Secretary–JCS relationship have arisen primarily from the activities that have taken place during the budget process.

The budgetary framework

The budget process of DOD is currently divided into planning, programming and budgetary cycles (PPBS) which last for 18 months.[7] Thus, work on the budget for fiscal year (FY) 1973 which was submitted to Congress in January 1972, and which became effective in July 1972, began in the summer of 1970. The use of PPBS and the 18-month cycle are not innovations of the Nixon administration. Both were introduced into the Pentagon by Secretary McNamara and have been operative since FY 1963.

The foundation of PPBS is the Five Year Defense Plan (FYDP). This document is the master plan for the budget process. It contains the approved programs of DOD with their estimated costs projected for five years. Each year the FYDP is updated by decisions made during the budget process.

The JCS inaugurate the annual process and the planning cycle by producing Volume I of the Joint Strategic Operations Plan (JSOP) and sending it to the Secretary. The JSOP is an enormously ponderous document that assesses the entire international situation,[8] United States' commitments and military strategy, and then prescribes the forces that the JCS believe are required to carry out the military strategy and meet national commitments. Volume I is the strategic assessment.

The Secretary of Defense reviews Volume I of the JSOP for about three months and then issues the "coordinated, complete and current strategic guidance document for the entire defense community," the Strategic Guidance Memorandum (SGM). This document is essentially the JSOP with some updating and enlargement and is issued in January; e.g., the SGM for FY 1973 was issued in January 1971.

Despite the time and effort expended in its preparation, the SGM is of very poor quality and thus nearly useless for budgetary purposes. It is replete with ambiguities and waffles the difficult questions. The SGM is so deficient that many non-defense officials within the National Security Council (NSC) system have endeavored to participate in its production in an effort to improve its quality. Melvin Laird resisted successfully all such attempts.[9]

Unfortunately, inadequate strategic plans for budgetary purposes are not unique to the Nixon administration. The JSOP, which was the only planning document produced under McNamara, was composed of unrealistic alternatives and not taken seriously by anyone outside of the JCS.[10] During the Eisenhower administration, the NSC produced annually a document known as BNSP (Basic National Security Policy), which whitewashed the sharp differences over what the strategic policy of the United States should be.[11] Prior to the Korean War, Truman's Chiefs were developing plans predicated upon defending the line at the Rhine, while budgetary constraints did not even allow them to maintain a line of communication in the Mediterranean.[12]

Each January, the Secretary also issues a Tentative Fiscal Guidance Memorandum (TFGM), projecting dollar constraints for the next five years. While the elements of DOD are reviewing the TFGM, the JCS complete the force structure portion of the JSOP, i.e., Volume II. This is prepared from a purely military perspective, without regard to the fiscal constraints of the TFGM.

The Secretary reviews the comments on the TFGM and Volume II of the JSOP and then completes the planning cycle by issuing a Fiscal Guidance Memorandum (FGM) in March. The FGM sets definite ceilings on the total budget and on each service.

The ceilings for the FGM are a product of the Defense Program Review Committee (DPRC), a subcommittee within the NSC system composed of the President's assistant for National Security Affairs, the Deputy Secretary of Defense, the Undersecretary of State, the chairman of the JCS, the director of the Office of Management and Budget, and the chairman of the President's Council on Economic Advisers. The task of this committee is to anticipate the political, economic and social implications resulting from changes in defense spending, budgeting and force levels.[13] This body was created in October 1969, and has become involved in the FY 1971 and subsequent budgets. The ceilings that it produces have been guided by a desire to keep the budget within certain limits and an anticipation of how much Congress will allocate for defense. The ceiling for FY 1971 was $75 billion, for FY 1972 it was $70 billion, and for FY 1973 it was set at $75 billion.[14]

Laird has claimed that the introduction of specific fiscal constraints early in the budget process was his most important innovation as Secretary and should help alleviate many of the problems that McNamara had with the JCS.[15] However, fiscal constraints are not new.

While it is true that from 1961 through 1968, McNamara steadfastly maintained that there were no arbitrary budget ceilings and that this nation could afford to spend whatever was necessary for defense,[16] this was rhetoric and not reality. McNamara's office told the service Chiefs how much they were going to receive each year.[17] Moreover, in the Truman and Eisenhower administrations, the Defense Secretaries gave the JCS explicit ceilings at the outset of the budgetary process and never deviated from these figures. The problem has never been that the Chiefs did not know how much they would receive. Rather, the difficulties have been caused by the fact that the JCS were not satisfied with their alloted shares. For example, in Eisenhower's last year the Chiefs asked for $41.73 billion when the ceiling was $37 billion. In McNamara's first year he gave them $44.86 billion, $3 billion more than they sought from Eisenhower. The next year the JCS sought $49.1 billion.[18]

The programming cycle begins in April, when the JCS draw up a Joint Force Memorandum (JFM) which presents the Chiefs' recommendations on force levels and support programs that can be provided within the fiscal constraints of the FGM. The FGM also includes an assessment of the risks in these forces as measured against the strategy and objectives of JSOP, Volume I, and a comparison of the costs of its recommendations with the FYDP. Finally, the JFM highlights the major force issues to be resolved during the year.

In May, each service submits to the Secretary of Defense a Program Objective Memorandum (POM) for each major mission area and support activity in the defense budget. These memoranda express total program requirements in terms of forces, manpower and costs, and must provide a rationale for deviations from the FYDP and the JFM.

Allowing the JCS to produce the JFM and the services to draw up the POM does constitute a major innovation. Under McNamara the program documents, then known as the Major Program Memoranda (MPM), were written by the Systems Analysis Division of the Office of the Secretary of Defense (OSD). The JCS and the services merely reviewed the work of Systems Analysis.[19] Permitting the JCS to highlight the major force issues to be resolved during the year is also a major alteration. McNamara solicited JCS approval only on those items he wished and never let the Chiefs set priorities.[20]

In July, the Secretary completes the programming cycle by issuing Program Decision Memoranda (PDM) for each budget area. These are based upon the inputs of the JSOP, JFM and POM and are then reflected in the FYDP. During July and August, the Secretary meets with the JCS to resolve any disputes over the PDM. Thus far, these disputes have concerned primarily two areas: production of controversial weapons systems, and a manpower-weapons tradeoff. In each of these areas JCS preferences appear to be prevailing. Laird rejuvenated such previously rejected JCS projects as the B-1 bomber, an expanded ABM, the F-14 and the F-15 fighter planes, and acceded to JCS desires to sacrifice manpower rather than the sophisticated weapons. For example, in January 1971, the Secretary projected a force of 2.5 million men in June 1972,[21] but by January 1972, despite an increase of $4 billion in the budget, he was projecting less than 2.4 million.[22]

The reason for the JCS success may be traced to two causes. First, the preceding steps place the initiative in their hands. Second, the JCS present the Secretary with a united front.

This unity of the JCS is a relatively new phenomenon. From 1947 through 1965, the JCS were their own severest critics. The Army constantly challenged the rationale for a large Navy; the Air Force considered infantry troops outmoded; and the Navy ridiculed the big slow bombers of the Air Force. Until the administration of Robert McNamara, this lack of unity did not harm the military's cause very much. However, McNamara capitalized on JCS splits to effect his own policies.[23] When the service chiefs realized what was happening, they began to work out their differences before confronting the Secretary. The man responsible for forging this unity was General Earl Wheeler, who served as chairman of the JCS throughout the Johnson administration and for the first 18 months of the Nixon administration. Admiral Thomas Moorer, who served as CNO for three years under Wheeler's leadership before assuming the chairmanship, has also been able to maintain this unity.[24]

The budgetary cycle commences on September 30, when each Service submits its budget to the Secretary. In Laird's first three budgets, JCS submissions and the final budget were quite close, within 10 percent. Laird was fond of pointing out that this is a major improvement over the McNamara years, and credits this improvement to the introduction of fiscal guidance.[25] However, four considerations indicate that Laird's optimism may have been premature. First, while it is true that during the last years of McNamara's tenure JCS submissions were as much as 28 percent higher than the final figure, it should be noted that during McNamara's first four years, i.e., prior to the Vietnam buildup, JCS requests averaged only 14 percent more.[26] Second, huge budget requests are not uncommon in a war; e.g., in FY 1952 the JCS asked for $81.9 billion and received only $55.4 billion, a reduction of $26.5 billion or 32 percent.[27] Third, the JCS have succeeded in raising the amount that they received above the figure originally established. The FGM projected defense spending for FY 1972 at $70 billion. The President requested $76.5 billion from Congress. For FY 1973 the FGM figure was $74.5 billion and the administration's budget $83.5 billion. This is the first administration that has raised its ceiling. Not even the communist victory in China, or the Russian takeover of Czechoslovakia could raise Truman's $15 billion ceiling in FY 1950.[28] Likewise, not even a Sputnik could convince Eisenhower to spend more than $35 billion.[29] Prior to Vietnam, Robert McNamara remained right around $46 billion.[30] Fourth, Laird permitted the services to divide the budgetary pie almost equally. In the first three budgets of the Nixon administration, the Army received $67.7 billion, the Navy $67.8 billion, and the Air Force $69.9 billion.[31]

The service budgets are reviewed jointly by OSD and representatives of the Office of Management and Budget. After their review is complete the budget is sent to the DPRC for a final inspection. This subcommittee of the NSC examines the budget several times from mid-November through the end of December.

In its several years of existence DPRC has reviewed three budgets. Because of the lateness of its involvement, its impact on these budgets has been limited.[32] Thus far, the DPRC has served primarily as a forum for the services to plead for additional funds for projects that could not be paid for within budgetary limitations. For example, in December 1970, the Army was able to obtain additional money to maintain troop levels in Europe.[33]

The use of outside bodies to review the defense budget is a change from the McNamara years, but not unknown to the Eisenhower and Truman eras. McNamara's final budgets were not subject to review by any outside agency. He was the first Secretary of Defense who could claim that his budgets were not changed by anyone.[34] During the Eisenhower administration the NSC reviewed the defense budgets quite thoroughly, while Truman used his Bureau of the Budget (BOB) for this same purpose.

What is different about the DPRC's actions is that they have recommended increases in the size of the defense budgets which they have examined. Eisenhower's NSC consistently excised items from the budget and reduced expenditures; for example, in December 1953, the NSC reduced the force level for FY 1955 by over 100,000 men from that proposed by Secretary of Defense Wilson.[35] Prior to the Korean War, BOB reduced the budget requests of Secretaries James Forrestal and

Louis Johnson about 9 percent annually.[36] Despite some almost heroic attempts, JCS were never able to convince Eisenhower's NSC or Truman's BOB to give them a larger share of the budget than they were originally alloted.

THE MEN

The JCS is composed of four men: a chairman, who may be from any one of the three services, and the chiefs of the individual services, the Army Chief of Staff, the Chief of Naval Operations (CNO), and the Air Force Chief of Staff. Although the Commandant of the Marine Corps attends meetings of the JCS when matters pertaining to the Marine Corps are being discussed, he is not a statutory member of the body and his tenure in office is governed by separate legislation.[37]

General William Westmoreland, the recently retired Army Chief of Staff, was appointed in July 1968. At the time of his appointment, he was 54 years old and had served 16 years as a general officer. The general is a graduate of West Point and his major commands have included the 101st Airborne Division, the United States Military Academy and the United States Forces in Vietnam.[38]

The career patterns of Westmoreland's eight predecessors as Army Chief of Staff are similar to his. The average age of these generals was 54. None of them was younger than 52, nor older than 58 at the time of his appointment. Their average time in flag rank was 11 years, with none less than seven nor more than 17. All except George Decker (1960-1962) [39] were West Point graduates. Each general, except Harold Johnson (1964-1968) had held a major combat command at the divisional level, and four of Westmoreland's predecessors had also held a major unified command. Even Westmoreland's service as superintendent of West Point was not unique. Maxwell Taylor (1955-1959) served in that capacity from 1945 to 1949.

The present Air Force Chief of Staff is General John Ryan. He received his appointment to the JCS in July 1969. At that time, Ryan was 53 years old and had been a general for 17 years. General Ryan is a graduate of the U.S. Military Academy at West Point, and his major commands have included the 16th Air Force, the Strategic Air Command and the Pacific Air Force. At the time of his appointment, he was serving as Air Force Vice Chief of Staff.

Ryan's career is nearly identical to that of his five predecessors. The average age of these men was 54. Only one, Hoyt Vandenberg (1949-1953), was under 54, and none of these aviators was over 57. Their average time in flag rank was 16 years, with Vandenberg and Nathan Twining (1953-1957) the only former members with less than 15 years. All of Ryan's predecessors, except General Curtis LeMay (1961-1965), were alumni of West Point. Each man who came before Ryan had commanded an Air Force; all except Thomas White (1957-1961) and John McConnell (1965-1969) [40] headed a major Air Command; and every Air Force Chief of Staff was serving as Vice Chief of Staff at the time of his appointment.[41]

Admiral Elmo Zumwalt is the current Chief of Naval Operations. He was appointed to that position in July 1970. At the time of his appointment Admiral Zumwalt was four months short of his 50th birthday and in his sixth year of service as a flag officer. The present CNO is an Annapolis graduate and has held only two flag commands: Commander Cruiser-Destroyer Flotilla Seven and Commander Naval Forces Vietnam. His appointment caused a great furor both inside and outside government, and it was widely believed that Secretary Laird had broken with previous patterns of recruitment in an attempt to "shake up the Navy." [42] While it is true that the career pattern of the first eight Navy members of the JCS is somewhat different from that of Zumwalt, the difference is not as great as one might imagine. The average age of the post-World War II CNO was 55. Admiral Forrest Sherman (1949-1951) was the youngest. He was three days past his 53rd birthday when he assumed the post. The previous CNOs averaged seven years as flag officers. Two of these, Arleigh Burke (1955-1961) and Louis Denfeld (1947-1949), had served approximately the same time in flag rank as Zumwalt. Burke was only a Rear Admiral and ranked

93 on the Navy's seniority list when he was appointed. Zum-walt was a Vice Admiral and ranked 38. All of the previous CNOs were alumni of the U.S. Naval Adacemy at Annapolis and all, except Arleigh Burke, had commanded at least one of the four Navy fleets. Burke's most notable command, Destroyer Forces Atlantic, was considerably smaller and less prestigious than Zumwalt's Naval Forces Vietnam.

Thus, although Zumwalt is somewhat younger than his predecessors [43] and lacks some of their command experience, his time as a flag officer is about average [44] and like his predecessors, he is a Naval Academy graduate. His appointment is certainly not any more of a break with established patterns than that of Arleigh Burke. In fact, Zumwalt is the first nonaviator since Burke to head the Navy.

The present chairman of the JCS is Admiral Thomas Moorer, who was appointed in July 1970. At the time of his appointment Moorer was 58 years old and had served for almost three years as CNO. The average age of Moorer's six predecessors was 58, and their ages varied only from 56 to 61. All, except Admiral Arthur Radford (1953-1957), had served as a service chief, with an average time on the JCS of 2.6 years. Moorer is only the second Navy man to serve as chairman. Four Army generals have held the post. General Nathan Twining (1957-1960) has been the only Air Force representative to be appointed chairman.

The relationship between the Secretary and the JCS has two dimensions. First, the relationship may refer to the activities performed by each party; for example, the JCS initiated policies and the Secretary reviewed them. Second, the concept may refer to the *propriety* of the activities discharged by each party; for example, the JCS dominated the budget process or the JCS were not allowed to make a sufficient input. Both dimensions are inextricably interrelated. A comment on the propriety of the activities, without full awareness of what was actually done, is meaningless. This chapter has attempted to provide a firm foundation for qualitative judgments.

Clearly, in the post-1968 period there have been few major

changes in the method by which the budget is produced and the activities performed by the Secretary and the Chiefs have not altered significantly. Many of the things that have been advertised as changes in the budget process are in reality only formal recognition of already existing practices or a return to previous procedures.

The SGM is as irrelevant to the budget process as the JSOP and the BNSP document.[45] The FGM is merely an explicit recognition of a constraint which, despite rhetoric, has always existed in DOD. The use of outside agencies to review the defense budget is a return to the procedures of the Truman and Eisenhower years.

Comparatively speaking, the JCS were somewhat more successful with Laird than his predecessors, especially McNamara. Under Laird, defense ceilings have been raised and certain weapons systems of dubious values, e.g., ABM and B-1, have been approved. However, three considerations must be noted. First, the ceilings were raised by agencies outside DOD and not by the Secretary of Defense. Second, Laird is not the first Secretary to give his consent to a controversial weapons system when faced with a unanimous JCS opinion. Even Robert McNamara hesitated to overrule a unanimous JCS opinion.[46] Third, the JCS success is only marginal. Defense spending as a percentage of the total budget and the GNP is at its lowest level since before the Korean War, and if one allows for inflation, lower than pre-Vietnam levels.

The recruitment process presents a similar picture. Generals Westmoreland and Ryan are almost carbon copies of previous Chiefs of Staff. Admiral Moorer is quite similar to the other chairmen. Only Admiral Zumwalt, the present Chief of Naval Operations, appears to deviate somewhat from previous patterns. But Zumwalt is not as much of a maverick as the last non-aviator to head the Navy, Arleigh Burke. Moreover, although Zumwalt has "shaken up" many of the frills of Navy life, such as length of hair, he has not had much effect on the essentials. For example, in the summer of 1970 Zumwalt proposed to reduce the number of carriers to 12.[47] The FY 1973 budget has funds for 16. Furthermore, the impact of Zumwalt on the Navy does not yet compare to that of Burke. Two days after he took office Burke demanded to see Eisenhower and persuaded the President to overrule the negative decision of Secretary of the Navy Thomas and Secretary of Defense Wilson on drafting men into the Navy.[48]

On the surface things appear quite harmonious in the Pentagon. There are none of the outward signs of tumult that have characterized previous eras. But there is evidence that Secretary Laird has felt some of the same frustrations as his predecessors. In his third annual report to the Congress in February 1972, Laird spoke of the need for a "new order of service partnership" and for "the courage to look anew at parochial and outdated roles and mission assignments." [49]

If the process of making decisions and the type of men making them were responsible for the past failures, then there is little room for optimism about successful adjustments to post-Vietnam realities on the part of DOD.[50] It is "business as usual" in the Pentagon, and changes will have to be the result of activities performed elsewhere in the political system.

NOTES

Interviews held with the following individuals provided substantial information for this chapter.

George Anderson, Admiral USN, CNO—September 5, 1968

Art Barber, Deputy Assistant Secretary of Defense—February 2, 1968

Arleigh Burke, Admiral USN, CNO—September 6, 1968

George Decker, General USA, Chief of Staff—September 4, 1968

John McConnell, General USAF, Chief of Staff—June 17, 1971

David McDonald, Admiral USN, CNO—August 27, 1968

Wilfred McNeil, Comptroller, DOD—December 13, 1968

G. Warren Nutter, Assistant Secretary of Defense—January 29, 1971

Arthur Radford, Admiral, USN, Chairman JCS—September 4, 1968

Arthur Sikes, Chairman of the House Subcommittee on Military Construction—August 14, 1968

Carl Spaatz, General, USAF, Chief of Staff—September 5, 1968

Maxwell Taylor, General, USA, Chairman JCS, Chief of Staff, Military Assistant to the President—September 4, 1968

Earl Wheeler, General, USA, Chairman JCS, Chief of Staff—October 8, 1971

Because the majority of the references cited come from the annual congressional hearings on the defense budget, a simplified system to reduce the citations to manageable proportions has been used. References to the hearings of the committees will be found in the following form: HCA or HCAS, 1965, I, 57 and SCA, 1965, II, 95. HCA and SCA refer to the House and Senate Appropriations Committees before which the hearings on the defense budget are conducted (HCAS—the House Armed Services Committee), the year refers to the fiscal year for which the money will be appropriated, and the Roman numerals signify the volume number.

1. Dwight Eisenhower, *The White House Years, v. 1 Waging Peace* (New York: Doubleday, 1965) p. 356.

2. For example: Representatives Sikes, Whitten, Flood, Ford, Arends, Laird, Minshall, Mahon, Rivers and Vinson; Senators Russell, Saltonstall, Cannon, Thurmond, Smith, Monroney, Jackson and Miller.

3. Admiral George Anderson and General LeMay were fired and General Lemnitzer was sent to NATO.

4. Past criticisms have centered primarily around these two areas. See Charles Hitch, *Decision-Making For Defense* (Berkeley: The University of California Press, 1965) pp. 3-21.

5. Bernard Gordon, "The Military Budget: Congressional Phase," *The Journal of Politics,* 23 (November 1961): 689-710.

6. Data for this chapter come from congressional hearings and interviews. A list of interviewees is provided above.

7. The budget procedures of the Nixon administration are outlined in HCA, 1971, III, 480-481.

8. For example, the JSOP has a long section dealing with Africa, an area which does not really affect force planning very much.

9. Interview with a member of the Defense Program Review Committee Working Group, April 1971.

10. Alain C. Enthoven and K. Wayne Smith, *How Much is Enough?* (New York: Harper & Row, 1971) p. 94. After 1965, members of the JCS did not even bother to work on it, but left the task to their deputies.

11. Maxwell Taylor, *The Uncertain Trumpet* (New York: Harper & Row, 1959) pp. 82-83.

12. SCA, 1950, 17. Walter Millis, ed., *The Forrestal Diaries* (New York: Viking, 1951) pp. 418-500.

13. Richard M. Nixon, *United States Foreign Policy for the 1970's: A New Strategy for Peace,* The President's Report to the Congress, February 18, 1970 (Washington, D.C.: GPO, 1970) p. 20; and Richard M. Nixon, *United States Foreign Policy for the 1970's: Building for Peace,* The President's Report to the Congress, February 25, 1971, (Washington: GPO, 1971) p. 228.

14. Interview: Member DPRC Working Group. All amounts in this Chapter refer to obligational authority.

15. HCA, 1971, III, 482.

16. HCA, 1963, II, 4-6; HCA, 1965, I, 305.

17. Interviews. This figure was usually communicated by the comptroller. As one Chief remarked, "We knew we did not have the key to the back door of the Treasury."

18. HCA, 1964, II, 585.

19. Enthoven and Smith, *How Much Is Enough?* p. 334.

20. Interviews.

21. *Fact Sheet* (Washington, D.C.: U.S. Department of Defense, February, 1971) p. 19.

22. The *New York Times,* January 25, 1972, p. 17.

23. Interviews.

24. Interviews.

25. HCA, 1971, I, 159.

26. HCA, 1964, II, 585.

27. Ibid.

28. HCA, 1951, IV, 1739.

29. HCA, 1959, 353.

30. HCA, 1964, II, 585.

31. *Fact Sheet,* Department of Defense, p. 22, and Enthoven and Smith, *How Much Is Enough?* pp. 334-335.

32. As discussed above, Laird has thus far successfully resisted attempts by the DPRC to become involved earlier. The SGM has been an effective mechanism for this purpose.

33. Interview. Laird has encouraged the Chiefs to go over his head. Press Conference, August 14, 1971.

34. SCA, 1964, 211-212.

35. Interviews. HCA, 1955, 43-45.

36. HCA, 1964, II, 585.

37. Every post-World War II Marine Commandant has served exactly four years. Other service chiefs have served for as little as 22 months and

as long as six years. Moreover, Marine Corps personnel are not eligible to become Chairman.

38. Data on the chiefs were obtained from the official biographies of the services. Westmoreland was not originally appointed by Nixon, but was reappointed by him in July 1970, when his two-year term expired.

39. The years in parentheses refer to the individual's time on the JCS.

40. McConnell was the Vice Commander of the Strategic Air Command from 1961 to 1962.

41. This is markedly different from the other services. No Vice CNO has ever moved up to the top position. Three Army men have advanced to Chief of Staff after service as Vice Chief.

42. Interview.

43. Zumwalt is not the youngest man ever appointed to the JCS. That honor belongs to General Hoyt Vandenberg, who was six months younger than Zumwalt.

44. Zumwalt's advance within the flag ranks is not especially rapid. His young age is attributable to the fact that he is the youngest person ever to be promoted to Rear Admiral. Interestingly enough, General Westmoreland was six years younger than Zumwalt when he was promoted to Brigadier General. Westmoreland was 38 and Zumwalt 42 when they reached flag rank.

45. Part of the blame for poor planning must be laid at the doorstep of the Administration. Every post-World War II president has been ambiguous about his strategic concepts.

46. Interviews. The JCS were much more successful vis à vis McNamara after 1965, when they presented a united front.

47. This was known as Project 60.

48. Interview. Burke's predecessor, Robert Carney (1953-1955), had acquiesced in the decision, and Thomas and Wilson regarded the matter as settled before Burke arrived on the scene.

49. Melvin Laird, *Defense Report* to the House Armed Services Committee February 17, 1972 (Washington, D.C.: Department of Defense, 1972) pp. 17-18.

50. According to Zbigniew Brzezinski, "Half Past Nixon," *Foreign Policy* (Summer, 1971), p. 19, the Nixon administration's defense policy rates only a "C," well below most other areas.

12

MILITARISM OR THE MILITARY VIRTUES: THE CHANGING ROLE OF MILITARY FORCE IN NATIONAL POLICY

Paul R. Schratz

The American professional military may be entering one of the critical eras of its history. Amid unprecedented demands upon national resources for outer space and the inner city, for the environment and national transportation, and for social welfare initiatives aimed generally at bettering life, the military leader finds himself disillusioned and discredited. Ominous references to Soviet challenges to American supremacy cannot overcome the unprecedented public revulsion against the professional military man, his image tarnished by an Asian war which he could neither leave nor resolve. The critical self-analysis which inevitably follows defeat may bring to a focus for the first time in U.S. history far-reaching deficiencies in military strategy and the military's isolation from national policy.

Depending upon the widely divergent views of critics, the war in Indochina will for years to come serve variously as the justification for delegating greater authority to military commanders in the field, and for the contrary; for greater restrictions on rules governing air bombardment, and the contrary; for newly developed strategies responsive to the needs of political warfare, and conversely for greater reliance on traditional military techniques. Above all, perhaps, it may evoke far-reaching changes in military doctrine to support the needs of foreign policy. Post-Vietnam analyses are likely to be more objective, more pragmatic and more uninhibited than those following other American wars, for the simple reason that the real lessons which war teaches become most apparent when the war is lost. But uninhibited criticism will not necessarily eschew subjective, moralistic and self-justifying judgments. The analyst must capitalize on the opportunity presented by the experience of Vietnam, working objectively and rationally, to insure that from now on the role of military force in national policy reflects both internal and international political realities.

THE AMERICAN APPROACH TO WAR

This changing military role calls for careful reexamination of several rather unique aspects of the American approach to war. The first of these is the American concept of the role of power in foreign policy and the traditional cleavage between military power and the goals of national policy. The widely held belief that a nation, even a great nation, has a choice between "power politics" and a foreign policy which is free from the taint of power, is no longer tenable. Such a belief finds expression in the idea that the United Nations is a viable alternative to traditional foreign policy and that a nation has a choice between traditional foreign and military policies on the one hand and a UN policy on the other. Many Americans, unlike less idealistically motivated Europeans and Asians, consider war not an instrument of policy as Clausewitz saw it, not an integral and unavoidable part of political revolution, but a lamentable aberration, a detour in the historical process, a moral evil.

The oft-cited but little-read principle of Clausewitz, and of Frederick the Great before him, holds that the purpose of military power is to achieve a political goal.[1] American statesmen and strategists, by contrast, insist upon the isolation of war from politics. Further, they also follow the moral tradition in American thought and reverse strategic doctrine in the relation of war and logic. Clausewitz claimed that war is merely another kind of writing and language for statesmen—a code with its own grammar but not its own logic. U.S. military leaders exhibit a clear tendency to give the war a dialogue of its own— "clearcut victory in military terms" or "unconditional surrender"—as the precondition for peace. The overcommitment to the means of war encourages technological domination of policy, spawning interservice rivalry which leads to militarism.

The difficult relation between power and policy is in some measure common to all democracies. A democratic people involves itself morally and emotionally with national policies and actions, and demands that the government reflect its sentiments. This inevitably inhibits a democratic government from acting with the kind of dispatch and calculation of ends and means which rational adjustment of power and policy requires.[2] Although America's military policies have been revolutionized during recent decades, her basic propensities formed during the long nineteenth century innocence remain in effect. Under Soviet, and to some degree Chinese tutelage, the American people are learning that military power is an essential element in foreign relations. But they are only beginning to learn that military power must be strictly disciplined by the concrete requirements of national policy, and the converse, that national policy can be effectively pursued only to the extent it can be supported by military resources. For many reasons, it will always be difficult for modern democracies to put the Clausewitz aphorism into practice, but Americans are bound to find it especially difficult to use military power as a rational and precise instrument of national power and influence. More than any other

great nation, the American experience in world politics encourages the dissociation of power from policy. The result is
apparent, not in the great success of American foreign policy
in gaining great power status at very low cost, but in the belief,
increasingly fallacious after 1945, that since the cost was low,
military requirements need not be carefully assessed when foreign commitments are made.

Lacking a close relationship between war and policy, the
United States has demonstrated an impressive ability to defeat
the enemy in the field, yet has been unable to prevent war from
occurring. It has been unprepared to fight war; and it has failed
to gain the objects it fought for, while its settlements of war
have not brought satisfactory peace.[3] War is something to abol-
ish; war is something to get over as quickly as possible; war is
a means of punishing the enemy who dares to disturb the peace;
war is a crusade. These conceptions are inherent in the American outlook.

The late Edgar Furniss claimed that such a view of war
arises also from the American conception of the state. Americans
view the state not as the unit of power in the commonly accepted sense, but principally as a device for the preservation
of human rights—hence by implication as an essentially passive
agent in international politics. Emphasizing the rights rather
than the power of the state, a natural harmony of interests
among states parallels and springs from the natural harmony
of interests among individuals. Conflict is an aberration and the
morality between states is idealized beyond the code of morality
of individuals acting in the name of the state.[4]

THE CLEAVAGE BETWEEN POWER AND POLICY

The cleavage in American thought in the relation of politics and power, of diplomacy and war, has unfortunate consequences. The stunted participation of the military in the policy
process contributes to strategic and doctrinal deficiencies which
prevent conceptualizing the use of force in other than military

terms. War becomes a contest of logistics rather than politics. On the civilian side, important political consequences inextricably imbedded in events are traditionally isolated from policy as "purely military matters." When national security increasingly depends upon military considerations, the theory of separation not only aggravates the evils of making political and military policy in a vacuum, but it tends to create such great reliance upon military considerations that national goals are subordinated to military policy. As Robert Osgood has observed, the deference of political leaders to military advice has not been matched by a corresponding capacity of military leaders to acquire political guidance, although military men have frequently been more conscious of the need for such reciprocity than the civilians.[5] The enigma therefore is a policy devoid of military participation yet dominated by military considerations.

In Vietnam, civilian deference to military advice is one of the prime causes of the overmilitarization of an essentially political problem, of attempting to fight a political or guerrilla war with conventional tactics, of measuring success in the field in engineering rather than political terms. Largely ignored is General Fuller's advice that we fight conventional wars to destroy the enemy capacity for war but that we fight guerrilla wars to convert him. At long last, perhaps, the bitter experience in the field may destroy America's ideological preoccupation in her international political dealings, and transform, finally, her traditional moralistic approach to policy. We cannot again allow ourselves, as we did in both World War II and Korea, to terminate a war yet remain scarcely more conscious of the interdependence of military power and national policy than we were when we entered the conflict.

Yet there are strong indications that military leaders will not accept the war as a strategic failure except as a direct consequence of overcontrol by civilians in Washington. In this view, the Vietnam tragedy is the responsibility of

> years of national fear aided and abetted by so-called intellectuals within and outside government circles. No amount of rhetoric expounded by self-styled pundits can erase the simple fact that we have not won this conflict only because

we or our leaders did not try to win . . . did not try to use
the power at our disposal. . . . We are victimized. We are
called upon to take abuse from the press and the public
for decisions in which we have taken no part.[6]

At heart, the cleavage between power and policy may be
the essence of what is generally understood within the term
"civilian control of the military," and the unique concept of
civil-military relations in the United States. Throughout its
history the United States has been uniquely free of any reason
to fear a coup by its military. Its uniformed leaders have invariably displayed a proper spirit of subordination to duly
established civilian authority. At no time did the officer corps
represent a threat of the kind which restored de Gaulle to power
in France or which troubles so many countries in Latin America, Asia and the Middle East. With varying degrees of influence
of military counsel, key national security decisions are made by
civilians. But under the cloak of subordination to designated
authority, American military leaders voluntarily and traditionally isolate themselves from full and normal participation in
the policy process to which their professional training and experience entitles them. In its place, they rationalize their isolation as the legitimate deference to civilian authority. Subordination to civilian control of policy is the apparent reason, but
deficiencies in strategic doctrine and the proper relation of
strategy to policy have been the real reasons. Civilian control in
itself carries no such connotation of isolation on either side.

Civil and military power in the U.S. system are carefully
balanced one against the other and fused in the person of the
President. The President as a civilian is the Commander-in-
Chief; as an elected official, he is subject to the control of the
people. The fundamental principle is popular power over both
the President and the military, balanced or shared power between all the branches of the government, and real military
effectiveness despite the checks and balances. This is not civil
control over the military as much as it is a balance of civil and
military authority with a fulcrum held by the chief of state. It
is a subtle relationship but an important one. "Civilian control" over the military, except through the legislature, was ex-

plicitly rejected by our founders. The framers of the Constitution were more afraid of military power in the hands of politicians than they were of political power in the hands of the military. Charles Pinckney of South Carolina had proposed that "the military shall always be subordinate to the civil power." This was stricken—the Constitution did not, in fact, provide for civilian control. But the remainder of his plan, for control over the military through the purse strings, was adopted in revised form.[7] In short, the Commander-in-Chief clause, insofar as operational authority over military forces is concerned, seemed designed no more to provide than to prevent civilian control over the military.

The danger in our system today is the enormous influence wielded by the various power centers, not because it is enormous but because it is uncontrolled. Uncontrolled power in any form can be hazardous to liberty and safety, whether it be the armed might under control of the military, political power under control of the diplomats, subversive power under clandestine control of intelligence officials, the power of economic strangulation under control of supranational corporate executives, the power over unsympathetic political systems under control of the arms merchants, or whatever. The principle, both historical and modern, is the danger of uncontrolled power anywhere in the state apparatus and the necessity for all forms of power to be subject to the ultimate sovereignty of the popular will.

The government of Guatemala fell in 1954, not through intervention by U.S. military leaders, but by the covert acts of the CIA and a palace coup led by the U.S. ambassador and the Guatemalan archbishop, each with a .45 caliber automatic strapped to his side. The invasion of Lebanon by 14,000 U.S. Marines in 1958 was not the consequence of aggressive plans by U.S. military chiefs, but the application of an erroneous political estimate in the implementation of the Eisenhower doctrine to protect the country against "international communist aggression." In fact, Lebanese President Chamoun was far more concerned about domestic Arab aggression. The Bay of Pigs disaster occurred in Cuba in 1961, not because of an attempt by the military to overturn a hostile political system, but because of a series of gross failures by nonmilitary officials in intelligence, logistics, operations planning and above all, in organization. It was not U.S. military power which toppled the Erhard government in Germany in 1966, but the financial and economic leverage exerted through arms purchases urged by Secretary of Defense McNamara to ease U.S. balance of payments deficits. Nor was it the particular urging of its military leaders which involved the 20,000 U.S. armed forces in the Dominican Republic in 1965. Partly because U.S. Ambassador Martin and other American officials were obsessed with the international communist danger, President Johnson ordered the Marines ashore in Santo Domingo 67 minutes after the new Director of the CIA stated that the rebel leadership included three communists. Lastly, U.S. military power has been used, as in Vietnam, not in attempts by U.S. military leaders to overturn colonial political systems, but more likely the reverse, in attempts to keep autocratic, unpopular regimes in power that support U.S. economic interests against the will of the masses as expressed in legitimate, national revolutionary movements.

The tragedy in Vietnam, as indicated above, ensued from the gross overmilitarization of an essentially domestic political crisis and major strategic and political failures by U.S. military and civilian leaders. The degree of personal control and subsequent tragedy in Vietnam in isolation from military advice is indicated by the fact that Defense Secretary McNamara, on each of his six inspection trips to Vietnam, reached his conclusions and meticulously prepared his position, including a draft of his report to the President, prior to his departure from Washington in every case.[8] In short, the abuse or potential abuse of power has not been in the past and can hardly now be a condition in America limited to competition for civilian authority by the military services. The traditional military "crisis-manager" is in eclipse behind the rise of appointive, i.e., nonaccountable, civilian officials to positions of authority in international crisis situations.

In principle, power rests ultimately with the people. Cause for concern should legitimately arise when power is not exercised through an elected official subject to the popular will but through an appointed official, whether a Secretary of Defense, a director of the CIA, a U.S. ambassador or a military leader, as in each of the cases above. The *reductio ad absurdum* is that civilian officials have no unique gift of prescience which enshrines their policy decisions, nor do military officials have a natural tendency to error.

Moreover, fewer and fewer policy recommendations of any consequence in the Pentagon or the State Department are developed by solely military or civilian officials. The State Department has extensive participation by military officers in responsible offices. The military departments and the JCS rely more and more upon civilian participation at all levels in developing their analyses. And the staff of the Secretary of Defense, including the Office of Systems Analysis, conversely, is composed almost half of military officers. Moreover, one does not always look upon congressional control of the military, whether on budgetary or policy matters, as "civilian control." Yet this was the control visualized by the founders, a sharing of power, a fragmentation of power over the military by the legislature and the executive.

Control by the Secretary of Defense, on the other hand, is best viewed as managerial control. It is the normal exercise of vested authority by the deputy Commander-in-Chief. It is not the equivalent of operational control, nor is it "civilian control" devolving to the Secretary as a civilian. But despite participation of civilian and military officials in many phases of the policy process, the basic and fundamental isolation of power and policy in the American value system is deeply embedded, especially among older and more senior participants. Integrated staffs have not produced integrated planning. It is at the operational level that a new approach to truly unified politicomilitary planning is clearly needed, not only as the natural development of the U.S. national security organization, but as the extremely important direction of change for the military in its own interest.

THE NEED FOR UNIFIED PLANNING

The crying need is for truly unified politicomilitary planning. Yet planning can neither be effective nor have proper leverage on the changing role of military force in national policy with current deficiencies in strategy and doctrine. Whether developing a doctrine for modern maritime power on the sea, a role for nuclear weapons in policy at one extreme of violence, or a satisfactory doctrine for partisan or guerrilla warfare at the other, the professional military has been neither effective nor persuasive. Strategic deficiencies will be a natural focus for the examination of post-Vietnam military policy, partly because of the increasing priority of domestic needs, partly because of negotiated reductions or agreed limitations upon so-called "strategic" nuclear weaponry, and partly through a re-examination of the rules of war governing unrestricted air and ground attacks upon civilian populations flowing from the bombing of Haiphong and Hanoi, the Calley case and the Mylai massacre.

A maritime strategy, which geography indicates should have been followed in Vietnam, was discarded by Admiral Sharp and unknown to General Westmoreland. Naval leaders the world over, inspired by Alfred Thayer Mahan, proclaim a doctrine of freedom of the seas yet fail to realize that the Mahan ideal of free seas under American-British hegemony meant control of the seas; American-Soviet domination portends something entirely different. Strategic problems with nuclear weaponry are no less muddled. Widely advertised concepts of nuclear war guaranteeing the capability to inflict "unacceptable damage" on an enemy while limiting damage to oneself, have little relevance and no historical tradition. The theory offers a further, curious contradiction. Limiting damage received virtually requires a first strike as a logical premise, which is not only contrary to public policy, but under the circumstances, is neither rational nor moral. The theory assumes indiscriminately that a crisis response must be "instant," which is an operational problem, and does not distinguish this from the executive response, which must be deliberate. For an instant response, one must assume a clear and unambiguous enemy challenge to which to respond, and hence an interaction in military rather than in political terms. It assumes a U.S.-Soviet interaction in isolation, rather than as an Armageddon within and shared by the community of nations. The dialogue envisions use of weaponry classes as "strategic" or "tactical" based arbitrarily on kilotonnage rather than on traditional strategic or tactical functions in warfare. It assumes that the balance between East and West is delicate rather than sturdy; and that nuclear war is survivable and is therefore "thinkable" as a persuasive political dialogue. The student of strategy must find all of the above questionable, casual or absurd, and the surrounding air of authority to be spurious.

The root error in all theorizing of this type lies in the attempt somehow to separate the analytical and logical components from the political and moral elements, which cannot be done. Policy proposals rest on assertions about politics, and such assertions consist primarily of complex and indissoluble political judgments. A judgment is an expression of belief based on one's entire training and experience and is inevitably both moral and analytical, technical and political, subjective and objective. "All we can do at present is to recognize that there are various kinds of inseparable evaluative elements in all political judgments, and not attempt to hide this frustrating fact under the camouflage of theoretical social science." [9] The development of modern strategy is not for consideration here, of course. Our concern is with the context rather than the content.

Why have military professionals not developed a plausible theory of nuclear strategy? The civilian scholar, drawn like a moth to the atomic flame, developed the current dogmas of deterrence in a political vacuum. But the civilian academician has moved on to new interests, to new faddism in ecology and the environment, leaving his uniformed colleague with an old testament hardly appropriate to the new test. Perhaps it would be only a little bit facetious to suggest that the military profes-

sional accept the current nuclear deterrence theory with the
same skepticism used toward counterforce theorists in colonial
days. Those God-fearing and honest forefathers of modern strategic thought undoubtedly argued that when Indian attacks
threatened, the men should be brought into the stockade and
the women and children left in the fields. The colonials had no
intention of harming Indian women and children, and the red-
skin warriors, in the mirror image of the frontiersman's beliefs,
could therefore be expected to guarantee the safety of the colonial women and children. Each was a hostage insuring the
safety of the other. The iconoclast may have found fault even
then with such a version of the doctrine of deterrence; his successor can hardly be less free of doubt today.

At the other extreme in warfare, the military professional
has long forgotten historical doctrines of revolutionary or partisan warfare developed in the Indian wars, the Philippine insurrection and in his own anticolonial war of independence.
Again, the cleavage in political and military elements of planning finds him prepared to fight only a conventional war against
his guerrilla opponent. The Viet Cong–North Vietnamese revolutionary doctrine represented a highly successful blend of military force to a political goal. The combination of nationalist-
communist seeds planted in the fertile soils of feudalism, colonialism and oligarchic tyranny surrounding the Saigon government found rampant growth in the countryside and
extensive support among the oppressed throughout the world.
Despite great suffering by the Vietnamese people on both sides,
despite thousands of American lives and countless billions of
dollars in support of the Saigon regime, the revolutionary movement maintained control of the momentum of the war into
phase three of the revolution, which began in 1965 and lasted
until the Tet offensive of 1968. Until that time the close ob-
servance of the basic principles of strategy by Hanoi was nearly
flawless. Subsequent to Tet, the revolution was set back to the
first phase, but the political success of the Tet offensive, despite
its tactical failure, and the disastrous erosion of American
morale which soon followed, may prove to have been the de-

cisive event prodding the U.S. toward a withdrawal from Vietnam.

American strategic planning in Vietnam, a clear example of the blind spot in the American ability to integrate military means toward a political objective, violated the keystone of strategy, the principle of the objective. The consequent loss of control could hardly have been better expressed than in the words of Sir Robert Thompson:

> The American failure in Vietnam . . . [resulted from] an obscurity of aim, a failure of strategy and a lack of control. It was never clearly understood by the American Administration, and certainly not by the army, that the whole American effort, civilian and military, had to be directed towards the establishment of a viable and stable South Vietnamese Government and State, i.e., the creation of an acceptable alternative political solution to reunification with North Vietnam under a communist government.[10]

The failure in the relationship of ends and means, in the connection between the objective of our foreign policy and the weapons technology for its implementation, is essentially the same issue which has marked the difficulty in nuclear planning and which appears, for example, in the strategic justification for the antiballistic missile system. The military planner traditionally errs on the high side of security—he cannot be faulted for this because he bears the responsibility for failure through underestimating his enemy. But security is involved on both sides of the argument. One has to do with the security of means, the other with the objective, the security of ends. Many students of national security feel that for three decades we have erred on the side of the security of means. By overconcentrating on the security of means, we have permitted the economic, political and moral consequences to our society to undermine our security in its broader dimension.

Senator Fulbright maintains that every nation today has a double identity: it is both a power engaged in foreign relations and a society serving the interests of its citizens. As a power the nation draws upon but does not replenish its people's economic, political and moral resources. The replenishment of wealth in the broader sense is a function of the domestic life, of the nation as a society. The United States is preoccupied with its role as the world's greatest power, to the neglect of its duties to society and at increasing net cost to the national security.[11] The dual identity of a nation emerges in the military professional in the overconcentration on national *power* which breeds militarism as opposed to the proper concentration on national *goals* which fosters the traditional military virtues. This difference is similar to the contrast described by Alfred Vagts between militarism and the military way. The latter emphasizes the efficient and limited use of societal resources to serve political purposes while the former transcends the limited purposes of military professionalism and, in effect, substitutes military means for social ends.[12] The military way is self-sacrificing; militarism is self-aggrandizing. Military professionalism serves society; militarism serves power.

In planning for modern war, the military services are not yet equipped to do the job which is necessary, because the kind of planning needed is to rise above militarism, to rise above the roles-and-missions-competition among the services and the engineering approach to strategy. The services have rarely been able to do this. The military organization, as a consequence, has institutionalized doctrinal development and strategic planning in the service staffs rather than in the JCS in direct contradiction to the law and the clear intent of Congress that the JCS be responsible. Strategy formation by law is a unified action, on the assumption that separate land, sea and air warfare are gone forever. Yet strategy and doctrinal development, in practice, are delegated by the JCS to the separate land, sea and air services. Strategic planning, therefore, remains the prisoner of parochially oriented, antiquated concepts of land, sea and air warfare. Critically needed planning as visualized in the statutes lacks a broad concept within which it can develop. The loyalty of the U.S. military man is to his service institution, where the technical means become superior to the national goals. His aim should be loyalty to the American people, and the means for carrying out the concept of service to his country should be his military branch of service, not the reverse.

Unified planning is defeated in practice by the void in unified doctrine, and the JCS functions, consequently, as a legislative body wherein service lobbies contest for power, rather than as a planning forum wherein truly national strategic doctrines can be developed. As long as the primary requirement of planners at both the service and the JCS levels is attainment and preservation of a military position which does not injure the interests of any service, the development of unified doctrine can only languish. Protection of short-term interests of the service through accommodation prevents the exposition of logical, fully analyzed and possibly divergent views on important national issues. The services train an officer to be a spokesman for a service rather than to be persuasive as a strategist, i.e., to be fluent in the language of his profession. The development of a viable body of joint professional doctrine, as a consequence, is the single important action which can increase the efficiency and effectiveness of the JCS organization.

In the backwash of the Vietnam War, the reexamination of the national security structure now underway should stress the serious planning deficiencies on both the political and military side. On the military side the question is whether or not the developing role of the military can submerge individual service values and subcultures in the joint planning body so as to allow the reduction or elimination of the highly selective and powerful strategic planning staffs which thrive in each of the services without specific statutory authority. Budgetary strictures may impel the military planner, through fear of strangulation, to rise above parochialism and to carry out the intent of the law. This will be the real test of the growing maturity of our military leaders which is vital to their changing role in national policy planning; this, in broad choice, is the military way as opposed to militarism.

On the civilian side, the vast and increasing area where policy and strategy overlap emphasizes once more the extreme need for fusionist planning in national security policy-making.

The aim here is to eliminate forever the long-standing and deeply embedded cleavage in government between political, military and related economic and social planning for national security. Military policy and military techniques cannot stand on their own; they have no inherent validity if the national objective is a free, peaceful and stable world. It is not a paradox that military policies can be directed toward nonmilitary ends; a coherent strategy requires a blend of military techniques with nonmilitary aspects of statecraft in a consistent plan. The present organization in the national security structure and in the State and Defense Departments political-military planning bodies, simply does not allow this kind of merger.

The formal organization has centralized steadily since the National Security Act of 1947. "General direction, authority and control" by the Secretary in 1947 became "direction, authority and control" in 1949, centralization of control in 1953 and direct operational control of combat forces in unified and specified commands in 1958. But centralization of planning did not follow centralization of authority. There was no transition to a higher level of sophistication in planning nor a doctrinal development suggesting vital and extremely necessary changes in value structures among the Army, Navy and Air Force.

The importance to the military arm in particular in regaining its professional stature is beyond question. The serious decline in the prestige of the military in the public mind is widespread. Five recent nationwide surveys conducted by the American Institute of Public Opinion show that since 1968 a fundamental change has taken place in the American attitude toward national defense policy.[13] Even in the face of the wholly believable and ominous increases in the Soviet maritime capabilities, the American public is rebelling against the military budget, against what it regards as a legacy of ill-considered and often domestically motivated acts by the defense establishment: Vietnam, unneeded ABMs, pork-barrel defense contracting and gross cost overruns. In the opinion surveys, antimilitary feeling is concentrated in that part of the populace most likely to vote, most likely to express its opinions, to make campaign contributions and to participate in some form of political activity.

Where in the past, approval of new weapons systems could be had for the asking, the new mood in Congress is not only discriminating, but public opposition to defense spending could become nearly as undiscriminating as was past approval. When programs are truly necessary for the security of the United States, it may be difficult to persuade the people—or their legislative representatives—to pay for them.[14]

There is little question that a new image for the direction of change will critically depend upon more effective and persuasive planning within the government at the national level, wherein the various autonomies, through economic and political necessity, may at long last join together. The JCS cannot isolate themselves, for there are no purely military decisions at JCS level. That was the reason the Joint Chiefs were legally constituted as an advisory body rather than a decision-making body. The aim of the unification statutes is not to isolate but to integrate the military dimension into policy problems involving the national security. The best in integrated planning and one of the most productive civil-military relations in our history was that of General George C. Marshall and President Roosevelt. Marshall avoided informal confrontations with the President and even took care not to laugh at F.D.R.'s jokes, since he thought such informality would compromise his ability to express professional disagreement.[15]

The planning involved in the Cuban missile crisis was a judicious blend of visible usable military power in the closest harmony with political goals and backed by the entire retaliatory power of the United States. The plan was a properly integrated, ascending program of political, economic and psychological moves carried out while the military completed final preparations in absolute secrecy.

In each case it was not the autonomy of the military adviser that was being preserved as much as his professionalism, expressed in the broadest possible consideration of the problems shared with the Commander-in-Chief. National planning must be responsive to the style of national leaders. The changing trend must be toward control with sufficient decentralization so that statutory authority of subordinate agencies is not usurped by concentration of power to the point that the system collapses in crisis. One must avoid both the Charybdis of overdelegation and the Scylla of overinvolvement. Above all it must avoid the peril of militarism cited by Joseph Schumpeter of the defense establishment of ancient Egypt: "created by the wars that required it, the machine then created the wars it required."

NOTES

1. The basic principle of Clausewitz and most complete expression of the theoretical relation between war and policy occurs and reoccurs throughout his *On War:*

> We know, of course, that war is only caused through the political intercourse of governments and nations; but in general it is supposed that such intercourse is broken off by war, and that a totally different state of things ensues, subject to no laws but its own.
>
> We maintain, on the contrary, that war is nothing but a continuation of political intercourse with an admixture of other means. . . . This political intercourse does not cease through the war itself . . . but that, in its essence, it continues to exist, whatever may be the means which it uses, and that the main lines along which the events of the war proceed and to which they are bound are only the general features of policy which run on all through the war until peace takes place. . . .
>
> Accordingly, war can never be separated from political intercourse, and if . . . this occurs anywhere, all the threads of the different relations are . . . broken, and we have before us a senseless thing without an object. See Karl von Clausewitz, *On War,* trans. Matthijs Jolles (Washington, D.C.: Combat Forces Press, 1953) p. 596.

2. See Robert E. Osgood, *Limited War: The Challenge to American Strategy* (Chicago: University of Chicago Press, 1957) p. 28.

3. Ibid.

4. Edgar S. Furniss, Jr., *American Military Policy: Strategic Aspects of World Political Geography* (New York: Rinehart, 1957).

5. Osgood, *Limited War,* p. 28.

6. Army officer quoted by Ward Just, *Military Men* (New York: Knopf, 1970).

7. The U.S. Constitution was modelled after the British constitutional arrangements to control the military, but the British Constitution, being unwritten, proved much more flexible. The UK Constitution today provides for extremely effective civilian political control and military planning within the Cabinet; the U.S. Constitution is frozen in an eighteenth century model.

8. Townsend Hoopes, "The Fight for the President's Mind," *Atlantic Monthly* (October 1969) p. 3. Also, *The Limits of Intervention* (New York: McKay, 1969) p. 163.

9. Philip Green, *Deadly Logic: The Theory of Nuclear Deterrence* (Columbus: Ohio State University Press, 1966) p. 259.

10. Sir Robert Thompson, *Revolutionary War in World Strategy 1945-1969* (London: Secker and Warburg, 1970) pp. 130-131.

11. J. William Fulbright, lecture to National War College, May 26, 1969.

12. Albert Vagts, *A History of Militarism*, rev. ed., (New York: Meridian Books, 1959) p. 13.

13. See Bruce M. Russett, "Deflating the Military," *New Leader* (June 28, 1971) p. 5.

14. Ibid.

15. Forrest C. Pogue, *George C. Marshall: Ordeal and Hope 1939-1942* (New York: Viking, 1966) p. 23.

13

BREAD, GUNS AND UNCLE SAM: INTERNATIONAL REALITIES AND THEIR IMPLICATIONS FOR U.S. RELATIONS WITH THE WORLD

Davis B. Bobrow

Nations are secure when they are free to determine their own fate unhampered by external powers. A nation's citizens are secure only when they are not afraid of losing life or property in war. Thus, national defense policies should be evaluated not in terms of absolute or relative military might or complex professional calculations of when one nation comes out ahead in a war, but according to whether each increment of defense effort produces more national autonomy and less fear than if the effort were not made. Increments of defense effort which do not have the beneficial consequences just stated are actually harmful because they divert resources which could be used to provide other social benefits.[1]

One can accept this view of national security and still not be sure of what policies are compatible with it. We can envision an international and domestic context which makes almost any policy suitable, indeed desirable, in the terms of our concept of national security. My view of the likely international and domestic context leads me to emphasize the relative importance of nonmilitary factors and instruments for national security. In such a perspective, the details of strategic debate and military planning have only tenuous implications for whether or not war will occur and for who will win at what level of carnage.[2] In the long run, the so-called soft factors of human welfare determine the levels of hostility and conflict in the world. I contend that governments can attend to long-run welfare problems without sacrificing elements of national security. Indeed to act otherwise is not pragmatic but merely dogmatic.

In this chapter I want to suggest one formulation of a national security behavior appropriate for the United States. Hopefully this will stimulate empirical and disciplined investigation of a fundamentally different national security policy and machinery for this country. My feeling is that most of the "defense debate" considers only a framework of military options which can account for relatively little variation in national security as I have defined it.[3] The goal should not simply be avoiding Vietnams and reducing the defense share of the federal budget or the GNP. There is no reason to accept post-Korea U.S. national security policy as something to recapture. Indeed, to do so is to take an unduly rosy view of the pressures operating in the world and the threats they generate. Simply because a particular security posture avoids the last war does not necessarily make it good. The experts' consensus on the values of an arrangement among the major powers—a "Congress of Vienna revisited"—seems to be an equally incomplete prescription. Even if the "big guys" of international affairs could establish sufficient commonality of interests, there is little obvious reason to expect everyone else to go along. After all the stable European system created after the Napoleonic Wars ended in convulsions. And the kinds of economic competition and regional lesser power conflict which preceded those convulsions are already present.

National security policies are of necessity highly anticipatory. Weapons research and development programs, procurements and deployment take a long time to complete (often ten or more years). Manpower elements of force structure also require a number of years to be readied for appropriately skilled and organized military capability. Programs to alter sharply the conditions of human life or modify social demand are not designed and do not take effect quickly. Relations between states also leave established patterns rather slowly. Accordingly, the relevant context is at least as much that of the future as it is that of the present. This requirement obviously raises the degree of uncertainty to a very substantial level. Yet there is no reason to believe that the uncertainty of broad-gauge environmental forecasts is any greater than that of forecasts of force structure equally far into the future.

ASSERTED RULES OF BEHAVIOR

The following assumptions concern the rules which govern the behavior of those agents involved in national security and the consequences of that behavior. Disagreement with these assertions warrants disagreement with much that follows.

1. Regimes are more concerned with continuing in office than with policy consistency. Accordingly, regimes are primarily responsive to those population groups which are most responsible for their stability and viability as rulers. Regimes pay great attention to the levels of satisfaction and dissatisfaction of such determining groups. As the identity and utilities of such population groups change, regimes often change their policies.

2. Population groups which determine whether a regime will be replaced are more concerned with preserving their leverage than with maintaining the regime or the consistency of its

policy. Faced with threats to their power position, key groups in a society will dump a regime or a policy if they perceive other alternatives which will maintain much of their status.

3. Regimes seek to satisfy demands across the board rather than within one issue area.[4] It follows that national defense policy outcomes are traded off against the outcomes from other areas of external policy, e.g., foreign economic policy and domestic policy.

4. Except when populations define the threat as one to national survival, military resources and programs are seen as a source of quasi-public or private rather than of public benefits and costs. Because the parties to an actual or potential conflict differ in their willingness to define the stakes as national survival, their willingness to support military costs differs. To the extent that the parts of a military budget have a differential relationship to national survival, support for them varies. Distant intervenors in local conflicts are unlikely to be able to mobilize the support at home that the parties directly involved can.

5. The nation which pursues a national security policy does not determine its consequences. International policies turn out to be efficient and wise only if the behavior of other actors can be accurately predicted. If the behavior of relevant others cannot be estimated, that is, behavior rather than capability, the policy is of unknown value. If the reasons for the behavior of others and the dynamics which change it are not well understood, the marginal value of the policy is unknown because we cannot say what behavioral difference it makes. And there is no sufficient reason to assume that the dynamics relevant to our conception of national security primarily involve technical military considerations.

6. Actors define the implications of the actions of others in terms of how they affect them, regardless of how the actions are labeled. No one actor can then define the terms of interaction unilaterally. For example, the U.S. government may find it useful to exclude nuclear weapons in Europe which can impact on the Soviet Union from our general war, assured destruction forces. From a Soviet point of view, the U.S. assured destruction

forces are comprised of weapons which can kill Russians at home however we choose to categorize them. Obviously, the Russians arrive at decisions in terms of their definition of the threat, not ours. To paraphrase Amrom Katz, an airplane can be strategic even if it does not belong to the Strategic Air Command.

7. External penetration is not measured solely on a military dimension, but includes all forms of foreign presence which limit a nation's autonomy. From a national point of view, the national security threat posed by external actors is an aggregate of military, economic, political and cultural penetration. Threat is attributed accordingly.

8. A nation's political leadership does not make decisions to go to war on the basis of finely hewed military calculations. McGeorge Bundy has written eloquently on this point:

> it is one thing for military men to maintain our deterrent force with vigilant skill, and it is quite another for anyone to assume that their necessary contingency plans have any serious interest for political leaders. The object of political men . . . is that these weapons should never be used. . . . Political leaders, whether here or in Russia, are cut from a very different mold than strategic planners. They see cities and people as part of what they are trying to help —not as targets. They live with the daily struggle to make a little progress—to build things—to grow things—to lift the quality of life a little—and to win honor, and even popularity, by such achievements. The deterrent that might not please a planner is more than deterrent enough for them. And that is why the deterrent does work, even at a distance, as in Berlin. *Maybe* the American nuclear commitment is not as firm as it seems—but what sane Soviet leader wants to put the whole Soviet society in the scales to find out? [5]

And as for the insane political leader, why would he be affected by technical assessments? Hitler, the favorite such example among U.S. strategic thinkers, certainly was not. In sum, complex professional calculations of deterrent forces and assured destruction percentages are largely irrelevant to basic choices of war and peace. Thus, force structure changes which have weight only in such calculations have no marginal utility for deterrence.

9. Threats to a nation often provide opportunities for its constituent bureaucracies. That is, up to the point of having to demonstrate its ability to handle the threat, the relevant bureaucracy benefits from perceptions of a threat which suggest that it is genuinely needed. As the possible threat lessens, so too does the bureaucracy's case for resources and priority. If the bureaucracy which benefits from threat also assesses the threat for the nation as a whole, distortion will be particularly tempting.[6]

To the extent that we accept the previous assertions, several lines of questioning and analysis are suggested. We will want to find out if regimes are going to find it increasingly difficult to satisfy those who determine their tenure; and if the identity and preferences of the determining population groups change in the future. If they do, in what ways? Will key population groups see more alternative foreign and defense policy positions as available to them? If military issues are but one part of the set confronting regimes, we will want to determine what the other might be and what constraints on military policy will be imposed by attempting to cope satisfactorily with the other problems. We will ask what sets of situations will be linked with national survival by different actors, and how disparate these sets will be? What force structure elements will seem relevant to national survival for various nations, and how will these elements differ? What dynamics will determine the future behavior of key nations? In order to build into our thinking the threat evaluations of others, we must find out how to change our modes of national security analysis. How should we alter our policy machinery in ways consonant with an understanding of the full spectrum of threats which nations attribute to one another? What does lessening the aggregate level of threat involve? How do we formulate alternative national security policies so that they get the attention of political leaders? Finally, we would have to ask what a sufficiently different U.S. policy would look like; and what interests should be involved in national security policy for accurate threat estimates and attention to nonmilitary options?

ASSERTED CHARACTERISTICS OF THE FUTURE ENVIRONMENT

As is frequently the case, the questions create expectations which answers will leave unsatisfied. It is possible, however, to suggest elements of answers as hypotheses for testing. This section is addressed to characteristics of the future national security policy environment. The emphasis is on its political, economic and social characteristics rather than on force structure. No claim is made that the world characteristics stated below will be reached through a linear evolution from the current state of international affairs or will be distributed uniformly. Rather, the claim is made that 10 years from now the world will be more like that sketched below than it is now. Finally, the discussion below assumes that the factors operating in what are called postindustrial societies will operate in the United States.

1. Most regimes will be subject to intense demands to deliver domestic goods and services rather than ideology and international status. This will be as true of postindustrial as of developing countries. In the former, substantial population groups will experience at best a slowdown in improvement and at worst a decline in their quality of life. Other population groups will be making vocal demands for redistribution, not only from the rich to the relatively poor but also from the middle-income sectors to the poor.[7] In the developing countries, demands on regimes will be fueled by a variety of secular trends and resulting information and organizational needs. Such trends include urbanization, education, and the development of media and a transportation infrastructure. In general, the domestic demands made on political systems will increase faster than their resources to cope with the demands. This does not necessarily imply a vast multiplication of internal violence. It does imply that regimes will find themselves working harder and harder to maintain themselves with increasingly little success. Turnover

rates will be high. Given the pressures at work, there will be little consistency in policy; and foreign policy will increasingly become an instrument to cope with domestic pressures or a matter of residual resources.

2. One effect of these developments will be to enlarge the number of population groups that can influence the replacement of a regime. Previously established power groups will feel increasingly pressed either to eliminate or form alliances with newly important groups. Such efforts at eliminating new groups will not produce lasting tranquility; rather, they will have the opposite effect. In part, this is because they do not deal with the basic causes of demands but divert resources from satisfying demands. In part, this is because coercive solutions impose burdens on the elite, since they increase its separation from the rest of society, which the elite usually will not wish to bear for long. In part, this is because the cohesiveness of the established power groups will be eaten away by intergenerational conflict. And finally, it is in part because the secular trends mentioned earlier which transform societies into increasingly interdependent systems will dramatically increase their vulnerability to small groups of dissidents. As the rates of change in the composition and power of those who affect regime replacement increase, policy consistency and regime tenure will decrease.

3. Most nations will be increasingly unwilling to commit themselves to any particular grouping or alliance of other nations. Why will this be the case? Regimes and power groups will find it increasingly important to maintain autonomy in order to cope with domestic demands. For the major powers, substantial commitments to lesser nations will entail high opportunity costs domestically. All major nations will recognize that each faces similar cost factors. The lesser powers will, in turn, recognize that the major powers are not likely to make the sustained and massive commitments necessary to meet their domestic and regional needs; they must also perceive that such commitments curtail their own autonomy.

4. The gap between the influence, on the one hand, of the United States and the Soviet Union and, on the other, of West-

ern Europe, Japan and China will further narrow. This does not require an absolute growth in the military power of the latter. Their ability to complicate the decisions of the current superpowers and to affect their domestic performance will suffice. The general effect will be to further constrain the latitude of the superpowers and to enhance that of other nations. The "not-so-little three" will increasingly be able to affect the policy and results achieved by the "big two."

5. Except in instances of regional conflict, interdependence and the transfer of political models and social styles will occur increasingly between countries at the same levels of development. Three consequences will be associated with this phenomenon. The military competition between the major powers will be constrained by other forms of interdependence, just as military cooperation will depend on cooperation in other issue areas. The leadership role of the industrialized major powers will decline concurrently as will their effective leverage on other nations. Exchanges between the less-developed countries will be conducive to increasingly active coalitions on various allocation and control questions. With the possible exception of China, these coalitions will exclude the major international actors.

Several joint effects of these long-run trends merit special attention. First, military policy will increasingly be determined by the performance of regimes in dealing with domestic demand. And that performance will depend in turn on nonmilitary international policies. Accordingly, national security policy must give substantial weight to such issues as trade equity, pollution, the sharing of energy resources and exploitation of the oceans. These issues are directly connected with the processes which determine domestic well-being.

Second, the ability of the major powers to impose solutions which sharply change regional political systems either by force or the threat to use force will further decline. It is important not to confuse the capability of a major actor to forestall decisive intervention by another major actor with the capability to reverse relationships between local actors. Superpower regional monopolies will be attenuated. At the same time that the major

powers must pay increased domestic costs for their regional
power, the amount of military power any one of them will have
to expend to dominate situations will increase.

Third, under the pressure of domestic demand, regimes
will increasingly be pressured to focus their military allocations
on items directly relevant to threats to national survival. The
force structure implications will vary with the nature of the
threat. The force structure of the geographically isolated major
nations will probably stress deterrence of general war. Conflicting parties with common borders will require forces which
match those of the threatening neighbor—conventional always
and nuclear if necessary and feasible. That contingent statement
implies that the force depends on the need to deter on two
fronts rather than on one and the extent to which a militarily
neutralized territorial buffer can be created. One implication
of these assertions is that all major nations will seek to acquire
some capacity to deter general war so long as others have it. As
that happens, the superpower margin of global control will
decline further.

Earlier we set aside instances of regional lesser nation conflict as a special case. The increase of domestic demand and the
weakened belief that any single major nation can dominate
the situation will increase pressures for resolution through
regional war, negotiation with multiple major nation guarantees, or international peace-keeping barrier forces which release
resources to meet domestic demand. Prolonged low-level violence will become increasingly intolerable. Sharp setbacks in
a nation's ability to meet domestic demands because of the
actions of regional competitors are particularly likely to trigger
regional conflict.[8] But negotiation and international peace keeping are viable only to the extent that they seem credible to relevant regional actors. Given the forecast we have made about
domestic pressures on major actors, their credibility will decline unless such regional commitments are compensated for by
at least equivalent reductions in military resource allocations.

GENERAL POLICY IMPLICATIONS

What do the preceding assertions imply for U.S. national security policy and policy machinery? At the very least, they imply that many commonly accepted assumptions that have served as the basis for policy no longer are tenable. The frailty of such assumptions can be indicated briefly. Then, I shall identify alternative premises that *should* serve as the basis for policy. The no-longer-tenable premises are as follows:

1. *Formal alliances reliably will produce collective action.* Such alliances will probably become increasingly attenuated. In order to continue at all, their process of decision-making will become more and more federal. The ties of their members with nonalliance major actors and lesser actors will increase. The result will be a decrease in the certainty of the outcomes of their decisions and an increase in the time required to reach decisions. If the alliances are primarily military, their solidarity increasingly will depend on nonmilitary interactions which are not coordinated by the alliance structure.

2. *Military commitments to others will increase our national security.* Instead, they clearly will involve a loss of decision autonomy. And the costs of honoring the commitments will rise sharply. As we do not honor them meaningfully, i.e., in ways which preserve the social system to which we are committed, the credibility of guarantees against regional conflict suffers.

3. *Commitments to regimes with dubious prospects for domestic performance provide a solid basis for long-range planning.* Such regimes give the United States little reason to expect that they will survive long, that they can maintain command and control in a war situation, or that they will really allocate their coercive capability to our purposes.

4. *The United States will maintain the predominant foreign presence (military or nonmilitary) in many foreign countries.* The desire for decision autonomy and the competitive

nature of the more complex international system will operate jointly to reduce the relative American presence. In the short run, the decline in the U.S. presence may seem to imply replacement in the predominant role by another country. This appears to underestimate the desires for autonomy of foreign nations and the constraints on other major nations.

5. *"Friendly" nations will probably over time increase their defense allocations and the efficiency of their use substantially.* By substantial, I mean sufficiently to alter a political leader's judgments about the usefulness of war or its actual outcome. This position seems contrary to recent experience, e.g., the increase in the contribution of the European members to NATO and the Cambodian buildup. Yet it still seems valid as a general proposition. In most countries demands for a larger share of resources for domestic purposes have a broader constituency than do those for military allocations. Those sectors which usually push hardest for increased military allocations are at best inhibited and at worst actively hostile to steps to alter radically the use of military resources. Nor is there any evidence that the NATO or the Cambodian buildups have altered political leaders' views of the probability or consequences of war.

6. *Other nations are deterred from war primarily by the United States.* If one accepts the previous assertions, the U.S. deterrent posture is only one consideration. Other important concerns are that nations are pursuing domestic goals, that they have other international considerations and that they do not believe the United States will pursue policies which require them to strike first.

7. *Deterrence of general war is so delicately tuned that it is necessary to continually adjust one's forces as those of others change and to maintain a high degree of certainty about assured destruction.* The political leader's calculus referred to earlier suggests that domestic demand and the problems and opportunities posed by a world of five major actors create skepticism about extrapolating short-run force improvements as if they were linear.

8. *National security policy is fundamentally a matter of*

managing military instruments. If domestic demand plays the future role that we assign to it, it follows that national security planning and implementation will not be effective unless they involve groups expert in domestic performances and international economic and natural resource policy.

9. *Private-sector foreign policy need not be coordinated with public-sector foreign policy.* By private-sector foreign policy, I refer particularly to the activities of the multinational corporation. Foreign actors concerned with autonomy do not treat the threat to their decision autonomy posed by American-based corporations as separate from their relationships with the U.S. government. Private-sector foreign policy can easily, though not necessarily, impede indigenous attempts to meet domestic demand and can unwittingly or purposefully increase domestic demands. Private-sector foreign policy which diverts resources from U.S. domestic well-being simply increases pressures at home to allocate resources to other than defense purposes.

In contrast to the above premises, U.S. national security policy should be based on the following:

1. The involvement of more than two major powers in each of the regions of the world is for the most part probable and desirable.
2. International coalitions among the major powers will change rapidly and from issue to issue.
3. Commitments to particular regimes and elites are valuable only so long as they meet domestic demands in their own societies.
4. U.S. force reductions will not be compensated for by the building of allied forces.
5. Decline in U.S. military striking power from current levels will not increase the probability of war.
6. A credible minimum deterrent can be planned with relative certainty.
7. U.S. regional projections of force will be effective only as instruments to checkmate other major powers or impose barriers between lesser international powers.
8. National security policy will have a desirable impact on international affairs as it affects levels of domestic

demand abroad and makes effective and compatible use
of nonmilitary relationships with foreign nations.

9. Pressures within the United States to restrict defense
   expenditures will continue.

SOME INITIATIVES

It seems useful to conclude by suggesting some initiatives
for national security policy and national security policy machinery. But first we should place in perspective what the Nixon
administration has done and the set of issues centering on force
structure and defense budgets.

Since 1968, U.S. policy has moved substantially in the same
direction as our previous argument.[9] The frozen relationship
with China has been broken. A SALT agreement can be expected in the near future to limit some nuclear arms acquisi-
tions. The Nixon Doctrine implies gradual decreases in U.S.
regional conventional force projections. The chairman of the
JCS has observed, and not with dismay, that American military
superiority will not be reestablished along previous lines.[10] The
Secretary of Defense has justified the FY 1973 budget request
in part on the grounds that it calls for almost record low Cold
War shares of the GNP and the federal budget.[11] Relevant numbers are given in Exhibit 1. Nevertheless, these steps are not
sufficient to meet the future situations we have sketched. The
Nixon Doctrine assumes a buildup in the military posture of
"friendly" nations, as does Secretary Laird's Total Force concept.[12] Neither calls for reexamining and reducing commitments.[13] The publicly reported pattern of arms control negotiations with the Soviet Union does not suggest that they will
lead to substantial reductions in current nuclear inventories
in the foreseeable future. The general war deterrent is still
treated as fragile and requiring substantial improvements in
three types of delivery forces—sea-based missiles, land-based
missiles and manned bombers. And the requested conventional forces, including the reserves, imply substantial capabil-

Exhibit 1. RELATIONSHIP OF DOD BUDGET
TO FEDERAL BUDGET AND GNP[9]

Fiscal Year		GNP	Federal Budget Outlays National Budget	Dept. of Defense	DOD as % of GNP	National Budget
1950	Lowest Year Since World War II	$ 263.3*	43.1	11.9	4.5	27.7
1953	Korea Peak	358.9	76.8	47.7	13.3	62.1
1964	Last Prewar Year	612.2	117.6	50.8	8.3	41.8
1968	Vietnam Peak	827.0	178.9	78.0	9.4	42.5
1971	Last Actual Year	1,008.0	211.4	75.5	7.5	34.5
1972	Current Estimate	1,090.0	236.5	75.8	7.0	31.0
1973	Budget Estimate	1,202.0	246.3	76.5	6.4	30.0

*Amounts are expressed in billions of dollars.

ity for waging conventional, limited wars overseas. More fundamentally, there is little emphasis on the nonmilitary aspects of national security policy and no reversal of the decline since 1965 in the nonmilitary portion of the foreign affairs budget.

Obviously, the assertions we have made imply a sharp decline in the force structure and the defense budget. However, the issues posed cannot be met solely by steps. Accordingly, rather than devote much attention to the force and budget alternatives it seems useful to summarize briefly one recent proposal limited to those issues but compatible with our perspective. Senator George McGovern, who proposed in his 1972 presidential campaign a FY 1975 defense budget of $54.8 billion, provided for a very substantial force despite the disparity between the total cost and that of the comparable FY 1972 Administration budget of $75.5 billion.[14] His suggested force structure is summarized in Exhibit 2. The strategic forces would be funded to the extent of $14.1 billion; the general purpose forces, to $40.7 billion. Included in those sums are substantial resources ($5.5 billion) for research and development hedging against an uncertain

Exhibit 2.
PROPOSED FY 1975 U.S. FORCE STRUCTURE

Forces	Number
Strategic Forces	
Minuteman Missiles	1,000
Polaris (submarines/missiles)	34/544
Poseidon (submarines/missiles)	7/112
Strategic Bombers (B-52's and FB-111's)	200
Manned Fighter-Interceptor Squadrons	5
Air Defense Firing Batteries	8
General Purpose Forces	
Land Forces	
Army Divisions	10
Marine Divisions	2
Tactical Air Forces	
Air Force Wings	18
Navy Attack Wings	6
Marine Corps Double Wings	2
Naval Forces	
Attack Carriers	6
Nuclear Attack Submarines	69
Escort Ships	130
Amphibious Assault Ships	56
Troopships, Cargoships, Replenishment Ships	80
Airlift Forces	
C-5A Squadrons	4
C-141 and Other Squadrons	14

END EXHIBIT 2-BABROW

future. McGovern arrived at this posture on the basis of assumptions about deterrence and regional power of the United States similar to those made earlier in this chapter.

What should the posture of the United States be in the world we have posited? The following initiatives represent policies which might operationalize our perspective.[15]

Commitments Contingent on Self-help. Although the United States should not abandon foreign countries to military aggression, we should no longer encourage them in the belief that we will bear the primary costs of their defense. We should no longer maintain a military assistance posture that assumes that attacks will come out of the blue; nor should we permit mobilization or transportation of military capability from the United States itself to the scene of the threat. For example, the United States should adopt these policies:

—Military aid to industrialized countries not to exceed the defense burden which they themselves bear. Useful comparative measures are percent of GNP spent on defense and percent of central government budget spent on defense.

—Military assistance to less developed countries only when they collect taxes from the most affluent 20 percent of their population on as heavy a taxation schedule as the United States applies to the most affluent 20 percent of its population.

—Security commitments to regimes only when their domestic performance is or promises to be strong. Useful measures are changes in mass standard of living and trends in the distribution of a variety of items of value, e.g., purchasing power, property, political access.

—Nonmilitary assistance, whether formal aid or a variety of other special privileges and status, to be made contingent on the extent to which recipients improve the quality of life for their people. Improvement will be measured by the UN through social statistics. In order to insure that aid allocations are based on these criteria, the United States would transfer its aid funds to the UN for allocation on the basis of domestic performance potential. Such a policy should, first, give the governments of the developing countries incentives for social development, and, second, make the demanding criteria for receiving aid more a matter of international norms than of U.S. interference.

If we apply these principles, we will modify our military subsidies to Western Europe and Japan, curtail our aid to regimes which oppress their people (e.g., Greece), and maintain a discreet distance from regimes which have little long-run viability (e.g., Laos).

Self-restraint. A central element of U.S. policy should be to prevent new situations in which the set of U.S. public and private relationships (e.g., military, economic and in communications) come to dominate local behavior, and to improve situations in which the United States is already dominant. The implication is an American policy of exhortation, coordination and regulatory disincentives on the private sector, to restrict the United States in these sectors in certain foreign nations.

From Arms Races to Welfare Races. We need to shift the focus of competition and peace-keeping in international relations from a military to a social-benefit focus. Toward that end, at least three developments are required: a reduction in perceived military threat; the involvement of powerful domestic forces in the relations between nations, forces whose incentives are met only when resources go for social benefits rather than military preparedness; and the creation of international institutions charted and adequately supported to move quickly to assist member states with nonmilitary problems. It seems helpful to provide an example of an appropriate policy for meeting each of these requirements more fully than they are now being met.

—U.S. policy should actively seek to create zones free of nuclear weaponry in Asia and Europe. Such zones lessen asymmetries in threat assessment caused by differences in military deployment between countries. They should reduce the utility of tactical nuclear weapons and increase the possibility of international agreements to reduce such weapons.

—U.S. policy should feature a unilateral initiative to conclude Good Life treaties with the Soviet Union and all other nations. Good Life treaties are formal international commitments by their signatories to achieve higher domestic performance in the quality of life. Elements in such treaties might include units of new housing per year, physicians trained per year, reduction in infant mortality per year. Full inspection would be part of the treaties. If arrived at, such instruments should provide powerful domestic program interests with a vehicle and motive to become involved in international policy. If implemented, they will *de facto* reduce resources available for arms budgets.

—U.S. policy should actively encourage the creation of international institutions directed towards problems which affect daily life. For example, the world needs a UN arm with general responsibility for the environment, a world environmental authority (WEA).[16] The WEA would: monitor the environment and provide statistics on which public awareness and policy depend; establish standards for environmental protection to be embodied in an environmental protection treaty; provide an environmental consultation service to assist less affluent members in determining the environmental costs and benefits of alternative modernization and development programs; and maintain a ready capability to react quickly to environmental disasters in order to limit damage and reclaim the environmental condition of the disaster region. The costs of WEA should be met by tax measures which themselves encourage environmental protection, e.g., taxes on polluters of ocean and air space.

With regard to the U.S. policy machinery, the following suggestions will illustrate desirable directions of change.

Make the Executive and the Congress Responsible and Accountable. In order to increase executive and congressional responsibility and accountability, the Congress must change its ways of dealing with national security and related policies. One form of change would be to establish a joint committee on the state of the world (JCSW). The JCSW would have as members the ranking member of each party in each House, the chairman and ranking minority member of the two military and two foreign affairs committees, of the Joint Committee on Atomic Energy and of the Joint Economic Committee. Like other joint committees, it would have a staff of sufficient size and analytic competence to critically assess presidential suggestions and policy performance and needs. The JCSW's responsibilities would be to: review all national commitments; consult with the President on all executive agreements; consult with the President

prior to any action which might involve the United States in
armed conflict abroad, other than those directly related to nuclear attack on America itself; determine the coherence of
international programs and military and nonmilitary plans;
evaluate the performance of major foreign and defense programs and policies, e.g., foreign economic policy; and hold annually a major set of hearings in response to the President's
State of the World message. The hearings will predictably provide a major forum to review the assumptions on which U.S.
policy is based and performance during the previous year. With
regard to executive agreements and war powers—the second
and third areas of JCSW responsibility—the committee should
have the authority to in effect call Congress into session and,
should Congress be in session, to immediately bring the issue
at hand up for debate. In order to perform its duties effectively,
the JCSW would have the authority to request estimates from
the intelligence community.

Coordinate National Security Policy with Domestic Needs.
In order to achieve national policies rather than domestic and
foreign policies the policy machinery must insure confrontation between comparative and vigorous analysis of alternative
sets of policies. By sets, I mean clusters of domestic and foreign
policies. Two organizational suggestions may clarify the implications of this requirement.

—The cabinet should be revitalized as a national opportunities board (NOB). NOB should be composed of the Secretaries of the major domestic and foreign affairs departments.
More specialized groups in the Office of the President, for
example, the National Security Council, the Domestic
Affairs Council, the Environmental Council, will report to
it. NOB's responsibilities will be to insure that the consequences of policies abroad on those at home, and vice-
versa, are faced and planned for. NOB should be expected
to determine the opportunity cost of allocations, considering national security vs. domestic programs before the
money is spent.

—Responsibilities for missions which, if vigorously pursued,
would channel resources away from military uses should be

assigned to powerful domestic agencies. Advocacy responsibilities should be assigned to units with the bureaucratic
incentives, constituency support and congressional clout to
pursue them effectively. The Arms Control and Disarmament Agency is in a very weak position. But if it were
located in the Office of the Secretary of Health, Education
and Welfare, it would have a position of strength from
which to advocate a position opposed to weapons procurement and in favor of releasing resources for other national
needs.

Net Assessment. The benefits from any of the policies or
mechanisms we have suggested depend on the supply of pertinent and sound information—information similar to that required to determine if the assertions earlier in this chapter
have merit for particular situations. In the broad sense, information availability is an intelligence problem. Yet the
information our assertions call for is not the kind of information on which most intelligence resources are spent. Accordingly, an additional and indeed necessary type of change is to
increase the production and decrease the bias in information
which bears on the variables central to our earlier line of argument. Succinct and relevant information must be made the job
of an agency with incentives to collect and analyze nonmilitary
and noneconomic war potential attributes of the external system: domestic social performance, the change in population
elements, the threat and opportunity perspectives of relevant
foreign actors. And such information must be matched with
ordered facts on the extent to which and the ways in which
previous and current U.S. behavior and alternatives for the
future impinge on the autonomy of other nations in the economic and cultural as well as military and political sectors.

NOTES

1. A particularly helpful analysis of the trade-offs between defense and
domestic expenditures is that of Bruce M. Russett, *What Price Vigilance?*
(New Haven: Yale University Press, 1970).

2. This point has been made with particular forcefulness by Morton H. Halperin, "The Good, The Bad, and The Wasteful," *Foreign Policy*, 6 (Spring, 1972): 69-83.

3. This is not to question the utility of the defense debate in making "questionable" those matters which were previously treated as sacrosanct.

4. According to Herbert A. Simon, individuals "satisfice" (i.e., seek satisfactory or "good enough" solutions to problems) rather than maximize (i.e., seek best possible solutions). See Simon, *Models of Man: Social and Rational* (New York: Wiley, 1957), pp. 204-205.

5. McGeorge Bundy, "To Cap the Volcano," *Foreign Affairs, vol.* 48, no. 1 (October 1969): 12.

6. For a perceptive analysis and several illustrations of the distortion effect, see Albert D. Biderman, "Social Indicators and Goals," in Raymond A. Bauer, ed., *Social Indicators* (Cambridge: M.I.T. Press, 1966) pp. 68-153.

7. This theme underlies much of the appeal of George Wallace to the American electorate and has recently been put forward as a major social challenge to Britain by Roy Jenkins, the former Labor Chancellor of the Exchequer.

8. A recent salient example is the influx of Bengali refugees into India, the problems it posed and the consequences it helped trigger.

9. For an overview, see President Nixon's State of the World messages: *U.S. Foreign Policy for the 1970's: A New Strategy for Peace* (Washington, D.C.: G.P.O., 1970); *U.S. Foreign Policy for the 1970's: Building for Peace* (Washington, D.C.: G.P.O., 1971); *U.S. Foreign Policy for the 1970's: The Emerging Structure of Peace* (Washington, D.C.: G.P.O. 1972).

10. Admiral Thomas H. Moorer, U.S.N., "United States Military Posture for FY1973," mimeographed (Statement before the Senate Armed Services Committee on February 15, 1972) p. 1.

11. Melvin R. Laird, *National Security Strategy of Realistic Deterrence*, Statement before the Senate Armed Services Committee on the FY1973 Defense Budget and FY1973-1977 Program, February 15, 1972 (Washington, D.C.: G.P.O., 1972) pp. 186-187, 199, 201, 203.

12. Laird, *National Security Strategy*, pp. 108-127.

13. For a particularly insightful critique of the Nixon Doctrine from this viewpoint, see Earl M. Ravenal, "Nixon Doctrine, Defense Policy and our Commitments in Asia," *Foreign Affairs*, 49, no. 2 (January 1971): 201-217.

14. George McGovern, "Toward A More Secure America: An Alternative National Defense Posture," mimeographed, April 1972.

15. I have benefitted in large measure from discussions with University of Minnesota colleagues Roger Benjamin, P. Terrence Hopmann and Enid C. B. Schoettle.

16. The reader will recognize the idea as one propounded by Richard Falk. See *This Endangered Planet* (New York: Random House, 1971).

CONCLUSIONS

14

THE GREENING OF THE BRASS: EMERGING CIVIL-MILITARY RELATIONS

Philip S. Kronenberg

Charles Reich, in *The Greening of America,* offers an interesting if somewhat naive analysis of a revolution of consciousness
in American society. He argues that a change in self-identity
and social concept among increasing numbers of our citizens
will lead to profound changes in the social structures and power
relationships of the society. The problem is that Reich has it
reversed, in large part. Structural changes precipitate changes
in self-identity and one's concept of society, not the other way
around. Structures reinforce norms, focus the exercise of power
and shape the patterns of information among individuals. This
essay proposes that our political and military leadership adopt
an alternative perspective about the structure of national security decision-making. The realities of power and structure
involved in the conduct of national security affairs have under-
gone real changes; but we have yet to see a concomitant revolution in consciousness among the leadership. It is time that we

had a "Greening of the Brass"; changes in the character of civil-military relations in the United States demand it.

The Security/Democracy Dilemma

Historically, the chief concern in civil-military relations was that the armed forces might compromise the constitutional order of the civilian government. Given the nature of contemporary American society, there is at least one issue of greater concern in civil-military relations than the unlikely possibility of a military coup d'etat: the relationship between security needs and democratic needs.

One of the more perplexing realities of America in the 1970s is the tension between the perceived needs of national security on the one hand and the perceived needs for improving the performance of our democratic institutions on the other. Some argue that this security/democracy dilemma is a social problem in which greater increases in national security must be purchased at the expense of democratic practices or that improvements in the quality of American democracy can be had only by reducing our security in international affairs. While the zero-sum quality of the security/democracy dilemma has an undoubted rhetorical appeal—it is a premise underlying much of the polemic surrounding contemporary foreign policy discourse—it vastly oversimplifies the political and social issues associated with civil-military relations in American society.

Micro/Macro Levels

The security/democracy dilemma must be examined at the micro-level, which focuses on the internal processes of the military institution itself, and the macro-level, which emphasizes the political processes of the total society. In terms of problems of civil-military relations, the concern at the micro-level is with the potential rigidity of the military institution in the face of technological and social change; at the macro-level the concern is with the militarist tendencies of the total society. These two levels are interdependent: problems at the micro-level are due in part to problems at the macro-level and vice-versa. One consequence of this interdependence is that micro-reforms must be supported by macro-reforms.

The micro/macro distinction can be clarified by making explicit some basic definitions. For any organized society, the primary function of the military institution is to protect the physical and territorial security of the society from external threats of violence. This protection is effected through the preparation and application of coercive violent force by agents of the state called armed forces.

The focus of attention at the micro-level is with the viability of the armed forces as an efficient and effective agent of the state, as an *instrument* of society which is intended to serve the military function. This means that the armed forces must have enough resources and be properly organized to perform their role adequately. The micro-level, then, emphasizes the efficiency of the internal processes of armed forces and the effectiveness of these processes for the military function of protecting the physical and territorial security of society from external threats. Efficiency is defined in terms of the economic and social values of the society; effectiveness is defined by the priorities of security determined by the political system. Armed forces are inadequate if they consume more material and human resources than needed to serve the military function, even when they "win." They also are inadequate when they lack the flexibility to reorient their organizational purposes in line with changes in the concept of security provided by the political system. Rigidities within armed forces which limit their ability to change their use of resources and organizational goals are a major problem at the micro-level.

At the macro-level, the problem of militarism is the central concern. Traditional confidence in the capacity of American institutions to hold in check the emergence of militarism has been subject to increased questioning in the late 1960s and early 1970s. Many observers of life in contemporary America have expressed doubts about the reliability of assumed restraints

on militarism. They share the fear, asserted by President Eisenhower in his much quoted farewell address, that the acquisition
of unwarranted influence in public affairs by interacting military and economic power contains "the potential for the disastrous rise of misplaced power . . . and will persist."

Alfred Vagts makes a basic distinction (noted also by Paul
Schratz in Chapter 12) in the patterns of behavior of armed
forces in their performance of the military function for society:
the military way vs. militarism. The military way "is marked by
a primary concentration of men and materials on winning specific objectives of power with the utmost efficiency, that is, with
the least expenditure of blood and treasure. It is limited in
scope, confined to one function, and scientific in its essential
qualities." [1] Militarism, for Vagts, is a very different phenomenon. It means "the domination of the military man over the
civilian, an undue preponderance of military demands, an
emphasis on military considerations, spirit, ideals, and scales
of value, in the life of states . . . also the imposition of heavy
burdens on a people for military purposes, to the neglect of
welfare and culture, and the waste of the nation's best manpower in unproductive army service." [2]

It is important to note that Vagts's conceptualization of
militarism is not concerned merely with the behavior of armed
forces. His seminal book is entitled *A History of Militarism:
Civilian and Military.* At a minimum, militarism would seem
to require that the civilian population or its political leadership
acquiesce to progressive military dominance in society. Civilians
would have to cooperate, even if unwillingly or unintentionally,
with the progressive societal emphasis on "military considerations, spirit, ideals, and scales of value" which is required for
the development of militarism. The roots and vigor of militarism must somehow be legitimated by civilian support. And the
initiatives in taking society down the path of militarism may
come from civilians rather than from military leaders.

At its essential core, militarism is a perversion of the legitimate organized instrumentalities of state violence. The pursuit
of a capability to apply limited violent means in the service of
discrete goals which center on maintaining the security of the

society is subordinated to the aggrandizement of the instruments themselves and their self-serving ideologies. This process of goal displacement which leads to perversion of the military function may be due to military or civilian initiatives—or the collaboration of both sectors—and may be quite unintended and deceptively latent. The macro-level focuses, therefore, on the societal causes and consequences of the political system's perverting the military function.

Components of the Dilemma

The tensions between security and democracy comprise a complex matrix of problems involving the development of consistent policy and the reliability of its execution, the degrees to which the norms of the military are representative of American society, the priorities allocated to military programs relative to other public needs, and the role of individual discretion and democratic political participation in the context of security requirements. For the purposes of this Chapter, the security/democracy dilemma will be discussed in terms of three component issues: system standardization vs. local autonomy, integration vs. isolation, and military needs vs. civilian needs. Each of these issues will be examined briefly and illustrated at micro- and macro-levels.

SYSTEM STANDARDIZATION VS. LOCAL AUTONOMY

The issue of system standardization vs. local autonomy is concerned with decision-makers' efforts to maintain consistency for implementing policy while at the same time providing the means to respond to local conditions in the field and to elicit useful innovations in policy implementation.

At the micro-level, as the professional military attempts to establish an all-volunteer armed force, these standardization/autonomy tensions reveal the limitations of the military in adapting to social change. The memory of fragging incidents and insubordination by units in the field and on shipboard, coupled with a continuing malaise among servicemen associated with the withdrawal of ground forces from Indochina, characterize some fruits of the standardization/autonomy issue. Attempts to apply traditional universalistic standards of discipline, inducements and sanctions are no longer effective, because of the vast differences in race, education and career ambitions among men in uniform.

The standardization/autonomy issue at the macro-level emerged in 1972 with the case of General John D. Lavelle. Lavelle, a four-star officer commanding Seventh Air Force fighter-bomber operations in Indochina, directed strikes against targets in North Vietnam in direct violation of superior orders initiated by President Nixon. He did this based on intelligence information available to him which revealed a buildup of North Vietnamese forces above the demilitarized zone. He directed that reports in his command be falsified in order to hide the violation of orders. After Lavelle's actions had been made public, he indicated that he would do the same thing again under similar circumstances, but would not falsify the reports. His rationale goes to the marrow of the standardization/autonomy issue: a violation of orders in order to protect his aircrews and to enhance military operations. This is a rationale very similar to the infamous insubordination of General Douglas MacArthur during the Korean War. Judgments of "military necessity" assume a logic superior to the political logic to which the military is presumably subordinate. Indeed, the "military necessity" concept proposes a substitute political logic: politics is the continuation of war by other means.

Integration vs. Isolation

The second component of the security/democracy dilemma is the issue of integration vs. isolation. Isolation—physical, political and social—of the armed forces from the mainstream of civilian society presumably promotes traditional military norms while broader integration into society dilutes these norms.

The integration/isolation issue at the micro-level continues to defy solution as the Army, for example, attempts to popularize its image as being consistent with civilian norms, life styles and haircuts while yearning to have the "lean and mean" combat capabilities of the Marine Corps. The near-ideological concept of the "fighter spirit" of the combat soldier does not fit easily with the utilitarian recruitment appeals of salary, travel and educational benefits.

The integration/isolation issue at the macro-level is intimately associated with the problem of militarism when a volunteer armed force is contemplated. In the 1960s Gene Lyons analyzed the interpenetration of civilian and military sectors which produced a civilianization of the military and a militarization of the civilian sector.[3] Given this interpenetration, "civilian control" loses much of its relevance for civil-military relations. The Lyons' thesis prompts questions about militarism which become more difficult with the emergence of a volunteer force. Without the inducement of the draft, and assuming reasonable vitality in the economy, one can expect the enlisted ranks to be populated largely by men and women from lower socioeconomic strata and the officer corps to draw its numbers from the ranks and from the ROTC programs at nonelite campuses. The upshot is that the U.S. armed forces will become increasingly less representative of the general population and perhaps prone to castelike inbreeding. The closer congressional scrutiny of the military in the past few years, together with the antimilitary and amilitary attitudes of many Americans, may further reinforce the isolation and alienation of the military from the larger society. Colonel Richard F. Rosser, head of the Department of Political Science at the Air Force Academy, views the growing apathy of American youth toward the military as a crucial factor shaping civil-military relations in the future.

> Thus is born the major security dilemma of the next decade—*not* how to live with the "delicate" balance of terror, but how to maintain an effective armed force in a democratic society where the mood among the young is amilitarism. Once a society begins to downgrade its armed

forces, a descending spiral seems to take hold. The less valued the military function by the public, the fewer good men join the military. The fewer good men in the military, the more derogatory the opinion of the public about the armed forces—and the less money appropriated. At some point, the spiral will stop.[4]

Military Needs vs. Civilian Needs

The third issue is that of military needs vs. civilian needs. The tensions raised by this issue derive from distinctions made between the claims on societal resources for weapons and trained military manpower and the resources which are required to cope with domestic needs such as housing, welfare and education.

An important part of the rigidity of the military institution rests on its inability to lay claim to the social legitimacy which in former times had let it build a persuasive case for military needs distinctive from the requirements of the domestic sectors of the society. At the micro-level, it has lost much of its important officer procurement base in the ROTC programs of many elite universities (as Peter Karsten has described in Chapter 5). In the technical specialties, its recruitment and retention efforts based on salary and other benefits for volunteers will probably fall short of military manning requirements—due in no small part to employment opportunities in the civilian economy. The military justice system is another example of this aspect of the security/democracy dilemma. Although efforts have been made to move military justice from its traditional role as a disciplinary instrument in the hands of commanders, the individual soldier still finds his personal autonomy severely abridged in comparison to his civilian peers. The military institution finds it very difficult to adopt the changes necessary to give individual justice as high a priority as "mission" or "convenience of the service."

The military needs vs. civilian needs issue at the macro-level is fueled by some of the same factors that reinforce the tendency toward isolation of the military from civilian society. Pressing domestic social and economic problems, especially in our cities, have undermined much of the legitimacy of military claims on resources and have disconnected the military in the minds of many Americans from its favored symbolic identity with national purposes. As Huntington argues, Americans increasingly will view military needs as the claims of a vested interest which will have to compete for resources along with other vested interests; military interests no longer will be equated with the public interest.[5] But the process which Huntington predicts is not irreversible; vested interests can be rewrapped in the cloak of public interest during periods of perceived crisis. The historical willingness of the American people to accede to the foreign policy initiatives of the White House is well documented (see Russett essay in Chapter 3). The President has much latitude for manipulating the symbols of legitimacy and the informational premises of decision-making in the national security field. Also, the all-volunteer force may be a mixed blessing. As Huntington speculates, when the military finds its national image shifting toward that of a vested interest, defense will go on the defensive: "As the military-industrial complex comes under attack, it is also likely to become more concentrated, more cohesive, more disciplined, and possessed of more of the obvious attributes of power at the same time that the substance of power declines." [6] During periods of foreign policy crisis, a more defensive, isolated and cohesive military institution may be prone—and capable—of unleashing illiberal reaction in the body politic similar to that which emerged with the detention of Japanese-Americans in the early 1940s and with the anticommunist frenzy of the early 1950s.

An approach to the dilemma

The security/democracy dilemma has become a chronic problem for American society. The features are imbedded deeply in the structures of decision-making of this nation. These decision structures define the channels of influence and the locus of power at the micro- and macro-levels of civil-military relations.

The key to understanding this dilemma and to fashioning the means to inhibit its persistence is to recognize that the decision-making processes within the military institution and the larger political system of the society are influenced by both the actual structure of decision-making and the perceptions which the individual decision-makers hold of that structure.

Decision-making occurs in organizational settings. More accurately, decisions are made in the context of cooperative and conflictive interactions of clusters of components from various separate organizations within the military and the political system. There is probably a difference between the actual structure of decision-making and the perceptions of that process by decision-makers because every decision-maker—even the President—is limited to the value and informational premises that are peculiar to his role in a given organizational cluster. No individual decision-maker has the cognitive capacity to see and evaluate all of the complex organizational and interorganizational forces which bear on his role in the decision-making process.[7] Yet the tendency of decision-makers is to ignore the reality of these complex patterns and to perceive their spheres of action as being essentially bureaucratic in nature. The bureaucratic design is an effort to simplify the organizational complexities which exceed the cognitive capacities of decision-makers. But bureaucratic design is more than a pragmatic concession by decision-makers to the complexities that surround them. Bureaucratic design is a normative matter, a preferred strategy for organizing human action which decision-makers have learned to accept due to their years of exposure to bureaucracy in public and private life and due to their socialization since birth by a culture which reinforces bureaucratic norms.

Organizational Behavior: The Monoplex Tendency

What is this bureaucratic design that is so widely assailed by decision-makers as they simultaneously perpetuate its application? Basically, it is an attempt to make the most efficient use of organizational resources in pursuit of specified goals by relying on division of labor, hierarchical authority, standardized procedures, career stability, and universal decision criteria and performance measures.[8] In other words, bureaucracy intends to extract maximum efficiency by imposing rational order on the use of human and material resources.

Given this intention, what are the results in terms of actual behavior in bureaucratically designed organizations? The theoretical literature concerning behavior in bureaucratic organizations is too vast to be summarized easily. However, several major conclusions can be derived in order to characterize some major consequences of attempting to apply a bureaucratic design.[9]

First, individuals in organizations prefer to avoid uncertainty and have low tolerance for ambiguity. Although individuals will pursue their self-interest on the basis of subjective priorities, they will tend to seek satisfactory (good enough) solutions to problems rather than maximum (best possible) solutions.

Second, organizations consist of coalitions of individual actors which tend to conform to the formal boundaries of organizational subunits. Every organization has one coalition that tends to be dominant. Composition of the dominant coalition will change in response to environmental and technological uncertainties which affect the organization.

Third, organizations engage in *quasi-resolution of conflict* because they are inclined to have internally inconsistent goals. Organizations typically subdivide overall organizational goals into subgoals and assign these subgoals to subunits. Because there is a high probability that, over time, subunits will acquire a degree of local autonomy, subunit goals will not be consistent with the overall goals of the total organization. Thus, latent conflict will persist within the organization and will never be resolved completely. Related to this is the tendency for organizations to engage in *problemistic* rather than *opportunistic* *search*. That is, organizations are neither curious nor do they seek to understand fully the changing circumstances with which they must eventually cope. Instead, they search for new alternatives or new information primarily to control what they view as deviant behavior or to solve pressing problems. In effect, they do not search until a "fire" breaks out.

Finally, organizations—reflecting the dislike for uncertainty of the individuals in them—tend to avoid uncertainty by focusing on short-term issues and crises at the expense of future planning and the development of long-term strategies. The processing of information used by decision-makers is characterized by *uncertainty absorption*. As information is passed from subunit to subunit, inferences are drawn from this information and the inferences, rather than the information, are then transmitted to the next subunit. These successive efforts to edit out the uncertainty in information involve selective perceptions shaped by individual and subunit goal commitments which can lead to considerable distortion when the edited "information" finally reaches key decision-makers. A related aspect of the predisposition of organizations to avoid uncertainty lies in their efforts to insulate the established technological means for accomplishing organizational goals from environmental contingencies or threats. The persistence of a commitment by the U. S. Air Force to manned bombers is an example of this tendency. The image of the heroic aviator persists in spite of the instrumental effectiveness of the strategic missile.

An obvious implication of these four consequences of bureaucratic design is that the use of bureaucratic structures often does not produce the results that are intended by decision-makers. Maximum performance is neither pursued nor achieved; subunits behave as shifting coalitions rather than as precision components of a well-tuned bureaucratic "machine"; organizational inconsistencies persist; crises accumulate without complete resolution; and decisions must be made on the basis of information that is distorted *and* incomplete.

These dysfunctional consequences are not intense in all organizations that adopt a bureaucratic design. They are kept at a minimum in many small organizations and in organizations which perform highly routine tasks using predictable technologies under stable conditions. But these consequences are quite typical of the large-scale complex organizations that mark the terrain of the military establishment and the political system. Given the presence of such consequences, one might assume that rational decision-makers would modify or abandon their reliance on the bureaucratic design. The reverse seems to happen, in fact. As the dysfunctions of bureaucratic design continue to manifest themselves, decision-makers contrive, through continuing cycles of reorganizing, to reduce these dysfunctions by additional applications of bureaucratic measures. Thereby they reinforce the sources of dysfunctionality. This tendency, which has been described in intraorganizational research as a "demand for control," [10] can be called a *monoplex perspective* in the interorganizational processes of military and political decision-making. The monoplex perspective is an extrapolation of bureaucratic norms and expectations into the vast complexity of interorganizational relationships found within the military institution as it interacts with the technological, social, economic and political spheres of society. Those who share the monoplex perspective view military affairs and national security policy as being essentially bureaucratic and mechanistic in nature.

The monoplex perspective minimizes two points which are crucial to an understanding of civil-military relations. First, there is a tendency to forget that the military establishment and the political system are multicomponent and multivalue structures. The monoplex perspective acknowledges that the military is large-scale and complex. But the implications of its complexity and scale are minimized. Instead, the perception of the military establishment is of a single, huge, relatively integrated bureaucratic organization. Second, the monoplex perspective promotes the application by and to the military of universalistic decision rules, monolithic structure and standardized leadership styles which are appropriate to smaller, integrated bureaucracies under routine conditions but quite inappropriate for multicomponent, multivalue, large-scale structures. The generation gap which insulates many senior military and civilian officials from the realities of the youth culture is an example of the flaws in the monoplex perspective. The resistance or outright inability of the military to respond to technological and social changes which require differential leadership styles (the commander of an infantry brigade and the chief of a military research lab require different leadership styles) and organizational structures is an important result of the monoplex perspective. The significance of this limitation grows as military and civilian leaders attempt to accommodate themselves to the sophisticated political and institutional roles thrust upon the military by the all-volunteer force concept.[11]

Orientation Toward Political Certainty

The preceding discussion has focused primarily on the effects of the monoplex perspective on the military institution and its linkages with civilian political leadership. As we extend the implications of the monoplex perspective to the larger political system of the society, we must return to the distinction between the micro-level concerns of the military institution and the macro-level concerns of the entire political system. Micro-level issues pertain to the efficiency and effectiveness with which the military function is performed. Macro-level issues relate to the quality of democratic performance of the political system, especially as it responds to the threat of militarism. The effects of the monoplex perspective at the macro-level are revealed when we examine the literature which criticizes the tendencies toward militarism in the United States. Of particular interest in this literature is what can be called orientations toward political certainty/uncertainty. These orientations—and their relationship to the monoplex perspective—hinge on how particular analysts define the nature of the problem of militarism and the types of solution they propose.

An orientation toward political certainty is a mechanistic notion of the political process in which stability is given high preference, norms are to be specified, articulated and sanctioned, relative power relationships are to be maintained, and change is to be accommodated by controlled centralized adjustments in public programs. An example is to be found in the civilian supremacy critique of militarism. This critique visualizes various social mechanisms (constitutional principles, civilian commander-in-chief, congressional control over defense appropriations and military organization, etc.) as the means to keep the power of the military at a minimum, consistent with security requirements. The threat of militarism is thought to emerge when these control mechanisms are subverted or fall into disuse. This would happen if the civilian control apparatus —executive and legislative—becomes coopted by the military elite or has to rely increasingly on military-based interpretations of threats to security or the means needed to cope with these threats. The civilian supremacist's solution is to increase the procedural checks and balances and to enlarge the formal authority of the controlling institutions over the military institution that is to be controlled.

An orientation toward political *uncertainty* is an organic notion of the political process in which change is given high preference; norms are to be specified and sanctioned as changing circumstances cause modifications to be articulated; power relationships are allowed to fluctuate; and change is accommodated by maximum feasible support of local rationality (i.e., decentralized decision centers are in a better position to understand and act upon local needs) with centralized rule-making at a minimum. A critique of militarism which approximates this orientation is found in the garrison state thesis of Harold D. Lasswell. Lasswell is not concerned merely with keeping the military "in its place" in a formal sense. Rather, he is anxious to prevent the total penetration of society by the military function, with its norms of violence and mechanistic organizational patterns. His "cure" for militarism is *civilianism,* which involves the absorption of the military by the multivalued orientation of the society. He sees the decision processes of such societies as functioning through "shifting coalitions composed of formal and tacit representatives of the plurality of groups and persons formed by exposure to and interaction with the complex symbolic and material subdivisions of our civilization." [12]

How well does the American political system satisfy the requirements for civilianism? To what extent are our politics supportive of an orientation toward political uncertainty in the society? The answers rest with the structure of power in the society.

One does not have to take a Marxian position or accept C. Wright Mills's power-elite thesis to acknowledge that political power is distributed unequally in America. That is, there are political elites. Robert A. Dahl and G. William Domhoff,[13] among others, have offered evidence and argument to support the thesis that these elites are unrepresentative of the population of the United States in terms of socioeconomic class. If we accept this conclusion, that still does not necessarily mean that elites are unable to represent the preferences of the nonelite components of the population and cannot reflect the multivalued orientation of the society.

Yet the political alienation of American youth and minorities, the social and political turbulence in our society, and the declining performance of governmental institutions offer at least some impressionistic evidence that nonelite preferences are not being well represented. Elites use political power, whatever their motives, to maintain the stability of decision structures and their own self-perpetuation as elites in terms of norms which reinforce their socioeconomic interests. In effect, their orientation is towards *political certainty.* The result is a tendency to restrict the access of alternative groups and norms to important decision roles in the political process; the political process is stabilized as a structure of power relations in which dramatic change is retarded and only marginal reform is probable.

It is in this setting of relatively static politics that large conglomerates like the national security bureaucracy described by Richard J. Barnet [14] are able to perpetuate policies such as the disaster of Vietnam long after many Americans have become outraged—then fatigued—over our inability to disengage in a reasonable period of time. The unrepresentative power structure provides the political bases for monoplex tendencies to deepen and strengthen the maladjustments of American society to the security/democracy dilemma. The point here is not that the unrepresentative power structure is a conscious conspiracy to deprive nonelites of access to power in order to contrive the growth of militarism. Rather, the monoplex perspective that is diffused throughout the network of political decision-making tends to reinforce the orientation toward political certainty, the upshot being that such rigidities that are found within the military institution and the political system are husbanded by a political elite structure that prefers stability to accommodating to the shifting claims of a multivalued society.

The Multiplex Perspective and the Emerging Civil-Military Relations

The thesis of this chapter is that the security/democracy dilemma is a result of distortions in the interorganizational decision structures that determine civil-military relations. These distortions are due to the tendency of elite decision-makers in the political system and the military institution to base their perceptions and action premises on monoplex conceptions of social reality where the actual social condition is *multiplex*. Put differently, the often excessive influence in society of the military, its supporters and military values are due in part to the actual power structure of society at a given point in time and in part due to the perspectives decision-makers use to define reality (i.e., the identification of occasions to act, the nature of problems and the nature of their solutions) which tend to reinforce dysfunctional bureaucratic norms.

The multiplex perspective rejects the notion that the military is a vast monolith and portrays it as a multiplex—a complex system of interacting individuals, groups and organizations in which groups of coalitions have different objectives, structures and leadership styles. Each is engaged in some degree of bargaining over its role vis-à-vis others.

The multiplex perspective requires comprehension of the existence of necessary conflict among the constituent organizational coalitions of our political and military structures in the national security field and recognition of the inevitable social and resource costs of trying to impose coordination on such a complex multivalued system. Efforts to suppress these differences with centrally contrived and universalistic solutions impede the prospect of moving toward more viable orientations of political uncertainty and postpone efforts to cope with the security/democracy dilemma in a dynamic social context.

The general officer sitting in a Pentagon staff agency is in a different world from the company commander in Germany (or the U.S. Senator or the black housewife in Harlem). The general's world is different not only in a personal sense but also in an organizational sense. His role and his organization are far removed in time, space and concept from the combat company. The multiplex perspective may help us anticipate these differences in concept and power and suggest some means for reducing their rigidities. The problem is not merely that the general is insulated, but that the captain and the senator and the housewife also are insulated in their own distinctive and problematic ways.

Although it is likely that the security/democracy dilemma will never be completely resolved, it is clear that the persistence of monoplex viewpoints will impede progress in that direction. The multiplex perspective will not solve racial, drug or other problems in any neat, technical sense. But it will provide a framework to better illuminate the relationships of power, communications and technology in the military and political spheres that are requisite to asking some better questions about the nature of our problems. It also may sharpen our appreciation for problems of conflicting human values and capacities that cannot be solved by means of rationalist analogies to the modification of weapons systems, an analogy we have been too prone to use.

There are hopeful signs for the emergence of multiplex orientations in the early seventies. The "Greening of the Brass" —military and civilian—is emerging at a number of points in the form of Young (and not so young) Turks who are challenging conventional wisdom and willing to live in multiplex realities. Green Beret detachments from Fort Bragg have experimented with domestic civic action programs in Appalachia which are intended to use the technical and organizational skills of these troops to enhance community self-help. In addition to the steps toward community development which this experiment may represent, it has had a very positive impact on morale among Green Berets, who find themselves engaged in constructive rather than destructive missions. The intercultural relations project of the Bureau of Naval Personnel has established field teams on a pilot basis at several overseas installations in an effort to ease the culture shock for seamen and their families during home-porting and to reduce the dysfunctional impact of the U.S. Navy presence on the host nationals at the grass-roots level. A rather senior Young Turk, Admiral Elmo Zumwalt, the Chief of Naval Operations, has initiated a number of reforms within the Navy to enhance its responsiveness to the needs of individual servicemen.

Efforts at reforms which reduce civilian hostility toward the military or which propel the military into a wider range of nonmilitary missions have to be evaluated with political criteria that are appropriate to society's conception of civil-military relations. But it is clear that various reforms—especially those of a relatively cosmetic nature—will do little to resolve the security/democracy dilemma unless basic orientations change within the political system. A "peacetime" military complex—because it is less visible politically—poses some real dangers in a post-Vietnam era. American politics is prone to be seduced by manipulation of style and symbols. Unless American political life can be made safe for diversity, the quality of civil-military relations will not become healthier. Reforms of the military institution and the national security policy process must be based upon structural changes which rest on the multiplex perspective. The landslide victory of President Nixon at the polls in 1972, coupled with the end of U.S. combat involvement in Vietnam, offer America a major opportunity to probe these changes. This opportunity is reinforced by the recent strong antimilitarist trend in the attentive public noted by Russett in Chapter 3.

Structural changes from the top, though necessary, do not provide sufficient conditions for multiplex reform of a lasting character. Grass-roots support is essential. The disposition of the powerful to experiment with political uncertainty must be stimulated and nourished by a growing preference among citizents for decision structures that respond to the diverse values of the society.

One major structural thrust consistent with a multiplex perspective would be to redesign the institutional arrangements for the defense and foreign policy communities. This could take the form of radical surgery on the Departments of Defense and State. The military services and the Office of Secretary of Defense are a vast complex of research, development and logistical agencies, many of which have little direct role in the active training and deployment of combat forces. Yet these defense agencies have become major sources of the cement which bonds together the military-industrial-university complex. Other than a Cold War tradition of reciprocal accommodations, there is no compelling reason why these functions cannot be performed efficiently by other civilian agencies which are not part of the defense command establishment. The apparent efficiencies of the present arrangements do not compensate for the massive concentration of political and economic power represented by the Pentagon. The General Services Administration, elements of the Department of Health, Education and Welfare, and the National Science Foundation, among others, could absorb many of these essentially civilian missions of DOD. Broader use of private firms and public enterprises also would be appropriate. Furthermore, the growing number of essentially civilian tasks within the military due to the increasing technological character of the military services and the movement toward an all-volunteer armed force could be performed by civilian agencies or private firms. A concrete proposal toward these objectives would be to establish a Department of Foreign Affairs which would incorporate the purely combat forces and the military command structure within the present DOD together with the diplomatic, arms control and disarmament, consular, cultural and foreign assistance functions of the present Department of State. Although this briefly stated proposal oversimplifies the organizational measures required and ignores the political impediments to its implementation, it does reflect the action premises of the multiplex perspective.

The point of this proposed reorganization is not to deepen the roots of the security/democracy dilemma by tinkering with the bureaucratic machinery so as to further spread its grasp. Instead, it is to alter the structural inducements and sanctions of the political and military institutions so that multiplex rather than monoplex tendencies will be promoted. This requires a breaking down of the central dominance of a single set of decision-makers over all aspects of policy in the national security field and the designing of structures to prevent recentralization. Students of metropolitan government have examined similar needs in an effort to develop alternatives to traditional patterns of organizing governmental services in metropolitan areas.[15]

A number of concrete issues flow from the implications of the multiplex thesis in considering the proposal for a Department of Foreign Affairs. Relations with Congress and interest groups, structure of the armed forces, role of the presidency and other civilian authorities vis-à-vis the armed forces, military unionism, military professionalism and return to the regimental system are just a few.

These issues exceed the scope of this essay. However, the relation of a new Department of Foreign Affairs—incorporating multiplex premises—to the security/democracy dilemma is germane. Some tentative concluding thoughts can be mentioned here. The tensions between system standardization and local autonomy would be reduced because of the enlarged tolerance for diversity of means and purposes which would accompany de-bureaucratization along multiplex lines. The integration/isolation issue would become less intense with the removal of many civilian-type tasks from the formal military structure. Combat forces alone would remain in uniform and be encouraged to maintain proficiency in their military skills; but they would be rather interdependent with the civilian structures that they require for support. This would facilitate the maintenance of skill-related military norms without wrapping them in the ideological garb of patriotism or moral superiority, and would help provide a vehicle to dissect Lyons' "militarization of civilians/civilianization of the military" syndrome without weakening the effectiveness of the armed forces. Finally, multiplexity would lower the perceived tensions between "military" and "civilian" needs because the successful reorientation of values and structures would induce a sharpened delineation of the costs and benefits of alternative policies. Military programs could be evaluated more effectively in terms of the military function alone and their utility for that function could be more readily distinguished from other utilities.

These estimates of the consequences of creating a Department of Foreign Affairs along multiplex lines should not distract our attention away from the important relationship between multiplexity and the security/democracy dilemma. Structural change alone is insufficient; perpetual cycles of reorganization are a fact-of-life in the history of governmental institutions. A new approach to civil-military relations requires new structural arrangements but new structures based on essentially monoplex assumptions will only reinforce the static tensions of the security/democracy dilemma. A "Greening of the Brass" which is rooted in a multiplex orientation and supported by greater tolerance for uncertainty on the part of American political leadership is essential. This is not the "greening" associated with the stereotypes of the drug culture or the youth culture; rather it is a counter-culture involving elites and citizens alike in new perspectives on power.

The grass-roots level of political activity in the early 1970s has gained increasing momentum. The aftermath of every major war produces an agony of collective self-assessment of national purposes and an effort to forget some of the wartime experiences which cannot easily be erased from the memory of a people. Americans are tired of rhetoric and tired of the many burdens of our power, but there is a different mood in this land from that found in the mid-1950s. We are less willing to accept the conventional wisdom of policy elites and we are no longer as tolerant of simplistic solutions to complex problems. There is growing demand for participation in the decisions that shape our lives. Americans are experimenting and learning to live in an uncertain world. They will ask as much of their leaders.

NOTES

1. Alfred Vagts, *A History of Militarism: Civilian and Military*, rev. ed. (New York: Meridian Books, 1959) pp. 13-14.

2. Ibid., p. 14.

3. Gene Lyons, "The New Civil-Military Relations," *American Political Science Review*, vol. 55 no. 1 (March 1961): 53-63.

4. Richard F. Rosser, "The Descending Spiral of Amilitarism," *Air Force*, vol. 55 no. 6 (June 1972): 69.

5. Samuel P. Huntington, "The Defense Establishment: Vested Interests and the Public Interest," in *The Military-Industrial Complex and United States Foreign Policy*, ed. Omar L. Carey (Pullman, Wash.: Washington State University Press, 1969) pp. 1-14.

6. Ibid., p. 14.

7. For discussions of the cognitive limits of rationality in organizational behavior, see James G. March and Herbert A. Simon, *Organizations* (New York: Wiley, 1958), and Herbert A. Simon, *Models of Man, Social and Rational* (New York: Wiley, 1957).

8. For two classic statements of the bureaucratic design see Henri Fayol, *General and Industrial Management*, trans. Constance Stours (London: Pitman, 1949); Max Weber, *From Max Weber: Essays in Sociology*, eds. H. H. Gerth and C. W. Mills (New York: Oxford University Press, 1946).

9. These conclusions are derived from a core of theoretical works on organizational behavior: Richard M. Cyert and James G. March, *A Behavioral Theory of the Firm* (Englewood Cliffs, N.J.: Prentice-Hall, 1963), March and Simon, *Organizations*, and James D. Thompson, *Organizations in Action* (New York: McGraw-Hill, 1967).

10. See March and Simon, *Organizations,* Chapter 3; also Robert K. Merton, "Bureaucratic Structure and Personality," *Social Forces,* 18 (1940): 560-568; Philip Selznick, *TVA and the Grass Roots* (Berkeley and Los Angeles: University of California Press, 1949); Alvin W. Gouldner, *Patterns of Industrial Bureaucracy* (Glencoe, Ill.: Free Press, 1954).

11. For a perspective that emphasizes the need for more political sophistication within the military profession, see Robert G. Gard, Jr., "The Military and American Society," *Foreign Affairs,* 49 (July 1971): 698-710.

12. Harold D. Lasswell, "The Garrison-State Hypothesis Today," in *Changing Patterns of Military Politics,* ed. Samuel P. Huntington (New York: Free Press, 1962) p. 66.

13. Robert A. Dahl, *Who Governs?* (New Haven: Yale University Press, 1961), and "A Critique of the Ruling Elite Model," *American Political Science Review,* vol. 52 no. 2 (June 1959): 463-470; G. William Domhoff, *Who Rules America?* (Englewood Cliffs, N.J.: Prentice-Hall, 1967).

14. Richard J. Barnet, *Roots of War* (New York: Atheneum, 1972).

15. For examples of one approach which focuses on "polycentric political systems," see Vincent Ostrom, Charles M. Tiebout, and Robert Warren, "The Organization of Government in Metropolitan Areas: A Theoretical Inquiry," *American Political Science Review,* vol. 55 no. 4 (December 1961): 831-842; and Vincent Ostrom, "Polycentricity" (Paper delivered at the 1972 Annual Meeting of the American Political Science Association, Washington, D.C., September 6, 1972).

CONTRIBUTORS

DAVIS B. BOBROW is professor of political science and public affairs and director of the Center of International Studies, University of Minnesota. Prior to that, he was Special Assistant for Behavioral Engineering, and Acting Director, Behavioral Sciences, Advanced Research Projects Agency. He has taught at the School for Advanced International Studies (Johns Hopkins University) and Princeton University and served as Senior Social Scientist at the Oak Ridge National Laboratory. In addition to numerous journal articles, he has written *International Relations—New Approaches,* and edited and co-authored *Weapons Systems Decisions, Computers and the Policy-Making Community* and *Components of Defense Policy.* His major current interests are in indicator systems for anticipating and evaluating international policy and in the design of public institutions.

VINCENT DAVIS is director and the Patterson Chair Professor of International Studies of the Patterson School of Diplomacy and International Commerce, University of Kentucky. He has taught at Princeton University, Dartmouth College and the Graduate School of International Studies (University of Denver), as well as serving for a year as a visiting professor in the Nimitz Chair of Foreign Affairs at the U.S. Naval War College. In addition to numerous articles and monographs, he is the author of *Postwar Defense Policy and the U.S. Navy, 1943-1946,* and *The Admirals Lobby.* He wrote "The Department of Defense," a special report project sponsored jointly by the Ford Foundation and President Johnson, published by the Institute for Defense Analyses. Currently he is continuing in greater detail the research on which the essay in the present volume is based.

EDWIN H. FEDDER is director of the Center for International Studies and professor of political science at the University of Missouri-St. Louis. A specialist in alliances, Dr. Fedder is the author of numerous publications, including *NATO: The Dynamics of Alliance in The Postwar World.* He is editor of *NATO in the Seventies.* Prior to joining the faculty at the University of Missouri, Dr. Fedder taught at the Ohio State University, University of Illinois, University of Pittsburgh and Hollins College. He also has engaged in postdoctoral research at the Oak Ridge Institute of Nuclear Studies and at the Hague Academy of International Law.

PETER KARSTEN is associate professor of history at the University of Pittsburgh. He is the author of *The Naval Aristocracy: The Golden Age of Annapolis and the Emergence of Modern American Navalism.* He has spent the 1972-1973 academic year in Portugal, writing a book that is to be entitled, "Contours of Culture: Patriot-symbols in the English-speaking World from the 17th Century to the Present." He also has written "The American Citizen Soldier," "ROTC, Mylai, and the Volunteer Army" and a number of other articles. After graduation from Yale and prior to his postgraduate studies, he spent three years in the Navy, including service as legal officer and deck officers on the USS *Canberra.*

LAWRENCE J. KORB is associate professor of government at

the U.S. Coast Guard Academy. Prior to that, he taught at the University of Dayton. He was on active duty in the Navy as a flight officer from 1962-1966 and presently is a lieutenant commander in the Naval Reserve. His extensive research on the Joint Chiefs of Staff has resulted in a number of scholarly publications, including articles in the *Aerospace Historian,* the *Naval War College Review,* in *The Military-Industrial Complex: A Reassessment* and a forthcoming book. Presently Dr. Korb is working on a long range projection of defense expenditures (1975-1980) for the American Enterprise Institute for Public Policy Research.

ROBERT M. KRONE is an Air Force colonel, serving presently as an International Staff Officer at Supreme Headquarters Allied Powers Europe in Belgium. His 21 years of service in the United States Air Force have been divided between jet fighter flying, serving on a variety of military staffs, and attendance at numerous military and civilian educational institutions. He holds a command pilot rating and a parachutist rating and has served in Korea, Japan, Turkey, Thailand and Belgium, in addition to assignments throughout the United States. His overseas tours include a combat tour in Vietnam. He holds a Masters of Public and International Affairs degree from the University of Pittsburgh, and a doctorate in political science from the University of California, Los Angeles. His professional interest lies mainly in the international political-military relations area with a policy sciences orientation. He has published articles in several military periodicals.

PHILIP S. KRONENBERG is assistant professor of political science at Indiana University, where he also has been director of the Institute of Public Administration. Dr. Kronenberg served three years as an Air Force officer, with assignments in the AF Logistics Command and as a member of the international relations faculty at the USAF Officer Training School. He is co-editor of *National Security and American Society: Theory, Process, and Policy* and has written chapters in several books concerning empirical theory of public administration, analytical approaches to the study of national security, and unconventional roles of militia forces. His current research interests stress the problems which national security policies and programs pose in a democratic society and the role of interorganizational behavior in public policy systems.

JOHN P. LOVELL is professor of political science at Indiana University. He is the author of *Foreign Policy in Perspective: Strategy, Adaptation, Decision Making,* editor of and contributor to *The Military and Politics in Five Developing Nations,* and author of a number of articles in scholarly journals and books. A West Point graduate, he served in the Army in Germany and the United States in the mid-fifties before resigning to begin an academic career. He spent the 1971-1972 academic year as a visiting professor at the U.S. Naval Academy. Currently he is working on a book-length study of "Organizational Adaptation and Change at the U.S. Service Academies."

RICHARD A. McGONIGAL, a commander in the U.S. Navy, is director of Intercultural Relations, U.S. Navy. Prior to that he was on the faculty of the Marine Corps Command and Staff College. He holds bachelor's degrees both from Cornell University and the Union Theological Seminary, and a Ph.D. from Michigan State University. His military career includes service in Vietnam, where he undertook extensive attitude surveys, results of which have been published in a number of journals. Presently he is concerned with continuing the investigation in the subject area of the essay for this volume, racism.

M. SCOTT PECK is a psychiatrist now in private practice in New Preston, Connecticut. He has had nine years' experience in the Army, including three as chief of the Department of Psychiatry of the U.S. Army Medical Center, Okinawa, where he was involved in the initiation of programs to counteract drug and interracial tensions. From August 1970 until November 1972, he was the Assistant Chief Psychiatry and Neurology Consultant in the Office of the Surgeon General, Department of the Army. In this position he was concerned with the initial planning and development of the Army's Alcohol and Drug Abuse Prevention and Control Program. Dr. Peck received his B.A. degree from Harvard and his M.D. degree from Case Western Reserve University.

JOHN R. PROBERT is professor and chairman of the political

science department at the U.S. Naval Academy. He is co-author of *Military Assistance Management: A Proposal for Change,* and author of "Streamlining the Foreign Policy Machine," *Public Administration Review,* and of "Pentagon Reorganization: Phase Three," U.S. Naval Institute *Proceedings,* among other publications. He served on active duty in the South Pacific with the Army during World War II, and continued during the post-war period in the Army reserves, from which he recently retired as colonel. His current research interests lie jointly in a focus on post-Vietnam civil-military relationships in policy-making, and in the role of the military reserves in the future.

JAMES M. ROHERTY is professor and chairman of the department of political science, University of South Carolina. During the 1971-1972 academic year, he was visiting professor at the National Defense College of Japan. During the previous year he served as a member of the research staff of the President's Blue Ribbon Defense Panel. He has served as American Society for Public Administration Fellow with NASA, and as consultant to NASA and to the Defense Department. He is the author of *Decisions of Robert S. McNamara: A Study of the Role of the Secretary of Defense,* and of numerous other publications. Currently he is working on the design of national security policy models, and on the study of post-Vietnam security patterns in the Pacific.

BRUCE M. RUSSETT is professor of political science at Yale University. He is editor of the *Journal of Conflict Resolution,* a council member of the Peace Research Society (International), and has served as consultant to the Institute for Defense Analyses, to the U.S. Arms Control and Disarmament Agency and to the Rand Corporation. He is the editor of *Peace, War, and Numbers* and of *Military Force and American Society.* He is author of *What Price Vigilance? The Burdens of National Defense,* of *No Clear and Present Danger: A Skeptical View of the United States Entry into World War II,* and of numerous other publications. Currently he is doing research on economic and ideological influence on U.S. foreign policy.

PAUL R. SCHRATZ is director of the Office of International Studies, University of Missouri. He is the author of "History of the Naval War College," a monograph, "The Nuclear Carrier in Modern War," the 1972 prize essay in the U.S. Naval Institute *Proceedings,* a contributor to *Growth and Development of Aerospace Power,* and other publications. An Annapolis graduate, he served 29 years in the Navy, retiring as a captain. His military career included extensive service on submarines, during which he set a world's record for submerged transit in conventional subs, from Hong Kong to Pearl Harbor. His career also included combat experience during World War II and Korea, and subsequent service on the Joint Staff, JCS; on the Policy Planning Staff, DOD/ISA; and with the U.S. delegation to the Disarmament Conference in Geneva. Currently he is writing a book on "Mahan in the Modern World." Other current research interests include a study of reorganization of the U.S. national security planning structure.

INDEX

NEW CIVIL-MILITARY RELATION
The Agonies of Adjustment
to Post-Vietnam Realities.
Edited by John P. Lovell
and Philip S. Kronenberg

Diminishing United States military involvement in Southeast Asia has brought this country to a new era of American foreign and national security policy. Because Vietnam and other domestic and global turbulences have had a traumatic effect upon all our institutions, the role of the military and the use of force as an instrument of foreign policy are now under particular scrutiny.

The common theme that runs through the fourteen original essays in this volume is that traditional concepts and descriptions of American "civil-military relations," like our domestic and foreign policies themselves, have become anachronistic. Because of Vietnam, current policy assumptions and priorities are being challenged from within government as well as from without, and the chances for evolving policies that are knowledgeably based and broadly responsive to the needs and desires of the nation have been improved.

With viewpoints ranging across the political continuum, the authors also write from the perspective of various social science disciplines. In addition to civilian scholars, active-duty and retired officers of the Army, Navy, and Air Force are represented.

The volume is distinctive in its treatment of civil-military relations, not only at top policy levels (NATO, the Joint Chiefs of Staff, and the Office of the Secretary of Defense), but also at the community and operational levels (civil-military racism, drugs in the armed services, ROTC, and the National Guard).